344,041 DEC

NUTSHELLS

MEDICAL LAW

IN A

AUSTRALIA
Law Book Company
Sydney

CANADA and USA
Carswell
Toronto

HONG KONG
Sweet & Maxwell Asia

NEW ZEALAND
Brookers
Wellington

SINGAPORE and MALAYSIA
Sweet & Maxwell Asia
Singapore and Kuala Lumpur

NUTSHELLS

MEDICAL LAW
IN A
NUTSHELL

SECOND EDITION

by

Peter de Cruz
Professor of Law Liverpool John Moores University

London • Sweet & Maxwell • 2005

Published in 2005 by
Sweet & Maxwell Limited of
100 Avenue Road, London, NW3 3PF
Phototypeset by
LBJ Typesetting Ltd of Kingsclere
Printed in Great Britain by Creative Print and Design
(Wales) Ebbw Vale

A CIP Catalogue record
for this book is available
from the British Library

ISBN 0–421–89170X

©
Sweet & Maxwell
2005

INTRODUCTION

Terminology: Medical law, Healthcare law and Medical Ethics

'Medical Law' was described by Professor Ian Kennedy in 1983 as a 'discrete area of law' despite not being 'marked out or accepted as having its own territory' (see Kennedy "The Emerging Problems of Medicine, Technology and the Law" in *The Cambridge Lectures* (1985)). Kennedy also defined medical law as 'a discrete area, concerned with the interactions between doctors and patients and the organisation of health care.' (Kennedy, Chapter 1 in *Treat Me Right* (1988)). As he pointed out, Medical law draws upon and is seen as a development of tort law, family law, contract law and public law.

'Healthcare Law' has become a more popular term particularly in nursing circles over the last decade or so, is wider in application and as defined by Montgomery, "not only embraces the practice of medicine but also that of the non-medical healthcare professionals, the administration of health services and the law's role in maintaining public health." (Montgomery, *Health Care Law* (1997))

'Medical Ethics', however, are closely linked with philosophical principles, and have been described by Professor Dunstan as 'the obligations of a moral nature which govern the practice of medicine.' (Dunstan, *Dictionary of Medical Ethics* (1981)). Doctors are not the only professionals who deal with the health of people and the delivery of healthcare in the United Kingdom is the responsibility of the National Health Service. Hence 'Medical Ethics' can cover not only choices made by doctors but also those made by other health care professionals such as nurses, pharmacists and health care administrators. Many disputes in Medical Law involve medico-legal dilemmas and competing principles.

Examples of situations involving competing principles

Abortion pits the notion of the absolute principle that says that destroying the foetus is inherently wrong and always wrong, against the utilitarian principle which says that the question of what is right will depend on the best results for society at large.

On *confidentiality*, the absolutist would argue that the duty of confidence is sacrosanct and should never be breached under any circumstances. However, the utilitarian would argue that it would depend on the particular situation and its particular circumstances. (Phillips and Dawson, (1985)).

Many more examples of conflicting principles can be found, as this book will illustrate.

STRUCTURE OF HEALTHCARE PROVISION IN THE UNITED KINGDOM

Britain has a system of state funded and private health care provision. The vast majority of patients are treated by the state-funded National Health Service although the number of patients who have signed up for and are having treatment on a contractual basis with a private physician (instead of an NHS doctor) is rising.

The National Health Service (NHS) in the United Kingdom

In the United Kingdom, the responsibility for providing health services to in-patients and outpatients at General Practitioners' surgeries and hospitals and for improving the health of the nation as a whole, lies with the National Health Service (NHS) founded in 1948 by Aneurin Bevan, then Secretary of State for Health of the British Labour Party. It was intended to provide free, state-run, health care for all, a central part of the welfare state. In current times, it still seeks provision of comprehensive care; the right of everyone in the UK to use it; and care to be provided according to people's clinical needs, not on their ability to pay.

At present there is no constitutional guarantee to healthcare treatment in English law.

Clinical governance and health governance

The government has developed the concept of Clinical Governance. As it states in para 6.12 of the Government White Paper, *The New NHS—Modern, Dependable* (1997):

> The Government will require every NHS Trust to embrace the concept of 'clinical governance' so that quality is at the core, both of their responsibilities as organisations and of each of their staff as individual professionals.

National Institute for Clinical Excellence (NICE)

A new National Institute for Clinical Excellence (NICE) has been established to promote high quality national guidelines for treatment based on the most up-to-date scientific evidence. It began its work on April 1, 1999. It is responsible for disseminating 'best practice' guidance to healthcare professionals working within the NHS.

Commission for Health Improvement (CHI)

A new national Commission for Health Improvement was formally established on April 1, 1999 to ensure that all parts of the NHS are brought up to the standards of the very best. It is an independent body for England and Wales with statutory functions. Its legislative basis is the Health Act 1999. Its programme of work began in April 2000. The role and functions of CHI have grown following the NHS Reform and Healthcare Professions Act 2002.

THE PRACTICE AND CONTROL OF MEDICAL ETHICS IN THE UNITED KINGDOM

The General Medical Council (GMC)-a disciplinary, regulatory and advisory body

This statutory body was established under the Medical Act 1858 and is empowered to govern the training of doctors and the practice of medicine in the United Kingdom. Its regulatory powers are regulated by s.1 of the Medical Act 1983 (as amended). It keeps the medical register, and its disciplinary committee has the power to suspend or strike a doctor off the register for serious professional misconduct. It does not purport to regulate day-to-day decisions of doctors but is really an overseeing and disciplinary body charged with maintaining professional standards. The GMC comprises members of the profession and lay-members and it occasionally issues ethical guidance on specific matters, especially if they have been the subject of debate, for example, it issued guidance on *Professional Confidence: Treatment of Persons under 16* in the 1980s following the House of Lords' ruling in the *Gillick* case. Unfortunately, this advice conflicted with the British Medical Association (BMA) Guidance at the time on the question of confidentiality. Nowadays, there is far more unanimity between the BMA and the GMC on guidance documents. The Nursing and Midwifery Council (NMC) is the equivalent body for nurses.

The Professional Societies

The medical royal colleges issue various ethical guidelines jointly and separately. The Royal College of Nursing is the equivalent of the BMA and also issues guidance, but it has tended to concentrate mainly on pay and employment conditions rather than on ethical issues.

The British Medical Association (BMA) is the organisation to which most doctors belong and has been a registered trade union since 1974, influential in formulating medical ethics for many years. It has a Central Ethical Committee and issues a *Handbook of Medical Ethics* which is updated from time to time. In certain controversial areas such as withdrawal of treatment in PVS cases and human organ donation, it has issued detailed and wide-ranging ethical guidelines, even referring to the law in other jurisdictions. The key difference between the GMC and the BMA is that unlike the GMC, the BMA has no powers to enforce any breach of ethics. The BMA has also been active in advising and giving evidence to bodies such as Royal Commissions and the GMC.

Relevance of civil law and criminal law to professional conduct

Apart from censure or removal by his professional regulatory body, if a doctor injures a patient while treating that patient, he could also be liable in *civil law* (in tort for battery) or for negligence (see ch.5) and the *criminal law* may also be of relevance. The doctor may be charged with battery at common law or under the Offences Against the Person Act 1861. If the patient dies as a result of the treatment attributable to the doctor, a charge in murder or manslaughter may be brought, depending on the *mens rea* (guilty intention) of the doctor. Doctors are not generally charged under the criminal law but *R. v Adomako* (1994) indicates that doctors do not belong to any special category and can be convicted for manslaughter. The doctor here was seen to be grossly negligent in his failing to notice that an oxygen tube had become disconnected, as a result of which the patient died.

Clinical Guidelines

The British Medical Association and the General Medical Council have issued guidelines over the years but only the GMC has any power to discipline doctors and therefore to enforce the observance of these guidelines. The legal status of guidelines has, to date, never been definitively clarified by the English courts hence their precise status must remain in doubt at this time. However, there is a school of thought that believes that such guidelines represent best practice. Hence, although not legally binding, deviation from them resulting in injury to patients would probably require justification and an application of the *Bolam* test and the *Bolitho* (1997) decision (in the sense of their 'logicality').

Medicine, Ethical Principles and Medical Decisions

What is a 'medical decision'?

The difficult question of what is a 'medical decision' is an important and often crucial one, because there are some situations that arise in which doctors may be faced with decisions which are not strictly 'medical' ones; for instance, deciding on whether a severely disabled newborn baby should be kept alive because of its poor 'quality of life'. If the doctors decide that the baby should not be kept alive with modern technology because it might then have a life as a paralytic, for example, this is arguably not really a 'medical' decision at all, except that it is usually made by a medical practitioner. Ian Kennedy has argued '[a] decision as to what quality of life is worth living is not . . . a medical decision and thus not for doctors alone to make.' (Kennedy, *Treat Me Right* (1998)) and he argues that 'failure to examine the question [of what is a medical decision] has resulted in decisions being taken by doctors which may not properly be within the unique or special competence of a doctor *qua* doctor to make'.

In *Medicine, Ethics and the Law*, Professor Michael Freeman remarked in 1988 that 'Decision-making cannot be governed by consensus for clearly there is none. There may be agreement on such fundamental principles as the sanctity of life but conflict remains on the content to be attached to such a principle. . .The ultimate decision cannot be left to doctors alone.'

In *Old Law, New Medicine* (1999), Professor Sheila McClean argues that while doctors are 'uniquely qualified to reach a medical prognosis', the 'outcome of that prognosis is a matter which has moral, ethical, social and political consequences which doctors' training and technical knowledge in no way equip them to address, far less to answer.'

ETHICAL CONCEPTS AND PRINCIPLES

Key ethical principles in medical law

There are several linking ethical concepts that run through various medico-legal problems, namely: *Autonomy, Consent, Pate-*

nalism, *Beneficence* (doing good), *Non-maleficence* (not doing any harm), *Respect for Persons*, *Preserving Life*, *The Sanctity of Life* and the *Quality of Life* and Justice. These concepts have derived from long-established tenets or principles of religious origin of various faiths such as Roman Catholicism, Protestantism, Judaism and Islam. Some of the concepts which are frequently referred to are utilitarianism and 'deontological' ethics. Nearly all the medico-legal dilemmas that have arisen from abortion, confidentiality, involuntary sterilisation, embryo research, surrogacy, children and medical treatment, through to organ transplantation and assisted suicide, involve the balancing of principles that conflict with each other.

Autonomy and consent

Raanan Gillon contrasts the conflict between 'the desire to do what is considered to be in the best interests of the patient and a desire to do what the patient says he wants. . .Ultimately, the conflict is between, on the one hand, *beneficence*, the principle that one should do good and/or non-*maleficence*, the principle that one should not do harm; and on the other hand, the principle that one should respect people's autonomy.' (see Gillon in Lockwood, *Modern Dilemmas in Modern Medicine* (1985)). This encapsulates the classic conflict in many medico-legal situations.

Women refusing caesarean section: lacking legal capacity?

A woman patient might refuse a blood transfusion or a caesarean section which is required to save her unborn foetus or her own life on religious grounds, but healthcare professionals might decide that, in the light of her particular state of mind, she lacked the capacity to decide whether to consent or not at that stage (being unable to weigh in the balance the risks and benefits of the proposed treatment) and they should proceed to give her a transfusion and save her life or perform a caesarean section which saves both herself and her unborn foetus. Several cases were decided in this way by the English courts, especially around 1996, and in 1997 the Court of Appeal reiterated the right of the adult of sound mind to decide for herself the medical treatment she will or will not receive (see *Re MB* (1997); cf. *Ms B's Case* (2002)). This right may be described as the right of self-determination or autonomy. However, although this principle has been reaffirmed by the judiciary, there is clearly scope for discretion in certain circumstances. So what is the 'principle' cf autonomy?

Definitions of autonomy

Ranaan Gillon in *Philosophical Medical Ethics* (1986)defines the concept of autonomy as 'the capacity to think, decide, and act (on the basis of such thought and decision) freely and independently'. Writing in Lockwood's edited collection *Moral Dilemmas in Modern Medicine* (1985), he distinguishes the *concept* of autonomy from the *principle* of autonomy which he describes as 'the moral requirement to respect other people's autonomy' and he later adds: 'to allow [people] to make their own decisions'. Hence, in his opinion, respect for autonomy is 'the moral principle that people should have their autonomy respected to the extent that such respect is consistent with respect for the autonomy of others. Part of what such respect for autonomy implies, in practical terms, is not interfering with people without their consent'.

Gillon highlights three aspects of autonomy: of thought, of will, and of action, and argues that the principle of respect for autonomy is intended to safeguard these three types of autonomy in all persons, except that limits to an individual's autonomy are necessary when it encroaches on someone else's autonomy.

Sheila McLean describes autonomy as 'rights to self-determination' (McLean (1999)), which is the preferred phrase of lawyers, and Phillips and Dawson in *Doctors' Dilemmas* (1985) state that the principle of autonomy 'means that individuals should be permitted personal liberty to determine their own actions.'

Respect for persons and autonomy

If one respects another person's autonomy, one will also observe another principle which is to have respect for persons. This principle has arguably been extended to *respect for persons* even after (and perhaps especially after) their death, because of the special significance given to a person's expressed wishes while alive or as contained in a will, not to deal with his body in a particular way, or, as in ancient civilisations, because of the special regard accorded to corpses in general.

Justifications for autonomy

Gillon (1986) identifies the two classic justifications for the principle of respect for autonomy:

(i) the Kantian argument that the nature of rational beings recognised that they were bound by a 'supreme moral law' whereby rational beings were 'ends in themselves' and recognised the autonomy of other such beings; and

(ii) The Utilitarian argument of John Stuart Mill, who argued that autonomy was an essential part of utilitarianism because autonomy was an essential part of the flourishing of the human subject.

Utilitarianism

Utilitarianism promotes the notion of 'the greatest good for the greatest number', strongly promoted by the philosopher John Stuart Mill and Jeremy Bentham, amongst others. It judges the value of an action in terms of its consequences. The utilitarian usually wishes to maximise the happiness and welfare of the greatest number and this is usually contrasted with deontological theories, which are duty-based (actions carried out because of duty or obligation) and the opposite of teleological theories which are consequences-based or consequentialist. Thus, teleological (or functional) theories are promoted by the utilitarians. Difficulties with utilitarian theories are: who decides what is good, how do we quantify well-being, is it always preferable to attempt to calculate the 'greatest number'? Johnson in *Pathways in Medical Ethics* (1991) argues: 'if medical care is spread too thinly, no one will benefit, so the greatest good conflicts with the greatest number.'

Deontological theories

Johnson in *Pathways in Medical Ethics* (1991) explains: 'The concept of rights and duties is classified as deontological theory' and he also reminds us that 'Deontological theory is usually associated with ethics that have a religious basis'. The word comes from 'deon' which means 'duty' in Greek.

Medical Paternalism

The word paternalism means to act as a father would towards his children. In the medical context, this is usually applied to the case where although the healthcare professional purports to act against the wishes of the patient, it is on the basis of wishing to promote the patient's 'best interests'. Fairburn has said that 'paternalism is most often defined in terms of one person's acting in what she takes to be another person's best interests even when that other might wish to act otherwise' (Fairburn in *Justified paternalism and suicide* (1991)). Fairburn discusses suicide and its moral connotations and in that context, argues that paternalism and therefore intervention may be justified in certain circumstances, namely:

i) where the individual in question is badly informed
ii) where the individual in question is lacking in rationality
iii) where the individual in question is going to die unless we intervene but where it seems likely that his intention is something other than to bring about his death
iv) where the person's autonomy interests are best served by intervention

Does medical paternalism remain part of English law? It is clear from cases dealing with sterilisation of mentally disabled persons, children with anorexia and (in the latter years of the 20th century), for pregnant women who appeared to refuse caesarean sections, that paternalism is very much in evidence as far as the English judiciary is concerned. Yet, in a lecture delivered after the *Sidaway* decision in which he had been on the Bench in the Lords, Lord Scarman could say that "Medical paternalism is no longer acceptable as a matter of English law; that has gone" (see Scarman 'Consent, communication and responsibility' (1986) *Jo Royal Soc of Medicine* 697). In 2004, Lord Steyn again remarked in *Chester v Afshar* (2004) that "In modern law medical paternalism no longer rules" (see ch.4). Nevertheless, as cases dealing with caesarean sections and children indicate, medical paternalism supported by judicial paternalism, continued to thrive in the second half of the twentieth century. In 1997, the Court of Appeal in *Re MB* made an attempt to curb medical paternalism for certain situations involving refusal of caesarean sections, echoed by the High Court decision of *B v NHS Hospital Trust* (Ms B) in 2002.

Doctrine of double effect

Doing good (beneficence) and not doing harm

This is based on the principle of 'above all, do no harm' and these two principles are probably the essence of what people might come to expect from doctors. However, there may be cases when one might have to perform an action which may lead to an evil although this is the result of doing something which is *prima facie* good-like prescribing pain-killer to someone in dire pain-but which, either because of the need to increase the dosage, or because of the patient's condition, leads to a 'bad' result, which might be a premature death. This is the Catholic *doctrine of double effect*, whereby acts done with the intention of doing good result in unintended or unforeseen and secondary, bad effects. The principle is that one is responsible for the intended results of one's actions rather than any consequences that may follow from the action as long as those consequences were not intended. This doctrine was developed by Thomas Aquinas (a 13th century Italian theologian) who formulated a concept whereby it is morally acceptable to cause or permit evil in the pursuit of doing good.

Dying patients

'Double effect' usually arises in cases of dying patients, arguing that provided it can be proved that the doctor administered the pain-killing drugs primarily to relieve the patient's suffering and not to cause that patient's death, he is morally and legally blameless. In case law, there has been a conflict of approaches but *R. v Cox* (1992) appears to have resolved any contradictory judicial pronouncements. Devlin, J's words in *R. v Adams* (1957) where he said that 'The doctor is entitled to relieve pain and suffering even if the measures he takes may incidentally shorten life' were approved by Lord Goff in the *Bland* case when he said: '[It is] the established rule that a doctor may, when caring for a patient who is, for example, dying of cancer, lawfully administer painkilling drugs despite the fact that he knows that an incidental effect of that application will be to abbreviate the patient's life. . . Such a decision may properly be made as part of the care of the living patient, in his best interests; and, on this basis, the treatment will be lawful'. (see *Airedale NHS v Bland* (1993))

Preserving life

Various medical ethical codes stress the doctor's obligation to respect life but they do *not* require doctors to preserve life at all costs. The distinction is often drawn between *actively killing* a patient and *letting that patient die*. The former is regarded as unlawful and morally unacceptable and the latter is regarded, in certain circumstances, as 'acting in the best interests of the patient'. The duty or obligation to preserve life may, in practice, conflict with another principle, to respect a patient's autonomy, if, for example, the patient has specifically asked the doctor to end his life. Hence, if the doctor does not accede to the patient's request, it may be argued that the doctor is overriding the right of the patient to decide what should be done with his body, but the patient cannot expect the doctor to break the law. If the patient is in great pain, and wishes the doctor merely to alleviate this pain, but the doctor knows that to prescribe an increasing amount of pain-killing drugs would kill the patient, what is the doctor to do? If the doctor refuses to prescribe the drugs, is that acting in the patient's best interests, especially when the patient says he only wants relief from his pain? As often cited in the context of euthanasia, in the famous couplet from Arthur Clough, the approach is: 'Thou shalt not kill, but needs't not strive officiously to keep alive.' (Clough, A. *'The last decalogue'*). The acts and omissions doctrine is relevant to this couplet.

The 'acts and omissions' doctrine

Gillon (1986) describes the acts and omissions doctrine as the situation where 'actions that result in some undesirable consequences are always morally worse than inactions, or failures to act, that have the same consequence'. Roman Catholic philosophers, theologians and secular philosophers have strenuously rejected the acts and omissions doctrine on three grounds which are discussed by *Gillon*, namely: (i) 'an omission by definition is not simply an inaction but a morally culpable inaction'; (ii) the Roman Catholics claim that 'not only does outcome matter when a moral judgment is made on a person's actions. But so too are preceding considerations, including pre-existing moral obligations and the understanding and intention with which the person acted'; (iii) 'certain sorts of action and inaction are absolutely forbidden, in particular, intentional killing of an innocent person, including bringing about death by omission, is absolutely forbidden.' (*Gillon* (1986))

The English courts appear to have resolved the question of 'physician-assisted suicide' as the Americans call it, by requiring proof that the physician acted *solely* to relieve the patient's pain and suffering (for example in prescribing pain-killing medication) in order to exonerate the physician's actions if the patient ultimately died from taking the prescribed medication. (see chapter 9).

Sanctity of life, respect for human life and quality of life

The 'sacredness' of life

The Declaration of Geneva mentions the 'utmost respect for human life' and some would argue that all life is sacred (both human and non-human) on purely religious grounds, on the premise that all life comes from God, the ultimate sacred Being. The phrase and concept is complex even if we confine ourselves to *human* life. In *Life's Dominion* (1994) Professor Ronald Dworkin discusses his notion of what 'sacredness' of human life may mean and ponders what the notion of 'intrinsically valuable' might mean and suggests things might be considered 'sacred' or 'valuable': by association, because of its history, because of intrinsic value, respect for God as the divine creator, or because of the wonder at natural and human creation. In a memorable passage, he says 'The life of a single human organism commands respect and protection . . . no matter in what form or shape, because of the complex creative investment it represents and because of our wonder at the divine or evolutionary processes that produce new lives from old ones'.

Arguments about the sanctity of life as opposed to the 'quality of life' tend to surface in the context of the proposed sterilisation of mentally incapacitated persons or in cases which require decisions about whether to save the life of a severely disabled newborn child or to allow a child who has a poor prognosis of life expectancy to die 'with dignity'.

How does one judge the 'quality of life' of a person? Is it ever possible to do so with rational justification?

Sanctity of life v quality of life

In the early 1980s, two English cases on disabled babies led Professor Glanville Williams to say that if he were suddenly told by a wicked fairy that he was about to be transformed into a Down's syndrome baby and whether he would want to die immediately, he would say 'yes'. This suggested the fallacy, as McLean says, 'that we could take our own life experiences and translate them into someone else's reality'. Thus, the *quality of life* approach focuses on *whether a particular patient has the capacity or potential to live a 'normal' life, i.e. experience all the five senses, and the life experiences that a 'normal' person would.* In the case of a disabled newborn, of course, such a child would never have known what a 'normal' life would be like, so it would be simply fallacious to impose a 'normal' person's life or developmental experiences on such a person and assume that this person would reject life on the basis that it would have a very poor 'quality of life'.

In *The Value of Life*, Professor John Harris argues that 'the ultimate question for medical ethics . . . is simply: what makes human life valuable and, in particular, what makes it more valuable than other forms of life? . . . When we ask [this question] we are trying to identify those features, whatever they are, which both incline us and entitle us to value ourselves and one another and which license our belief that we are more valuable (and not just to ourselves) than animals, fish or plants . . . It is important to realise that it is the capacity to value one's own life (and those of others) that is crucial . . .' (Harris (1985)).

According to Harris, therefore, embryos, newborn babies, and the severely disabled would not have lives that were 'valuable' by his criterion. Indeed, if we look at the English court cases involving severely disabled newborns, the courts have appeared to have moved from a 'qualified' sanctity of life position to a quality of life position with the proviso that only lives which, if prolonged by artificial means or technology, were going to be 'demonstrably awful' could be seen as not worth preserving and should be 'allowed to die' with decency and dignity. Indeed, in *Re T* (1997) (the liver transplant case), a senior judge of the Court of Appeal (Butler-Sloss, L.J.) said that it was *not* the function of the [English] court to preserve life at all costs. However, post-*Re T* cases appear generally to have endorsed the 'qualified' sanctity of life principle again and were not guided by parental wishes (but see the *David Glass* case (2004) (European CHR) as a recent exception)

In the 'real world', as McLean reminds us in *Old Law, New Medicine* (1999): 'An absolute commitment to the sanctity of all life is absent in every community. Whether through laws about self-defence, engagement in war, the imposition of the death penalty or our failure to save everyday life that could be saved, we already concede that lives may be balanced and some may be lost.'

The notion of justice and QALYs

The Hippocratic Oath also mentions the importance of the doctor's duty towards the individual patient. In a society of

limited resources, the 'principle of distributive justice, under
which those in greatest need have their needs met first . . .
conflicts with the principle of autonomy, under which every
individual is entitled to an equal share of the health care provided
by the community. If services have to be rationed, how equal can
the share-out be?' (Phillips and Dawson, *Doctors' Dilemmas*, 1985).
In the context of allocation of scarce resources, difficulties have
arisen as to how to mete out distributive justice and it is in that
difficult area where 'hard choices' (Calabresi) have to be made
and where the economic notion of QALYs (Quality Adjusted Life
Years) have been utilised so that some calculation can be made of
evaluating health care outcomes according to a generic scale by
asking (i) to what extent and for how long will a particular
treatment improve the quality of a patient's life, and (ii) how
much will that treatment cost? As Lockwood explains 'What
economists who favour the QALY approach do . . . is to take a
checklist of health factors that are likely to affect the perceived
quality of life of normal people, and assign weightings to them'
because 'the assumption is that there is some rational way of
trading off length of life against quality of life, so that one could
say, for example, that three years of life with some degree of
discomfort, loss of mobility or whatever was worth two years of
normal life'. As he also points out, there is 'an inescapable
element of arbitrariness here, both in the choice of factors to be
taken into account and in the relative weightings that are attached
to them which . . . would differ markedly from patient to patient.'
(Lockwood in '*Quality of life and resource allocation*' in *Philosophy
and Medical Welfare* (eds. Bell and Mendus (1988))

1. CONSENT TO TREATMENT

General Principle-valid consent must be obtained before medical treatment can commence

The general legal and ethical principle (for adult patients of sound mind) is that legally valid consent must be obtained before a doctor or other healthcare professional may start treatment or physical investigation or providing personal care, for a patient (*see Reference Guide to Consent for Examination or Treatment*, 2002, Department of Health). Children under 16 or those not sufficiently 'mature' (see *Gillick* competence: ch. 2), would normally need the consent of their parents or carers before medical treatment could proceed; some teenagers whose refusal of consent to treatment could result in serious harm to themselves or cause their death, could have their consent overridden by those who have parental responsibility for them or by the courts.

Adult patient's right to refuse must be respected

In the case of terminally ill patients, the latest GMC guidance (2002) states that if they are adults who can understand information and make an informed decision, being able to choose how much weight to attach to the benefits and risks of treatment, then their decision to refuse treatment should be respected. The guidelines say that such patients 'have the right to refuse treatment even where refusal may result in harm to themselves or in their own death and doctors are legally bound to respect their decision.' It advises that if doctors decide not to follow any part of the Guidance, they must be prepared 'to explain and justify their decisions, to patients and their families, to colleagues and, where necessary, to the courts and the GMC'.

Autonomy and medical treatment

In the *Report of the Select Committee of Medical Ethics* (1994), para.40 states that "Alongside the principle that human life is of special value, the principle is widely held that an individual should have some measure of autonomy to make choices about his or her life. Such autonomy has become important in relation to medical treatment, as the relationship between doctor and patient has changed to one of partnership. As the law stands, medical treatment may be given to competent adult patients only with their informed consent, unless in an emergency." However, the notion of consent is by not always straightforward in its scope or application. Autonomy and consent are fundamental to an understanding of the basic notions of Medical law.

The ethical framework

The notion or principle of consent to treatment to medical treatment is often stated to be the prerequisite to treatment of adults of sound mind. This is sometimes described as the 'doctrine' of informed consent but this notion more accurately describes the American rather than English version of consent to medical treatment. The requirement of consent has several functions: first, to promote individual autonomy; secondly, to encourage rational decision-making, both of which derive from the basic principle of the right to self-determination, which has been reaffirmed by the English courts. Lord Donaldson, MR, stated in 1989 that "The ability of the ordinary adult to exercise a free choice in deciding whether to accept or refuse medical treatment and to choose between treatments is not to be dismissed as desirable but inessential. It is a crucial factor in relation to all medical treatment." (see *In Re F (Mental Patient: Sterilisation)* [1990]) Finally, the rules on consent were intended to impose on health professionals *'an obligation to make appropriate disclosure of relevant information to the patient, so that the exercise of autonomy was meaningful.'* (McLean, *Consent and the Law. Review of the current provisions in the Human Fertilisation and Embryology Act 1990 for the UK Health Ministers.* (1997)). The underlying ethical principle is self-determination, complemented by the principle of respect for persons.

INFORMED CONSENT

Is there a legal doctrine of 'informed consent' in English law?

In 1981, Gerald Robertson in 'Informed consent to medical treatment (1981) LQR 102, remarked that any writer attempting to examine the status of the 'doctrine'(sic) of informed consent in English law "must do so with a considerable degree of caution". Habiba, in the Journal of Medical Ethics, published in 2000, in the context of medical ethics, could still justifiably remark that this notion of consent is 'relatively new'.

The classic legal statement

The classic legal statement is found in an American case where Cardozo, J, in *Schloendorff v Society of New York Hospital* (1914) 105 NE 92(NY), said:

> "Every human being of adult years and sound mind has a right to determine what shall be done with his own body; and a surgeon who performs an operation without the patient's consent commits an assault."

If a valid consent has not been given to any medical procedure, the patient usually has the right to sue. There are, of course, exceptions, for example, *incompetent patients, children, treatment under public health legislation, and the unconscious patient needing life-saving surgery.*

But what does 'informed consent' actually mean in English law? The term has been called 'tautologous' by Mason, McCall Smith and Laurie in *Law and Medical Ethics* (2002), because, they argue, 'to be ethically and legally acceptable, 'consent' must always be 'informed'and consequently they argue that the first element of the phrase is redundant.

In *'Informed consent and other fairy stories'* (1999) Med LR 103, Michael Jones argues that "Technically, English law does *not* have a concept of informed consent except in the *very limited form* accepted in *Chatterton v Gerson* [1981] where the patient only needs to be informed 'in broad terms of the nature of the procedure which is intended." (emphasis added). Yet, as a concept it is certainly a basic requirement for medical treatment to proceed. The nature of the term and the variability of the medical context makes it a concept that adapts to the particular set of circumstances. In English case law there are fairly well-established sets of rules which govern the English version of informed consent.

There is a need to define one's terms carefully and be wary of judicial pronouncements such as those of Dunn, L.J. when he says in *Sidaway*: "The concept of informed consent forms no part of English law" (*Sidaway v Board of Governors of the Bethlem Royal Hospital* [1984] 1 All ER 1018 at 1030) where he was almost certainly referring to the subjective patient (American-derived) approach-judging what needs to be disclosed by what the individual patient would have needed to know rather than by an objective standard of disclosure i.e. what a doctor or judge thinks a patient ought to be told, as a minimum, in nearly every case.

Lord Donaldson in *Re T ((adult) (refusal of medical treatment)* (1992), said "English law does not accept the transatlantic concept of informed consent" but he was probably referring to some form of the American 'doctrine' which conforms to some 'subjective' standard that would vary from patient to patient; yet the majority of the American jurisdictions appear to support some form of objective standard of disclosure.

Kennedy and Grubb in *Medical Law* (1994) argue that 'informed consent' is not synonymous with 'valid consent' because it gives only a partial view, and because the requirement that consent be 'informed' is only one of the ingredients of a valid consent (although it is a very important one).

THE 'RULES' OF CONSENT TO TREATMENT

Must the patient's consent be 'real?'

English law has said that in order for the consent to be valid it must be 'real' meaning the patient must know what he or she is consenting to. This means that the 'nature and purpose' of the proposed treatment must be understood by the patient, but in the leading English case, it was said that 'once the patient is informed in broad terms of the nature of the procedure which is intended, and gives her consent, that consent is real': see *Chatterton v Gerson*[1981] QB 432, at 442B-C; so that treatment which is then carried out is not seen as trespass to the person. So the level of understanding under Chatterton would not have to be very great. This approach was approved by the House of Lords in *Sidaway* [1985]. (see also *Freeman v Home Office* (No.2) [1984]).

But the terms 'real' and 'nature' also require interpretation and clarification in individual cases.

Re C, (the 68-year-old man with the 'gangrenous leg') [1994] which has become the most recent leading case on this area, suggests the requirements could be more demanding. It suggests a three-part test and also illustrates that the fact that someone is mentally disordered does not render that person incapable of making a legally competent medical decision.

Re C affirmed a three-stage approach as a test for legal capacity to consent:

(1) Could the patient comprehend and retain the necessary information?
(2) Did the patient believe this information?
(3) Had the patient weighed the information, balancing the risks and needs, to arrive at a choice?

Types of consent

Consent may be express or implied. Consent need not be expressly stated or written to be valid in law. An implied consent could be simply offering one's arm for an injection in a surgery. Indeed, a signed consent form is merely evidence that the patient signed the form but does not mean that he necessarily understood the significance or implications of the treatment which was being proposed in the Form. In 2002, the Department of Health issued a new Form for consent-to-treatment which requires the risks and benefits of a procedure to be clearly spelt out. However, despite 750,000 leaflets being printed, there are apparently insufficient numbers of them to be used by all hospitals in the UK.

Patient must know the specific treatment that he is consenting to

English law has also established that in order for the consent to be valid it must be 'real' meaning the patient must know what *specific treatment* he or she is consenting to. This means that the 'nature and purpose' of the proposed treatment must be understood by the patient. In the absence of genuine consent, the defendant could, in certain cases, also be guilty of indecent assault (in criminal law).

What needs to be disclosed?

Patients have to make their choices based on the information given. Does the *Bolam* case which requires compliance with 'standard procedure' apply to both diagnosis and treatment? *Sidaway* [1984] *suggests material risks must be disclosed*, subject to *therapeutic privilege*; if a patient asks certain questions, these would usually have to be answered truthfully. Therapeutic privilege could be claimed for withholding some facts if there is the real possibility of psychological damage being suffered by the patient if all the facts were revealed (see *Sidaway* (1984)).

Some legally problematic areas

1. HIV testing—should specific consent be obtained for HIV blood tests?
2. Pregnant women refusing Caesarean sections. There have been several recent cases involving women in labour refusing Caesarean sections. Their wishes have been over-ruled and an enforced Caesarean section has taken place. The Court of Appeal in *Re MB* (1997) has laid down guidelines in this difficult area.

Consent to testing for HIV infection

The issue here is: does HIV testing exceed the bounds of consent which the patient has already given to therapeutic or diagnostic investigation?

The GMC have rejected HIV testing in the absence of specific consent except in the 'most exceptional circumstances' i.e. where it has not been possible to obtain consent and the health of persons other than the patient is endangered.

The BMA have said non-consensual testing is not permissible and might even constitute assault. The Central Committee for Hospital Medical Services has been advised that the doctor may exercise his clinical judgment unless the patient asks specifically about HIV testing.

The Medical Defence Union obtained a legal opinion which said that assault was not committed provided permission for venepuncture had been given but that specific consent for HIV should usually be obtained except where, perhaps, there was a very low expectation for a positive result.

Which persons are unable to give legally valid consent to treatment?

There are various exceptions to the rule concerning consent. Certain persons lack the capacity to make competent decisions with regard to medical treatment because they are:

- incompetent patients-those temporarily unconscious; permanently unconscious through disease, trauma, injury, mental impairment, mental handicap, dementia or illness

- children-who are below the age of maturity or at least not 'Gillick competent' i.e. who have not reached the level of 'sufficient age and understanding' (cf. the phrase used in the Children Act 1989) although it not always clear what this means in every situation.

Additionally, there is public health legislation-i.e. legislation passed for the good of the community as a whole without prior consultation of the public.

Necessity

Under the doctrine of *necessity*, e.g. the unconscious patients needing life-saving surgery. Treatment must be immediate and life-saving: see *Marshall v Curry* [1933]; *Devi v West Midlands AHA* [1980]. The two requirements for necessity to apply are: that it is impossible for medical staff to communicate with the patient and the action taken must be what a reasonable person would have done in the circumstances: see *Re F (Sterilisation) (Mental Patient)* (1990); What if the doctor knows in advance of treatment, that the patient would have refused life-saving surgery? See *Malette v Shulman* [1988] (Ontario) where the court held the doctor was not entitled to ignore the patient's clear statement refusing any blood transfusion, despite the fact that it appeared to be medically indicated. *Re T (An Adult) (Refusal of Treatment)* [1992] merely confirmed that English courts were, in certain cases, prepared to accept some form of advance directives (see ch. 9).

Consequences of proceeding without consent

Prima facie, the patient may sue for damages for the battery which is committed if non-consensual treatment, involving touching of any sort, is carried out. A claim in civil and criminal law may be available. However, a claim also may lie under the tort of negligence (see ch. 4).

An action for battery arises when the plaintiff has been touched in some way by the defendant without the defendant's consent, express or implied, to such touching. The crucial point here is: there is no need to establish loss as a result of the touching so long as the plaintiff can establish that the defendant wrongfully touched him. Where there has been *no consent whatsoever* to the physical contact, a civil action for *battery* would be appropriate.

If the patient consented to certain medical treatment, and something else was done while, for example, the patient was under anaesthetic, albeit in the belief that it was in the patient's interests, this might constitute negligence.

An action for negligence would have to establish that the defendant wrongfully touched him and that the negligence of the defendant in touching him without consent has led to the injury for which damages are sought. Thus, *there is a need to establish factual causation in an action in tort for negligence*. Such an action would be appropriate where the plaintiff consented to an act of the general nature of that performed by the defendant but there was no consent to performing certain features of the act of which the plaintiff was unaware and to which he did not consent. Thus, the doctor might be liable in negligence if he performed an act quite unconnected with the procedure to which the plaintiff did consent: see *Marshall v Curry* (1933); *Murray v McMurchy* (1949) (Canadian cases).

Measure of damages different for battery and negligence

In battery, all direct damages are recoverable. In negligence, only reasonably foreseeable damages are recoverable.

Criminal law

Charges would also lie against healthcare professionals in Criminal Law for criminal assault and battery; and under the Offences Against the Person Act: ss.18 and 20. If medical staff carry out procedures or operations with the intention of killing a patient, and do so, this, if proven, would constitute murder. If a doctor carries out a lawful act in a reckless manner, this could constitute 'gross negligence manslaughter': see *R. v Adomoko* (1995).

The best interests criterion

There have been cases where the courts have sanctioned the treatment that a doctor has carried out even where the patient was incapable of understanding the nature of the treatment, provided the doctor established that s/he acted in that patient's *best interests* (see e.g. *F v West Berkshire* [1989] which confirmed that if a responsible body of opinion would agree that the treatment was in that patient's best interests, the treatment would be sanctioned by the court-thus confirming the *Bolam* test's applicability).

PREGNANT WOMEN, CONSENT AND CAESAREAN SECTIONS

Ethical dilemmas

The common dilemma in caesarean section cases is: if the doctors do not act to save the pregnant woman's life and the life of the unborn foetus, they might be accused of negligence or failing to discharge their professional duty to save lives and act in the best interests of the patient; they would also appear to contravene the sanctity of life principle. If they do act, they will run the risk of being sued in trespass to the person or battery for acting against the will of the patient who has refused her consent thereby breaching her individual autonomy or right of self-determination. In addition, because it is women who are involved in these cases, issues of gender inequality, domination and exploitation of a woman's right to choose could be raised.

In 1996, a spate of cases reached the courts dealing with Caesarean sections being performed on women who allegedly refused their consent to the operation. Despite this lack of consent, the doctors proceeded anyway and in every case, the Courts upheld the doctors' actions.

Mother's rights v foetal rights?

The caesarean section cases, culminating in a Court of Appeal ruling in *Re MB* [1997] have highlighted the apparent ethical dilemma between a mother's rights and foetal rights. The appellate court reviewed the case law and gave clear guidance on whether there are circumstances where it is lawful for doctors to perform a Caesarean section even though the patient concerned has refused to consent to the operation. Subsequent to that case, the Court of Appeal then decided the Collins case (*St George's Healthcare NHS Trust v S, R. v Collins and others ex parte S* (1998) [1998]), which resulted in further guidelines.

Background

It is only in the 1980s that English appeal judges have begun to be more explicit in their statements about any general rule relating to consent to treatment as in the case of *Re F (Sterilisa-*

tion: Mental Patient) [1989] and *Re T (An Adult) (Consent to Medical Treatment)* [1992] when Lord Donaldson, MR declared that 'An adult patient who. . .suffers from no mental incapacity has an absolute right to choose whether to consent to medical treatment, to refuse it or to choose one rather than another of the treatments being offered.' Yet his Lordship then added, obiter: 'The only possible qualification is a case in which the choice may lead to the death of a viable foetus.' Serious doubts have now been cast on the correctness of this statement in *Re MB*.

English law on consent to medical treatment of mentally capable adults is by no means as easily applicable as might have been assumed. In the context of Caesarean sections, obstetricians have tended to argue that the life of the unborn child is paramount and others have reiterated that it is up to a pregnant woman to decide on the kind of medical treatment she should receive. Despite the academic criticism stirred up by the earlier case of *Re S (Adult: Refusal of Medical Treatment)* [1992], a High Court judge in the Family Division, granted two separate orders permitting NHS trusts to perform caesarean sections despite the absence of consent from the patients involved, in *Norfolk & Norwich v W* [1997] and *Rochdale v Choudhary* [1997]. In *Re L (An Adult: Non-consensual Treatment)* [1997] a Family Division judge also ruled that a Caesarean section could be performed lawfully despite the patient's objection if that patient lacked the competence to make a rational decision.

The earlier Caesarean section cases

Re S [1992] (Family Division—High Court)

The 30-year-old patient (a 'born-again Christian') was in labour with her third pregnancy, having been admitted to hospital with ruptured membranes and six days overdue beyond the expected date of birth of her unborn child. The medical staff recommended a Caesarean section operation which they regarded as vital as her medical condition was regarded as 'desperately serious' as was the situation of her unborn child who was in a 'transverse lie' position with the elbow projecting through the cervix and the head on the right side. The Health Authority asked Sir Stephen Brown, P. for a declaration to authorise the doctors to perform a Caesarean section, which they argued was warranted in the vital interests of the patient and the unborn child, when S refused consent to the operation on religious grounds, a decision which was supported by her husband. The application was received at 1.30pm, the hearing commenced shortly before 2pm and the President made the declaration which was sought at 2.13pm. The desperate nature of the application was emphasised but the Court of Appeal case of *Re T* was cited as 'having left the matter open' on the issue of authorising an operation despite the patient's refusal, but the American case of *Re AC* [1990], whilst not binding, was cited as a persuasive authority for the proposition that an American court would be likely to grant a declaration in these circumstances. This was clearly dealt with as an emergency situation.

The Tameside case [1996]

The 41-year-old-year patient in this case (*Tameside and Glossop Acute Services Trust v CH* [1996]) was a paranoid schizophrenic who was detained in a hospital under s.3 to the Mental Health Act 1983. Having found the patient lacking the capacity to consent to or refuse medical treatment concerning the management of her pregnancy, Wall, J. made an order under s.63 to the 1983 Act, justifying delivery by caesarean as constituting medical treatment of her mental disorder. He stated that it was an assault to perform invasive treatment without the patient's consent and that a mentally competent patient has an absolute right to refuse treatment for any reason, rational or irrational or for no reason at all, even where that decision will lead to her own death. Where the patient is incompetent, treatment should be given in accordance with the principles enunciated in *Re F* [1989], namely that it is lawful to provide treatment which is in the patient's best interests, such as that which is necessary to save the life or preserve or prevent deterioration of the physical and mental health of a patient. He followed the test of mental competence to make decisions as laid down in *Re C (Adult: Refusal of Medical Treatment)* [1994], namely the ability to:

(a) comprehend and retain treatment information;
(b) believe such information;
(c) weigh such information in the balance to make a choice.

The Rochdale case [1997]

Mrs. C arrived at hospital fully dilated and in the last stages of pregnancy but in a state of arrested labour. She objected to

Caesarean section. At approximately 4.30pm the consultant obstetrician treating Mrs C contacted a solicitor because in his opinion, the patient's uterus was rupturing and unless he was able to deliver the baby by caesarean within an hour, both child and mother would die. Johnson, J. was already hearing another emergency Caesarean case (the *Norfolk* case, below) but he regarded the present facts as sufficiently urgent for him to consider this case immediately. In a two-minute hearing, the judge heard that the patient's objection to Caesarean section was that she had previously been delivered in this way and had suffered backache and pain around the resulting scar. She told the consultant that she would rather die than have another caesarean section. The consultant asked the patient what would happen to her first born child after she was dead and the patient replied that her own mother would look after her. The Trust's solicitor sought an urgent psychiatric opinion as to the patient's competence because there were only 15 minutes or so remaining for the operation to be carried out successfully. The only information the judge had as to her competence came from her consultant obstetrician. Her view was that the patient's mental capacity was not in question and that she seemed to him to be fully competent.

Given the extremely short time available for consideration, Johnson, J. applied the test of legal competence laid down by Wall, J. in *Tameside* (see above) and found that although Mrs. C was not suffering from a mental disorder, she lacked the mental competence to make a decision because she was incapable of weighing up the considerations that were involved and could not weigh up even considerations of the most trivial kind. Thus, he found her incapable of comprehending, retaining and weighing-up the information she had been given, particularly because she was 'in the throes of labour with all that is involved in terms of pain and emotional stress.' The court granted the declaration sought.

The Norfolk Case [1997]

The patient, Miss W, aged 32, arrived at the Accident and Emergency department of the hospital at 9am, in the last stage of the pregnancy, apparently without having had any ante-natal treatment. She was fully dilated and physically ready to deliver her baby. However, she denied she was even pregnant. She had a history of psychiatric treatment and had had three previous pregnancies, all terminated by Caesarean section. The consultant obstetrician sought authority to terminate the patient's labour by forceps delivery and if necessary by Caesarean section. Otherwise, there were two risks to the patient: (a) if the foetus was not delivered it would suffocate within the patient; (b) the patient's old Caesarean scars would reopen with a consequent risk to the life of the foetus and the health of the patient. A consultant psychiatrist interviewed the patient and formed the view that she was not suffering from a mental disorder within the meaning of the Mental Health Act 1983 but was unable to say whether she was capable of comprehending and retaining information about the proposed treatment nor whether she was capable of believing information given to her about the treatment. However, he took the view that she was not able to balance the information given to her.

In the *Tameside* case (above) Wall, J. had specifically left open the question whether the court had the power at common law to authorise the use of reasonable force as a necessary incidence of treatment or whether the power was limited to cases which fell within s.63 to the Mental Health Act 1983. That section reads: "the consent of a patient shall not be required for any medical treatment to him for the mental disorder from which he is suffering . . . if the treatment is given by or under the direction of the responsible medical officer."

Johnson, J. held that in these circumstances the court had the power at common law to authorise the use of reasonable force. He applied Lord Goff's principle in *Re F* (above) namely that there must be a necessity to act and 'the action taken must be such as a reasonable person would in all the circumstances take, acting in the best interest of the assisted person.'

He ruled that:

- although the patient was not suffering from a mental disorder she lacked the mental competence to make a decision about the treatment that was proposed because she was incapable of weighing up the considerations that were involved.

- Termination of labour would be in the best interests of the patient. It would end the stress and the pain of her labour, avoid the likelihood of damage to her physical health which might have potentially life-threatening consequences, and it would avoid her having any feeling of guilt were she, by her refusal of consent, to cause the death of the foetus.

- The situation was one where 'there was a necessity to act.' Johnson, J. stressed that the patient was called upon to make a decision about whether to have a caesarean 'at a time of acute emotional stress and physical pain in the ordinary course of labour' which was made even more difficult because of 'her particular mental history.'
- His main attention was focused on the patient's interests not the interests of the foetus yet he also declared that 'the reality was that the foetus was a fully formed child, capable of normal life if it could only be delivered from the mother.'

Re MB [1997] (The Needle Phobia Case)—the leading Court of Appeal case

Miss MB, aged 23, first attended an antenatal clinic when she was 33 weeks pregnant. Then and later she refused to allow blood samples to be taken because of her fear of needles. When she was 40 weeks pregnant it was discovered that the foetus was in the breech position. The risk to the unborn child was assessed at 50 per cent, although there was little physical danger to the mother. However, it was explained to the patient that vaginal delivery would pose a serious risk of death or brain damage to the baby. It was recommended that delivery should be by Caesarean section. Miss MB agreed to have a Caesarean section and was admitted to hospital where she and her partner agreed to the operation and signed a consent form. However, when successive attempts were made to carry out the operation, she panicked at the last moment because of her needle phobia and withdrew her consent. Finally, when the patient was in labour and not responding to the midwife or the consultant and had again consented to and then refused to agree to the anaesthesia, the health authority obtained a declaration from the High Court that it would be lawful for the consultant gynaecologist to operate on her, using reasonable force if necessary. The declaration was granted at 9.55pm and 65 minutes later that night, the Court of Appeal was hearing the appeal, and dismissed the patient's appeal from that order in the early hours of the next morning, reserving its reasons. On the following morning the patient co-operated in the operation and delivered a healthy baby boy.

The Court of Appeal judgment

The Court of Appeal (Butler-Sloss, Saville and Ward, L.JJ.) provided guidance for future cases involving refusal of surgery and guidance concerning caesarean section cases.

General principles

(i) In general, it is a criminal and tortious assault to perform physically invasive medical treatment, however the invasion might be, without the patient's consent;

(ii) A mentally competent patient has an absolute right to refuse to consent to medical treatment even where that decision may lead to his or her own death;

(iii) The only situation in which it is lawful for the doctors to intervene is if it is believed that the adult patient lacked the capacity to decide, the treatment was a necessity and what was done was no more than was required in best interests of the patient;

(iv) The court does not have the jurisdiction to take into account the interests of the unborn child at risk from the refusal of a competent mother to consent to medical intervention;

(v) In an emergency situation treatment could be given even if no consent had been obtained, so long as the treatment was essential and achieved the minimum that was required in the patient's interests.

On the facts of the case, the Court held:

(i) Miss MB did consent to the caesarean section;

(ii) She accepted the incision of the surgeon's scalpel but not the anaesthetist's needle; and

(iii) She could not bring herself to accept the caesarean section because her fear of needles dominated her thinking to the extent that she could think of nothing else.

Consent to a Caesarean section

On caesarean sections, Her Ladyship noted that all the recent decisions dealt with urgent or extreme situations, the evidence was limited in scope and the mother had not always been represented in the proceedings. In all but one of the recent cases, it had been held that the woman concerned did not have the mental capacity to make the decision.

• In *Re MB*, the evidence of the obstetrician and the consultant psychiatrist was that the patient could not bring herself to undergo the Caesarean section she desired because a panic fear of needles dominated everything and at the critical point she was not capable of making a decision at all. Consequently, it was clear that she was at the time suffering from an impairment of her mental functioning which disabled her, and was temporarily incompetent. The tests in *Re C* (above) were applied.

• Since the mother and father wanted the child to be born alive and the mother was in favour of the operation, subject only to her needle phobia, and was likely to suffer long-term danger if the child was born handicapped or dead, medical intervention in this case was in the patient's best interests, with the use of force if necessary for it to be carried out. In these circumstances the judge had been justified in granting the declaration sought.

• The court suggested that an 'irrational' decision was one which was "so outrageous that no sensible person could have arrived at it", but *panic, indecisiveness and irrationality did not necessarily amount to incompetence.* However, these factors might be evidence of incompetence and the gravity of the consequences of the decision was commensurate with the level of competence required to make the decision.

• A person would lack the capacity to make a decision if rendered unable to do so by some impairment or disturbance of mental functioning. Capacity might be eroded by shock, fatigue, confusion, pain or the effect of drugs, *but only if the ability to decide is absent as a result.* (emphasis added)

• Panic induced by fear could influence a woman's decision. However, the evidence needed to be scrutinised with great care in every case because in some circumstances the fear of surgery can be rational, but in others fear could paralyse the will entirely, thus destroying capacity. That was the position in the present case and the woman was found to be incapable of making any sort of decision.

- On the earlier cases, the Appeal Court observed that although some of them had been decided on the issue of lack of consent to Caesarean section, the mothers involved were subsequently very glad that the operation had been performed successfully. However, the Court also emphasised that however desirable a successful outcome might be, and however important it was for a child to be born alive, this consideration was *not strictly relevant*. Hence, while doctors could lawfully attempt to persuade a woman to undergo medical treatment, if that attempt proved unsuccessful there would be no further steps which could be taken, even though the mother might regret her decision if her child died or was born handicapped.
- Accordingly, the *only* situation in which medical intervention against a woman's wishes was justified was where an adult patient *lacked the capacity* to make the decision. (emphasis added)
- The Court rejected the submission that it should weigh in the balance the rights of the unborn child. Although the dicta of Lord Donaldson in *Re T (an adult) (Consent to medical intervention)* [1993] supported that submission, there were many other decisions denying any rights to the foetus "which were more persuasive". These were cases applicable by analogy for instance *C v S* [1988] and *Re F (in utero)* [1988]. In effect the foetus "up to the moment of birth did not have any separate interests capable of being taken into account when a court had to consider an application for a declaration in respect of a Caesarean section operation. The court did not have the jurisdiction to declare that such medical intervention was lawful to protect the interests of the unborn child even at the point of death."

Several important points may be derived from *Re MB*:

(i) Consent remains a necessary prerequisite to medical treatment for adult patients of legally sound mind;

(ii) Consent was, of course, eventually obtained from the patient in *Re MB* before the operation;

(iii) The interests of the unborn foetus would not normally take precedence over those of its mother unless she was incapable of making a reasoned choice regarding her medical treatment by reason of an impairment of mental functioning caused by a variety of factors of which the Court gave examples;

(iv) The unborn foetus does not have a legal status until it is born. Otherwise, an interested party could seek to obtain court orders to curtail the lifestyle of the mother or even prevent her from having a legal abortion on the basis of protecting the rights of the unborn foetus.

The Collins case (*St George's Healthcare NHS Trust v S*)

On April 25, 1996, S, a single 29-year-old woman, approximately 36 weeks pregnant but who had not sought ante natal care, was diagnosed with severe pre-eclampsia, severe oedema extending to her abdomen and proteinnuria. She was told that her condition risked the life of both herself and her unborn foetus. She was also advised that she therefore needed urgent attention, and the only treatment was medication, bedrest and admission to hospital for an induced delivery. Without this treatment her health and life and the health and life of her baby were in real danger. She fully understood the potential risks but rejected the advice. She wanted her baby to be born naturally, i.e. by natural vaginal delivery and refused to be admitted to hospital. She was seen by an approved social worker and two doctors and was compulsorily admitted under s.2 to the Mental Health Act 1983 to Springfield Hospital as the two doctors had signed the necessary written recommendations.

Section 2 to the Mental Health Act 1983 states:

> 'An application for admission for assessment may be made in respect of a patient on the grounds that (a) she is suffering from mental disorder of a nature or degree which warrants the detention of the patient in hospital for assessment (or for assessment followed by medical treatment) for at least a limited period; and (b) he ought to be so detained in the interests of his own health or safety or with a view to the protection of other persons.'

Shortly before midnight, against her will, S was transferred to St George's Hospital. She continued to refuse consent to treatment, so an application was made *ex parte* to Mrs Justice Hogg on behalf of the hospital who was told, incorrectly, that labour had commenced, that S had been in labour for 24 hours, and that her life and the life of the foetus were in danger ; that 'every minute counted and this was a matter of life and death.' In fact, S was *not* in labour at the time and had recorded her objections in an articulate letter which she wrote while at Springfield Hospital. Mrs Justice Hogg granted a declaration which dispensed with S's consent to treatment. Later that evening, medical procedures were carried out and at 10pm, S was safely delivered by Caesarean section of a baby girl. When she recovered, S developed strong feelings of revulsion towards the baby and at first rejected the child. Fortunately, she later bonded with the child and is reportedly now looking after her quite happily

S's compulsory detention under the Mental Health Act was later terminated. During the period when she was a patient, no specific treatment for mental disorder or mental illness was prescribed.

S, a veterinary nurse, appealed against an *ex parte* decision of Mr Justice Hogg sitting in Chambers on April 26, 1997, in which it had been decided that the consent of Ms S to a Caesarean section could be dispensed with. The Court of Appeal was also asked to consider granting judicial review against a social worker, Louize Collins, Pathfinder Mental Health Services Trust, and St George's Healthcare NHS Trust as Ms S had been admitted to and detained in hospital for assessment under s.2 to the Mental Health Act 1983. Judicial review was sought of the application to Hogg, J. itself, the medical procedures which culminated in the birth and her return to and treatment at Springfield Hospital.

The Court of Appeal decision

The Court (per Judge, L.J.) concluded that virtually every stage in the medical and legal procedures could be criticised. The Court's view was that even when a person's life depended upon receiving particular medical treatment, as long as that person is an adult of sound mind, he or she has the right to refuse such treatment. This view reflected the ethical principles of the autonomy of the individual and the right to self-determination, and was supported by case law. In their Lordships' opinion, although pregnancy increased the responsibilities which a woman had, it did not diminish her right to refuse medical treatment, as long as she was of sound mind. Nevertheless, the Court of Appeal thought it appropriate to consider the position of the foetus, and Lord Justice Judge stated that although an unborn child was human and was protected by law in some instances, it was not a separate person from its mother, and its need for medical treatment or assistance did not prevail over the rights of the mother. She could not, therefore, be forced to submit to treatment against her will, even if her life and that of the foetus depended upon her receiving such treatment, and even if her decision might appear to be morally repugnant.

The mother's compulsory detention under the Mental Health Act 1983

The Court took the view that the Act could not be deployed in order to detain a person, even if her thinking appeared bizarre and irrational, and contrary to that of the vast majority of people in the community. Even if compulsory detention were justified, it could only be used to force a person to have treatment for mental disorder. Any compulsory medical treatment unconnected with medical disorder was contrary to law and could not be justified, unless the patient's capacity to consent to such treatment was diminished. This was a matter which required consideration in the light of all the available evidence in each case.

Application of the Mental Health Act 1983

With regard to s.2 to the 1983 Act in the instant case, the Court of Appeal decided that the cumulative grounds for compulsory admission set out in s.2(2)(a) had not been established, and although the grounds specified in s.2(2) (b) might well have been satisfied, they had to be considered in the light of the cumulative grounds which preceded them. The compulsory admission of S to hospital was therefore unlawful. However, s.6 (3) of the Act operated to allow Springfield Hospital to escape liability for unlawfully accepting Ms S as a patient, because the documentation would have given the authorities there the impression that the application for admission had been made correctly.

Was admission to St George's Hospital's Lawful?

The admission to St George's Hospital was unlawful as was S's period of detention there. Although this was conceded by the hospital and was due to an administrative oversight, the Court of Appeal concluded that it should not be dismissed as a technicality, since the truth was that S would have been entitled to an application for habeas corpus and to her immediate release from hospital. Her admission to St George's and her subsequent detention for treatment had therefore been unlawful.

MAIN PRINCIPLES OF *COLLINS*

The Court of Appeal affirmed that

(1) a mentally competent adult woman has the right to refuse a Caesarean section even if it means that she and her unborn foetus are in danger of dying as a result of this decision.

(2) The Mental Health Act 1983 cannot be deployed to achieve the detention of an individual against her will merely because her thinking process is unusual, even apparently bizarre and irrational and contrary to the views of the overwhelming majority of the community at large. S was entitled to have the order to subject her to have surgery against her will set aside. The order to have S transferred back to Springfield Hospital and her final period of compulsory detention there was also unlawful, as was her discharge from there, which was based upon the original unlawful s.2 application.

Comments on the Collins case

(i) The *Collins* case confirms that the foetus is unprotected by law in these kinds of situations. Although the foetus is regarded as human and is protected by the law in certain ways, as described in *Re MB*, the foetus is not a being which is separate from its mother, and as such, its need for medical care and assistance cannot prevail over that of the mother. It would seem that the problem here is that it is impossible to achieve a compromise between foetal and maternal rights. The Court forced to choose between mother and foetus will now decide in favour of the autonomy of the mother. Thus the foetus which has no status in law, has no legal protection in these sorts of situations.

(ii) This approach is consistent with the law on abortion but becomes more difficult to justify the closer the foetus is to term and will logically give way to emotional response when the obstinate refusal of medical assistance by the mother means probable death or serious injury to the foetus?

(iii) The Court of Appeal stated that 'in the present case there was no conflict between the interests of the mother and the foetus: no one was faced with the awful dilemma of deciding on one form of treatment which risked one of their lives in order to save the other. Medically the procedures to be adopted to preserve the mother and her unborn child did not involve a preference for one rather than the other. The crucial issue can be identified by expressing the problem in different ways: e.g. if human life is sacred, why is a mother entitled to refuse to undergo treatment if this would preserve the life of the foetus without damaging her own?'

Postscript to the Collins case: further guidelines

After giving judgment on the *Collins* case, in a case relating to treatment without a pregnant woman's consent, the Court of Appeal received further written submissions from counsel who had taken soundings from the midwives, nursing and medical professions and from patients' organisations, and issued new guidelines superseding those given in the original judgment, in *St George's Healthcare NHS Trust v S (No.2); R. v Collins and Others ex parte S (No.2)* [1998] Fam Law 662. These were mainly pre-emptive and procedural, eg that if possible, doctors should try to prevent the situation arising where there was uncertainty about the patient's intentions over consent by seeking to clarify the presence or absence of consent.

In *Re MB*, the Court of Appeal concluded that none of the earlier cases lent support to the proposition that the court should take into account the interests of the unborn child at risk from the refusal of a competent mother to consent to medical intervention. Lady Justice Butler-Sloss therefore stated:

" The law is . . . clear that a competent woman who has the capacity to decide may, for religious reasons, other reasons, or for no reasons at all, choose not to have medical intervention, even though the consequence might be the death or serious handicap of the child she bears or her own death."

This was Her Ladyship's conclusion after a review of the earlier case law which suggested that an unborn foetus might be protected by the law both at common law and indeed by statutes such as the Offences Against the Person Act 1861 which makes it an offence to procure an abortion and the Infant (Life Preservation) Act 1929 which makes it a criminal offence for the intentional destruction of a child, capable of being born alive, before it has an existence independent of its mother.

Her Ladyship observed:

> ". . . it might seem illogical that a child capable of being born alive is protected by the criminal law from intentional destruction and by the Abortion Act from termination otherwise than as permitted by the Act, but is not protected from the (irrational) decision of a competent mother not to avert the risk of death [but] this appears to be the present state of the law."

Further points to note from Collins

- *Collins* might well be regarded as unexceptional ir view of the law on abortion but as the foetus approaches full term, the judicial comments in that case may be used to argue that it might well become more difficult to accept that the unborn foetus should receive no legal protection or indeed warrant no special consideration.
- The court in *Collins* appeared to confirm that the principle of the sanctity of human life should be subordinate to that of self-determinism or patient autonomy; that the Mental Health Act should not be used to justify admission, detention and treatment of individuals unless its conditions have been fulfilled.
- Pregnant women may not necessarily be held to be temporarily incompetent in certain circumstances, as courts have declared in previous cases but the test of competence is that laid down in *Re C (Refusal of Medical Treatment)* [1994] (comprehension and retention of the information the patient is given, believing the information and the capacity to weigh and balance the information and to make a reasoned choice).
- On the status of the unborn foetus before birth, the court also referred to *AG's Reference (No.3 of 1994)* [1997], where the House of Lords disagreed with the Court of Appeal, which had said that the foetus should be treated as an integral part of the mother in the same way as any other part of her body, such as her foot or arm. Lord Mustill regarded the mother and the foetus as two distinct

organisms living symbiotically, not a single organism with two aspects. The foetus is a unique organism and the Court of Appeal in the present case confirmed that the interests of the foetus cannot be disregarded.

CONSENT AND THE PATIENT LACKING CAPACITY

There will always be people who, for one reason or another, are *incapable* of deciding whether they should have medical treatment either because they are: (i) temporarily incompetent; or (ii) permanently incompetent through disease or trauma or as a result of mental handicap or illness; and (iii) those who have not yet reached maturity; and (iv) those suffering from dementia and (v) those who are incompetent because of mental impairment or injury. In legal parlance, such persons lack the 'capacity' to make competent decisions with regard to medical treatment.

The test of legal capacity

Broadly, this is said to be *the ability to understand the nature and purpose of the proposed care and be able to weigh the risks of that treatment* as stated by the House of Lords in *F v West Berkshire Health Authority* [1989]. Yet the leading case containing a comprehensive definition of capacity is only a first instance case from the High Court, namely, *Re C (Adult: Refusal of Treatment)* [1994] although it has also been approved by an appellate court (see *Re MB*).

To avoid being liable in battery, all the doctor needs to do is to explain the nature and purpose of the treatment in broad terms (*Chatterton v Gerson*). Once the patient is informed in broad terms of the treatment, the consent then given is 'real' in law. But the requirements are more exacting for determining whether the patient had capacity to consent, as seen in *Re C* [1994] which, as we have seen, required the patient to comprehend and retain the necessary information, believe the information and be able to weight the information, and balance the risks and needs in order to reach a decision.

Note that *Freeman v Home Office (No.2)* [1984] ruled that whether or not consent had been given by a patient was a question of fact in every case. A valid consent can also be withdrawn.

Can anyone consent on behalf of an adult lacking capacity?

The current legal position is: **No one can consent to medical treatment on behalf of an adult lacking capacity**. This is because the *parens patriae* jurisdiction of the court was revoked (inadvertently) in 1960; thus, once a patient is over the age of 18, English law has no provision for proxy consent (i.e. on behalf of a patient) where the patient is unable to consent for themselves. However, the courts may validate the actions taken by a health care professional *ex post facto*, (i.e. after the event) by means of a declaration, provided they were carried out in the patient's best interests. However, the courts can manage property issues relating to such an adult patient.

Patients who may be treated under the Mental Health Act 1983

As Margaret Brazier in *Medicine, Patients and the Law* (2003) points out, the mentally incompetent patient is in legal limbo because no one can decide on medical treatment for such persons. However, Part IV of the MHA 1983 contains some provisions dealing with persons *detained* under the Act. The Act allows treatment of such people without their consent. Such patients can be given most forms of medical treatment without their consent. But only a small percentage of patients are detained under the Act; most cases fall outside their scope.

Detention in hospital and consent

In principle, a person may remain competent notwithstanding detention under the Mental Health Act 1983 (see *Collins*, discussed above). Further, the 1983 Act cannot be used to authorise treatment of a mentally disordered person which withholds his consent unless he is detained in hospital or has first been detained and been given leave of absence under s.17. See: *R. v Hallstrom* (1986).

R. v Hallstrom [1986] High Court

This case involved two chronic paranoid schizophrenics who had been admitted to hospital several times. The Court held:

(i) There is no power under the 1983 Act to give treatment to a mentally disordered person who withholds his consent unless he is detained in hospital or has first been detained and been given leave of absence under s.17.

(ii) Unless clear statutory authority to the contrary exists, no one is to be detained in hospital or to undergo medical treatment or even to submit himself to a medical examination without his consent. This is as true of a mentally disordered person as of anyone else.

(iii) Section 3 [which lists criteria for detention for treatment] only covers those whose mental condition was believed to require a period of in-patient treatment.

(iv) It was unlawful to recall to hospital a patient on indefinite leave of absence when the intention was to prevent him from being on leave for absence for six months continuously; s.17 only empowered the medical officer to recall the patient when it was necessary for the patient's health or safety or for the protection of other persons and therefore the purported recall of the patient in this case would have been unlawful even if he had been 'liable to be detained.'

It was stated that there is a difference between being 'detained ' in a hospital and being *liable* to be detained. Someone on leave of absence from a hospital cannot be regarded as detained in a hospital. But the *Barker* Case (1998) (see below) decided subsequently by the Court of Appeal says the detention can be renewed, pursuant to s.20.

In *B v Croydon HA* [1995] a 24-year-old patient was suffering from borderline psychopathic disorder with a compulsion to self-harm. She cut and burned herself several times and was admitted to hospital for assessment where her mental disorder was diagnosed. She was later compulsorily detained and then refused to eat as a means of inflicting harm on herself and only accepted food under threat of feeding by nasogastric tube. The plaintiff 's case was that the forced feeding was unlawful. The issue here was: was tube feeding 'treatment given to her for the mental disorder'? The first instance court held that the patient's application for an injunction to restrain the force feeding could not be granted because the nasogastric feeding was treatment for the mental disorder and therefore, because of s.63, did not require her consent.

The Court of Appeal agreed, holding that the term 'medical treatment' included a wide range of acts 'ancillary to the core treatment' so that nasal feeding was a form of medical treatment designed to alleviate the symptoms of mental disorder and therefore fell within the scope of s.63. The refusal of food and drink was the product of the patient's mental disorder and so the tube feeding could be seen as treating her mental condition which was therefore lawful and legally permissible even without the patient's consent. Relieving symptoms is just as much a part of treatment as relieving the underlying cause.

Widening the scope of 'medical treatment'?

This case appears to widen the range of procedures which may be administered without the patient's consent. The first instance court found that the patient did have the capacity to refuse medical treatment, but the Court of Appeal questioned this. It was accepted that because of the patient's condition, it would not have been lawful to detain her unless her condition was treatable. However, not every act could be said to form part of the treatment as defined under s.145(1) (whereunder 'medical treatment' includes nursing . . . care, habilitation and rehabilitation under medical supervision'). In practical terms, some form of restraint might foreseeably be exercised in order to keep a disruptive patient quiet and make life more peaceful for the other patients within proximity. Yet, if the patient in this case was able to object to the nasal feeding, she might well have possessed sufficient capacity to refuse medical treatment but the whole point of patients who are compulsorily detained under the Act is that their consent is dispensed with and this wide definition of treatment appears to justify non-consensual treatment which does not alleviate the mental disorder of the patient. The Code of Practice (para.15.4) strongly suggests that despite s.63, the consent of the patient to treatment for the mental disorder should at least be sought in the first instance.

We have already considered the *Tameside* case where 'treatment' was given a wide meaning in circumstances where the court believed that a statutory justification was required in order to override a refusal of consent in order to save the life of the mother and the unborn foetus.

Does a Caesarean section constitute 'medical treatment' for mental disorder?

The Tameside case (Tameside & Glossop Acute Services v CH [1996])

The court in *Tameside* held that the Caesarean section performed on a schizophrenic pregnant patient could be 'treatment' of her mental disorder within the meaning of s.63 to the Mental Health Act 1983. This is a somewhat curious decision in terms of the court's usage of s.63 not least because the Code of Practice advises that treatment for physical disorder cannot be given under this section unless 'it can reasonably be said that the physical disorder is a symptom or underlying cause of the mental disorder'. *Tameside* falls outside this situation because it could not be said that the woman's pregnancy was a 'symptom or underlying cause' of her schizophrenia.

However, the woman's doctor presented the court with a stark choice, as Bartlett and Sandland (2000) put it: 'between a psychotic patient and a dead child on the one hand and a mentally healthy mother and child on the other.' (Bartlett and Sandland *Mental Health Law: Policy and Practice* (2000)). Consequently, the judge preferred the second option and adopted the 'holistic' approach of the *Croydon* case (see *B v Croydon HA* [1995] discussed below under Detention and Consent) so that he could argue that if the proposed treatment was administered (which was the caesarean section), it would be beneficial to the mental health of the patient. The court said that it would not be stretching language to say that 'achievement of a successful outcome of the pregnancy is a necessary part of the overall treatment of her mental disorder'. Consequently, Wall, J held that the treatment fell within s.63.

In Re Barker (1998) Court of Appeal

This case disapproved of the interpretation of the court in the *Hallstrom* case with regard to the possible meaning of 'detained' under the Mental Health Act.

The Court of Appeal held (*inter alia*) that:

A patient who was detained under section 3 of the Mental Health Act 1983 could have her detention renewed pursuant to section 20 of the MHA even though, at the time of renewal, she had been granted lengthy leave of absence from the hospital where she was detained and only returned periodically for her progress to be monitored.

In an emergency, medical staff may rely on a defence of necessity. What is the situation where a patient suffers from a disability which renders them permanently incapable of giving consent?

The legal basis for discussing this issue is *T v T* [1988], wherein Wood, J. held that doctors could lawfully proceed with an abortion and sterilisation of a severely handicapped 19 year old girl. As he put it "In these exceptional circumstances where there is no provision in law for consent to be given and, therefore, no one can give consent, and where the patient is suffering from such mental abnormality as never to be able to give such consent, a medical practitioner is justified in taking such steps as good medical practice demands."

Barker was approved and followed in *F v West Berkshire HA* [1989] which disapproved of the *Wilson v Pringle* 'hostile intent' test, (see *Wilson v Pringle* [1987] which held that battery could only be established if there was 'hostile intent' on the part of the defendant).

In the case of abortions, there is no need for a declaration from the court: Re *SG* (*Adult mental patient: Abortion*) [1991]. It was stated by the court here that regulation by the Abortion Act 1967 provided adequate safeguards; however, this is at least questionable as far as this incapacitated adult patient was concerned.

For sterilisations, court approval is usually required (see ch. seven) For abortions, one might have thought court approval should normally be required as well but Re *SG* (above) suggests otherwise.

Other cases

Re H (mental patient: diagnosis) [1993]

The court in this case ruled on an application as to whether relatively intrusive diagnosis procedures could be performed on an incapacitated patient, on the basis of *F v West Berkshire* (1989) and held that it could, as long as treatment was in the patient's 'best interests'.

Re GF [1992]

The woman suffered from severe menstrual bleeding. A hysterectomy was performed with the court saying there was no need for a declaration as it was a 'therapeutic' sterilisation.

Return of the therapeutic/non-therapeutic distinction?

As Stauch et al (2002) point out, the provisions of the Abortion Act 1967 are not an adequate safeguard for a mentally incapacitated woman. They argue "There is something highly distasteful about forcing [an incompetent woman] to submit to an abortion". Ironically, the very therapeutic/non-therapeutic distinction so summarily dismissed by Lord Hailsham in *Re B* (the Jeanette case) on the basis that the patient would not be able to understand the nature of the sterilisation, has now been resurrected to justify invasive treatment, either on the basis that it was purely to deal with menstruation problems or to authorise an abortion because it is now seen as 'therapeutic'. There has to be the same safeguards for an abortion as exists for a proposed sterilisation.

Re S -Court of Appeal did not authorise hysterectomy

In *Re S* (2000), the Court of Appeal did not authorise an operation that was invasive—a hysterectomy—on a mentally incompetent 28-year-old woman; an intra-uterine device was preferred as less invasive. The position seems to be that non-invasive contraception would be the preferred option rather than surgery such as hysterectomy. However, if contraception proves unsuccessful, the question of abortion would become a serious alternative and this is not necessarily adequately safeguarded under the Abortion Act 1967. In future cases, the courts might take the view that an abortion would have to be the last resort or the only option (as opposed to a less invasive procedure such as insertion of an intra-uterine device) before an English court would approve it for a mentally incapable woman.

Court's supervisory jurisdiction over incapable adults at risk of harm: can the doctrine of necessity co-exist with the statutory regime?

The leading case in the area is *Bournewood* (*R. v Bournewood Community and Mental Health NHS Trust ex parte L*) [2005] which involved L, a profoundly retarded 48-year-old autistic man unable to speak. He was never capable of consenting to medical treatment, did not possess a sense of danger, with a history of self-harming behaviour. In 1994, he was discharged from the hospital in which he had lived for over 30 years, and went to stay with paid carers, Mr and Mrs E. L was not finally discharged from hospital and the relevant Trust remained responsible for his care and treatment. He attended a day centre. In July 1997, while at the day centre, he became agitated and began to harm himself, hitting his head and banging it against the wall. The carers could not be contacted, and he was sedated and taken to hospital. The consultant considered that he should be admitted as an in-patient, and, since he appeared to be compliant, he was admitted informally (not compulsorily) under s.131 to the Mental Health Act 1983.

The carers began proceedings in L's name against the Trust for judicial review of the decision to detain him, a writ of *habeas corpus*, and damages for false imprisonment and assault. Although dismissed at first instance, the Court of Appeal upheld the claims.

The Trust appealed to the House of Lords and in the meantime, the Trust committed L compulsorily under s.3 to the 1983 Act. In November 1997, L applied for discharge from the hospital, and he was discharged in December 1997.

The House of Lords *allowed* the Trust's appeal and held:

1. Patients admitted under s.131 may be classed as either voluntary patients if they have capacity to consent and give their consent to admission; or as informal patients who, though lacking capacity to consent, do not object to admission.
2. The treatment and care of such informal patients who lack the capacity to consent can be justified on the basis of the common law doctrine of necessity.
3. The re-admission of L to the hospital did not constitute the tort of false imprisonment because he was not kept in a locked ward and, since he had made no attempt to leave, he had not actually been deprived of his liberty.
4. All the steps taken had in fact been taken in the best interests of L and in so far as they might otherwise have constituted an invasion of his civil rights, had been justified on the basis of the common law doctrine of necessity.

Lords Nolan and Steyn considered that L had been 'detained' but regarded such detention as justifiable under the doctrine of necessity. However, Lord Steyn drew attention to the consequences of their decision. The main problem was that the decision left compliant incapacitated patients without the safeguards enshrined in the Mental Health Act 1983.

The case went on *appeal* to the European Court of Human Rights in October 2004 which *overruled* the House of Lords on the basis of a breach of Human Rights. (**see below**).

Effect of the earlier House of Lords judgment

This case was seen as exposing the failure of the mental health system to protect some of the most vulnerable members of society. At present, compulsorily detained patients' cases are reviewed by Mental Health Review Tribunals. The effect of the judgment is that mentally incapacitated patients can be treated when they lack capacity without the protection of review by an independent body which is afforded to compulsorily detained patients. The Mental Health Commission, which has responsibility for the oversight of the care of patients in hospitals, gave evidence that on any given day there would be 22,000 patients in hospital in the same position as Mr L. During a year a further 48,000 persons could expect to be admitted. The consequences for Mental Health Trusts in having to assess every patient, was seen by some as heralding an administrative nightmare. (*but see now the European Court decision, below*)

Bournewood followed by Court of Appeal in *Re F*

In *Re F (Adult: Court's jurisdiction)* (2000), decided by the Court of Appeal in June 2000, the principle was affirmed that the court has jurisdiction to supervise an incapable adult who is at risk of harm on the basis of the doctrine of necessity, which had been laid down in the *Bournewood* Court of Appeal decision.

Bournewood Lords' decision overruled by the European Court of Human Rights

Following the House of Lords' judgment, L and his carers applied to the European Court of Human Rights (ECHR) alleging a violation of Art.5 on the basis that L had *not* been lawfully detained in accordance with the requirements of Art.5(1) and (4): detention on grounds of unsoundness of mind and limited opportunities to challenge the detention before the courts, respectively.

Both these submissions were accepted by the European Court of Human Rights which ruled:

- The informal admission of a compliant adult patient who lacked capacity to decide about his psychiatric care, constituted an arbitrary detention that fell foul of Art.5(1).
- The absence of effective legal procedures to review such informal detentions was in breach of Art.5(4).

- The detention of this particular patient was not in accordance with the procedure prescribed by law.
- The doctrine of necessity was insufficiently precise in its scope to prevent arbitrary application of its criteria.

COMMENT

Despite this judgment, which overturns the House of Lords' ruling, the Department of Health issued a statement after the ruling that the judgment did not automatically mean that it was unlawful to admit incapacitated patients to hospital for mental health care informally. Nor did it mean that such patients must invariably be admitted under the Mental Health Act. It declared further that the breach of Art.5(4) had now been addressed by the Human Rights Act 1998, which had come into force on October 2000, after the House of Lords' judgment, before the European Court decision had been made.

Meaning of non-consensual treatment under the Mental Health Act broadened by House of Lords-The Ashworth Case

Section 63 of the Mental Health Act 1983 Act deals with the treatment of compulsory patients in hospital:

> "The consent of a patient shall not be required for any medical treatment given to him for the mental disorder from which he is suffering, not being treatment falling within section 57 or section 58 above, if the treatment is given by or under the direction of the responsible medical officer."

The Ashworth Case (2005)

The patient was convicted of manslaughter in 1987. At the time of his offence he was acutely mentally ill with symptoms of a psychotic illness. The court made a hospital order with a restriction order of indefinite duration under the 1983 Act and he was classified in the order as suffering from mental illness, namely schizophrenia. The doctors also noted features of personality disorder and he was later transferred to a ward to address the traits of personality disorder. This was different in a number of respects from the regime of wards designed to treat mental illnesses. A Mental Health Review Tribunal later concluded that he was still suffering from a 'schizo-affective disorder' (a mental illness) but did not, however, reclassify him to show both mental illness and psychopathic disorder. In August 2001, his solicitors contacted the hospital arguing that he should never have been transferred to a ward for patients with psychopathic disorder. The hospital's response was that, his mental illness having been successfully controlled by medication which he continued to take, the current ward was appropriate to address the remaining problems of his personality type. Judicial review proceedings were started early in 2002, seeking an order to quash the decision to place him on the ward, a declaration that the placement was unlawful, and a declaration that his treatment for personality disordered behaviour was unlawful. That claim was dismissed by Sir Richard Tucker in July 2002 but his appeal was allowed by the Court of Appeal, which made the following declaration (see *R (B) v Ashworth Hospital Authority* [2003] 1 WLR 1886):

> "The treatment without consent of the claimant for a psychopathic disorder is unlawful unless and until the claimant is classified as suffering from such disorder by the Mental Health Review Tribunal under section 72(5) of the Mental Health Act 1983."

The Hospital appealed to the House of Lords.

Baroness Hale observed: "The issue for us is whether. . . the only treatment which [such patients] may be given without their consent under section 63 is treatment for the particular form or forms of mental disorder from which they are recorded as suffering in the application, order or direction under which they are detained. There are a great many reasons for thinking that section 63 is not so limited." The learned judge held that the words of section 63 "authorise a patient to be treated for *any* mental disorder from which he is suffering, *irrespective of whether this falls within the form of disorder from which he is classified as suffering in the application, order or direction justifying his detention.*" (emphasis added).

The earlier Court of Appeal decision in *Ashworth* (2003) was *overruled* by the House of Lords.

COMMENT

This decision suggests that the House of Lords has now broadened the scope of s.63 so that a compulsory patient can be treated for any mental disorder from which he is suffering, *irrespective of whether this falls within the form of disorder from* which he was originally classified as suffering in the application order or direction justifying his detention. Thus, while compulsory patients are a vulnerable group who deserve protection from being forced to accept inappropriate treatment, restricting their treatment to that which is designed for their originally 'classified' disorder was considered by the Law Lords to be so haphazard as to be 'scarcely any protection at all.'

Principle of necessity used by courts to safeguard mentally incapacitated patients

The general principle currently adopted by the courts is that if an adult patient lacks the capacity to consent and no one can strictly consent on her behalf, it is still possible, by invoking the doctrine of necessity and the best interests of the patient approach, to exercise supervisory control over such a patient on a day-to-day basis, to safeguard that patient's welfare, care and protection. (and see comments in the *Bournewood* case in the House of Lords, above).

2. CHILDREN AND MEDICAL LAW

The medical treatment of children will often be decided by their parents and carers but, as with adults, it should be carried out according to the professional standards which would be supported by a responsible body of medical opinion, in accordance with the *Bolam* principle, as currently interpreted, although a particular procedure might be challenged if it is not necessarily 'logical' (*Bolitho*). The courts have consistently ruled that a child's treatment should always be in the 'best interests' of the child. This is a concept that takes its content from the nature of the cases it governs. A 'child' or 'minor' in English law, refers to a person who has been born and under 18 years of age. In English law, children are regarded as coming within the category of those who are legally incompetent to give consent, being unable, at least in the early years of their life, to decide on what medical treatment they should have, until they reach 15. The guiding principle for older children under 16, since 1985, has been the so-called *Gillick* principle, (after *Gillick v Wisbech &*

West Norfolk AHA (1985) House of Lords) whereby a minor of 'sufficient age and understanding' (a phrase open to interpretation) is prima facie, entitled to make her own decisions and give valid consent in relation to medical treatment. This is reflected in various provisions of the English Children Act 1989, in force since October 14, 1991. One basic principle is that the consent of a child who is 16 is (generally) effective under s.8 of the Family Law Reform Act 1969.

However, there are several difficulties associated with child patients:

(i)   very young or younger children cannot usually decide on their medical treatment for themselves, i.e. they cannot exercise autonomous choice (because of their level of comprehension) or give their consent, so parents or their caretakers would usually have to decide for them, giving proxy consent especially when children are very young.

(ii) 'consent' as a pragmatic and legal concept presents special issues, particularly for older child patients;

(iii) how does one delimit the scope of parental choice and parental opinion?

(iv) whose consent should be effective where there is disagreement over what is in the child's best interests: the parents', the courts, the local authority if the child is in care, or the 'mature' child who claims to be 'Gillick competent'?

(v)   Despite s.8 of the Family Law Reform Act 1969, case law suggests that a child's refusal of consent may sometimes be overridden, even if she is aged 16 or 17. Is this ethically justifiable?

Functions of consent

Lord Donaldson in *Re W* (1992) appeared to identify two functions of consent:

(i) the legal function: to provide a justification for care.

(ii) The clinical function: to secure the patient's trust and co-operation.

Without such consent, the crime of battery would be committed on the child and healthcare professionals who touch their patient unlawfully would also be liable in tort for trespass to the person.

When can a child consent?

Legally, a child is a person who has been born (as opposed to a foetus *in utero*) but under the age of 18, yet under s.8 of the Family Law Reform Act 1969, consent to treatment of a child aged 16 is as effective as if she or he were an adult, 'Treatment' includes diagnosis and procedures such as the administration of anaesthetics which are ancillary to treatment (see the *Gillick* case and *Gillick*-based statutory provisions in the Children Act 1989). Caselaw in the mid-1980s and 1990s has established the concept of '*Gillick* competence': a level of maturity, as ascertained by a court, which is possessed by a child 'of sufficient age and understanding' to make its own decisions. Lord Donaldson, MR in *Re W* mentioned the 'flak jacket' of consent to protect healthcare professionals from any liability for assault or battery.

Gillick v West Norfolk and Wisbech AHA and the DHSS (1985), the *cause celebre* of children cases in the 1980s, was seen as heralding a new era in children's rights, and hailed as a landmark case in delineating some parameters of a parent's responsibility. It has led to statutory recognition of a child's right to refuse consent to a medical assessment or examination, in the Children Act 1989.

THE *GILLICK* CASE

A 1980 DHSS guidance (memorandum) stated that although parents should normally be involved in cases of children under 16, in 'exceptional cases', it was for a doctor to prescribe contraception without informing the parents of that child's request for contraceptive advice or treatment. Mrs Gillick had several daughters under that age and sought a declaration that that the guidance gave unlawful advice which adversely affected parental rights and duties. She lost the first hearing in the High Court, then won a unanimous decision in the Court of Appeal, but ultimately lost 3:2 in the House of Lords, the highest appellate court in Britain.

Lord Fraser formulated five criteria (based on the original DHSS memorandum) for doctors contemplating whether to provide such an under age girl with contraceptive advice and treatment without reference to her parents. He stressed that the doctor should always seek to persuade the girl to tell her parents or to agree to the doctor informing her parents. However, if the girl still refused to agree to either of these suggestions, the doctor could give advice and treatment provided, in the doctor's opinion, the following conditions were satisfied:

(i) the girl understood the advice;
(ii) the doctor could not persuade her to inform her parents or to allow the doctor to inform her parents that she was seeking contraceptive advice;
(iii) she was very likely to begin or to continue having sexual intercourse with or without contraceptive treatment;
(iv) unless she received contraceptive advice or treatment her physical or mental health or both were likely to suffer; and
(v) that it was in the best interests of the child for the doctor to give her contraceptive advice and treatment or both without parental consent.

Confidentiality should be respected, provided the five conditions have been satisfied

Put another way, the doctor would be expected to preserve the confidentiality of the consultation provided the preceding conditions were satisfied; conversely, if these conditions were not fulfilled, the doctor (it could be argued) would be entitled to breach the duty of confidentiality and inform the parents.

Level of understanding required

Under condition (i) there is some scope for interpreting the level of understanding but how deep should the understanding be? Should it cover psychological and emotional implications of the treatment? Should she be able to understand the impact on the family? Lord Scarman's judgment provides some indication of the answers to these queries. He spoke of the parental right to determine medical treatment terminating when the child below the age of 16 achieved 'sufficient understanding and intelligence' to be able to understand fully what was being proposed. He also expected the girl to understand: moral and family questions relating to the treatment especially the girl's relationship with her parents; long term problems associated with the impact of a pregnancy and its termination; risks to health of sexual intercourse at her age. This appears to require an extremely deep and perceptive understanding of the consequences of the proposed [contraceptive] treatment, which is arguably more demanding than that possessed by most adults who decide to decide to use contraception.

Lords Templeman and Brandon dissented from the majority judicial opinion and Lord Templeman memorably said "There are many things a girl under 16 needs to practise but sex is not one of them."

'Gillick' provisions in the Children Act 1989

Several provisions have been included in the Children Act 1989 which are a clear recognition of the *Gillick* principle. The provisions are:

s.43(8); 44(7): which give the child the right to refuse to submit to medical assessment or examination;
s.39: whereby the child may apply for discharge of care orders;
s.45(8): gives the child the right to challenge Emergency Protection Orders
s.10(8): gives the child the right to apply to court for leave to apply for a s.8 order dealing with specific issues.
In the aftermath of the *Gillick* case, some commentators believed that the case was a harbinger of children's rights but in the 1990s, (see the post-*Gillick* cases) the courts ruled in a number of cases that a child's refusal of consent could be overridden by the courts in certain circumstances and this applies even to those girls aged 16 as well. In medico-legal terms, a strong tendency towards judicial paternalism was emerging which has continued to manifest itself in the 1990s and in the early 21st century.

Post-Gillick cases

Re W (1992)- Child of 16 does not have absolute right to veto her medical treatment

W, an anorexic 16-year-old wished to remain in the specialist adolescent unit rather than move to a clinic specialising in eating disorders. Lord Donaldson, MR said that s.8 of the Law Reform Act 1969 'conclusively presumed' that a 16 or 17-year-old was competent but the section did not confer an absolute right on a child to refuse treatment. Thus, the presumption could be rebutted if a child, although 16 or 17, suffered from a mental disability which affected her understanding and capacity to give a valid consent to surgical, medical or dental treatment decisions. In view of the deterioration in W's condition and the likelihood of suffering permanent damage to her brain and reproductive organs, 'the point had been clearly reached when the court should be prepared, in W's own interests, to overrule her refusal to consent to treatment'. The court ordered that she be treated by the appropriate hospital.

Thus, the Court held that neither s.8 nor the *Gillick* principle gave the child of 16 an absolute right to veto medical treatment. Hence, where the 16-year-old child was seen to be suffering from a mental illness which affected her ability to give a valid consent, the court could overrule the child's wishes. However, the Court also held that a 16-year-old minor's consent cannot be overridden even by those with parental responsibility for the minor (see *Re P* (1982) where the court allowed a 15-year-old girl, who already had a baby, to have a termination despite her parents' objections). Again, a *Gillick* competent minor (i.e. who might be under-age but found to possess the necessary maturity and understanding) also has a right to consent to medical treatment which cannot be overridden by those with parental responsibility. However, this consent can also be overridden by the court.

Somewhat confusingly, the Court of Appeal also said that despite having the right to consent, the child had no right to refuse treatment and that both its parents and the court can override even a competent child's refusal of treatment.

Legal Position after Re W

Hence, the legal position, after *Re W*, seems to be that:

- Children aged 16 have the statutory right to consent to surgical, medical or dental treatment by virtue of s.8 of the Law Reform Act 1969. Such consent cannot be overridden by those with parental responsibility for the minor but it can be overridden by the court. The statutory right does not extend to consent to the donation of blood or organs.
- Consent to treatment of a minor is analogous to a legal 'flak jacket' which protects a doctor from litigation for trespass to the person (battery) regardless of whether

consent has been obtained from a minor over 16, or a 'Gillick competent' child under that age or from another person having responsibilities including a right to consent to treatment of the minor (i.e. usually a parent or someone with parental responsibility).

- A practitioner will be liable to a minor of any age in negligence if he fails to advise with reasonable skill and care and to have due regard to the best interests of his patient.
- No minor of whatever age can refuse consent to treatment when consent has been given by someone with parental responsibility or a court. In other words, both parents and the courts can override a minor's refusal to consent in certain circumstances, even where the minor is competent to make such a refusal of consent. Nevertheless, such a refusal is a very important consideration in making a clinical judgment and for parents and the court in deciding whether themselves to give consent.

The Court's approach seems to seek to protect such children from doing (potentially life-threatening) harm to themselves especially if this results in death or permanent damage.

Re K, W and H (1993)

Three adolescents had been admitted to a specialist adolescent unit because of their highly disturbed behaviour and each had been making commendable progress since admission. They complained about the treatment they had received at the unit but only one complaint related to the medication (tranquillising drugs). Children were only admitted to the unit if their parents or the local authority having care of them consented in writing to the regime adopted by the unit, including the emergency use of medication. The committee's report recommended that in cases where there was doubt about a child patient's consent, the hospital was advised to seek s.8 orders under the Children Act 1989, if there was doubt as to a child's patient's consent. In all three cases, there had been full parental co-operation and consent to the treatment regime.

Thorpe, J. held:

(i) The applications under section 8 to the Children Act 1989 were misconceived and unnecessary. The decision of the Court of Appeal in *Re R* [1991] made it plain that a child of *Gillick* competence could consent to treatment but that if he or she declines to do so, consent can be given by someone else who has parental rights or responsibilities.

(ii) Where more than one person has power to consent, only a refusal of all the parties who have that power will create a veto.

(iii) None of the three children in this case were *Gillick* competent. Even if they had been, it was evident that their refusal of consent would not have exposed the doctor at the unit to the risk of civil or criminal proceedings if he had proceeded to administer medication in an emergency and in the face of such refusal since in each instance he had parental consent.

South Glamorgan CC v W and B (1993)—*Court can override child's objections by invoking its inherent jurisdiction*

A 15-year-old girl suffered from severe psychiatric disturbance since she was seven. She had received virtually no schooling since the age of 11, had been seen by five child psychiatrists and been the subject of 22 court appearances. She was approaching the end of her first year as a recluse in a room in her home. She was verbally abusive to her family and effectively controlled them, dictating who could enter her room or cook her meals, and threatening suicide or harm to herself if they failed to comply with her demands. Psychiatric advice recommended that she be removed to an adolescent unit, where she had previously received psychiatric assessment and treatment, as she was clearly beyond control but there was no attempt to place her in care until a psychiatrist stated that her behaviour was likely to 'seriously impair her mental health in the future and limit her ability to function reasonably'. The local authority applied for care proceedings, asking for the court's consent to assessment and treatment and removal from her home. Her mother supported the application but her father did not.

Douglas Brown, J. held that the court should give leave to the local authority to do what they requested. He was not prepared to recommend secure accommodation for the girl but noted that although the girl was not going to a secure unit, a doctor's report suggested that the hospital authorities would not let the girl leave unaccompanied. It was therefore imperative that the court give clear permission for this to be enforced. The court could override the child's objections by invoking its inherent jurisdiction.

Court has powers for compulsory detention for feeding if necessary

Re C (Detention: Medical Treatment) (1997)

An anorexic 16-year-old girl had a history of persistent absconding; she refused to eat to the extent that her weight became dangerously low. The court authorised detention for feeding although she had refused this treatment. It needs to be pointed out that although this case made the headlines because of the compulsory detention element, Wall, J., stressed that it was unlikely that detention would in fact be enforced but confirmed that this was within the court's powers if necessary. (See de Cruz (1999) 62 Mod LR 595 for a detailed account of this case.)

Re L (Medical Treatment: Gillick Competence) [1998] Fam Law 591

A 14-year-old girl accidentally suffered very serious burns. She needed a blood transfusion to save her life and without it a horrible death would have ensued. The girl was a staunch Jehovah's Witness who had signed a 'no blood card' in which she expressed her wish not to receive a transfusion if she suffered injury. The surgeon had not given her full details of the horrible consequences of failure to receive treatment on the ground that it would have been too distressing to her. The NHS Trust applied for a declaration that surgical intervention including blood transfusion was lawful.

Sir Stephen Brown, P held that (i) the girl was not *Gillick* competent in respect of the proposed treatment. She had led a sheltered life in the context of her family and their religious community. Her limited experience of life necessarily limited her understanding of matters as grave as her situation. It had been appropriate to withhold from her details of the likely manner of death which would have been necessary to the making of the decision; (ii) The proposed treatment was not only in her best interests but vital to her survival. The court also said that treatment would also have been declared to have been lawful even if the patient had been found to be *Gillick* competent.

Comments on Re L

- it suggests that the determination of *Gillick* competence does not depend simply on the cognitive powers and maturity of the child in question but also on the seriousness of the decision to be taken.
- the court appears to have followed the Lord Donaldson, MR line of argument in *Re R*, that the court can override the '*Gillick* competent' child's refusal to receive treatment which is in her best interests.

The court followed previous decisions such as *Re E (A Minor) (Wardship: Medical Treatment)* (1993) and *Re S (A Minor) (Consent to medical Treatment)* (1994), where Jehovah's Witness adolescents aged 15 were held not to be *Gillick* competent. Both these cases are notable for the courts emphasising that the children there were unable to appreciate the consequences of not receiving the proposed treatment.

Child's refusal of treatment can be overridden in heart transplant case

Re M (A Minor) (Medical Treatment) (1999) The Heart Transplant Case

In 1999, a High Court judge ordered that an afflicted teenager be treated, despite her refusal of treatment. The patient, M, aged fifteen and a half, had been perfectly fit and well until about three months previously, in May, when she developed heart failure. Her condition deteriorated and by June 29, 1999, her doctors' opinion was that the only medical option possible was a heart transplant within the next few days otherwise her condition would deteriorate to the extent that she would not have been well enough to undergo the operation. The situation now was that she had only about a week to live. Her parents had already consented for her to undergo a heart transplant operation. On learning that her only chance of survival was the operation to which they had agreed, M refused her consent. M stated that "she would rather die than have the transplant and have someone else's heart" and that she did not wish to take medication for the rest of her life. She said that she did not wish to die but that the idea of being different from other people and living with someone else's heart made her feel very depressed.

Mr Justice Johnson insisted that M should speak to a solicitor to explain her views. The Official Solicitor believed that M was too overwhelmed at the discovery of her fatal illness and the seriousness of her situation to make an informed decision. He recommended that the surgery should take place and the judge accepted this recommendation on the basis that the surgeons should act in accordance with their clinical judgment. Mr Justice Johnson considered that the "imposition of a heart transplant on a young woman who objected seemed to be very serious." However, he also held: (i) The power to override M's refusal was undoubted; (ii) The court was very conscious of the great gravity of the decision which it was being asked to make in overriding M's wishes. (iii) Nevertheless, whatever the risks, both in short and long term of authorising the operation against M's wishes, such risks had to be matched against the certainty of M's death if the operation was not carried out; (iv) Consequently, it seemed to the court that seeking to achieve what was best for M required, on balance, for the court to give authority for the operation.

English courts paternalistic when dealing with teenagers with life-threatening conditions

The English courts thus continue to adopt a paternalistic approach when it comes to teenagers who are either afflicted with cyclical psychotic illness or are in danger of imminent death, as with anorexia or because of serious heart problems that could ensue when no food has been consumed for a certain length of time. There does not appear to be a 'right to die' as far as these teenagers are concerned but the courts rationalise their decisions on the basis of acting in the 'best interests' of the children concerned, which, incidentally, is the same rationale for authorising sterilisations of mentally incapacitated adults or teenagers. In potentially life-threatening situations, there is also no autonomous 'right to refuse' treatment for the older child, despite the *Gillick* principle, because the courts have held that even a *Gillick* competent child can have his or her refusal to consent overridden (by courts and parents) if the court believes that this approach would better protect the child and certainly, on the facts of the cases themselves, to preserve those children's lives.

When is no consent needed?

Cases of 'necessity' have been identified as exceptional. Lord Templeman (in *Gillick*) mentioned cases of urgency, abandonment and child abuse cases where it would presumably be necessary to proceed without consent. Apart from cases where death may be imminent without treatment, there is some uncertainty in knowing when to proceed without consent. It might be justifiable to do so pending taking further action such as contacting social services. On blood transfusion cases, the courts have so far not seen fit to abide by the wishes of teenagers who have refused consent when the possible outcome of complying with those wishes might be imminent death: see, e.g., *Re E (a minor)* (1993) where Ward, J. was prepared to override the refusal by the 15-year-old boy's parents who were devout Jehovah's Witnesses, and sanction a life-saving transfusion where the boy was suffering from leukaemia.

The general position

When presented with a child of 16, the health professional may presume capacity to consent to treatment, but this may be rebutted if the child is then found to be not in fact competent under the law; (under the *Re C* (1993) tests, which require comprehension, retention and belief in the information being given as well as the ability to weight the pros and cons of treatment). For children under 16, if it involves something other than treatment, then an assessment of the child's maturity must be undertaken but it remains unclear what the criteria might be. As far as the Court of Appeal is concerned, the 'best interests test' will be cited, as interpreted, to justify the court's opinion and the court remains the ultimate arbiter: see e.g. *Re P* (1992).

Parental consent

In order to deal with this aspect of consent, it is necessary to ask: who is a parent? Under the current law, it is any person with 'parental responsibility' (PR): s.3(1) Children Act 1989 (CA). In addition:

(i) married parents and all mothers have PR 'automatically';
(ii) unmarried fathers do not have PR automatically; they have to make an application under s.4 of the Children Act 1989. Alternatively, they may enter into a Parental Responsibility Agreement with the child's mother or may make an application to court that the child reside with the unmarried father: s.12(1): CA 1989; or they will have PR if

the birth of their child has been registered jointly with the mother and the birth took place after December 1, 2003: s.4: CA 1989, as amended by the Adoption and Children Act 2002.

(iii) In addition, if a person has care of a child (i.e. the physical care) but no PR, it is permissible to do what is 'reasonable in all the circumstances of the case for the purpose of safeguarding or promoting the welfare of the child.' : s.3(5): CA 1989 (e.g. foster parents)

Under s.12(2): CA 1989 a person acquires PR for the duration of the residence order. Note that under s.1(1): CA, the general rule is that the child's welfare is the paramount consideration in any matters involving the child's welfare and upbringing.

What if parents disagree amongst themselves?

Under s.2(7) to the Children Act 1989, one parent can act independently of the other, but is it safe to assume that a 'responsible body of medical opinion' (under the *Bolam* test) would support a hospital acting without consulting both parents, if they were both available but in dispute? The matter is unresolved. Under the law, doctors can probably proceed on the basis of one parent's consent or the mature child's consent but the problem would arise if the doctor's disregard of a child's refusal was something no responsible practitioner would have disregarded, as judged by experts in the medical profession, i.e. following *Bolam*.

Under the wardship jurisdiction it is possible to make a child a ward of court; once a wardship order is made and remains in force, nothing can be done unless the court gives its consent to major matters affecting the child such as education, health and immigration. (see, below, distinction between wardship and inherent jurisdiction)

What if parents disagree with an older child?

According to the *Gillick* case (1985) and comments from Lord Scarman, parents lose the right to consent on their child's behalf once s/he becomes *Gillick* competent. Lord Donaldson did not agree with this in *Re R* [1991] which was a Court of Appeal decision involving a cyclically psychotic child whose medication was causing her nausea. The question arose as to whether she was '*Gillick* competent'. Lord Donaldson in *Re W* opined that parents do not lose the right to consent on behalf of their child when their child becomes competent to make a decision. This meant that doctors could get the consent they needed from either the child or the parents. Under s.2(7) to the Children Act 1989, it would appear that either of the parents could consent to authorise the treatment, provided they were both in agreement that treatment should proceed, unless it was an emergency and one parent could not be located in time. A court order declaring that one parent objected to certain medical treatment would have to be respected except in cases of necessity.

The limits of parental consent under Criminal law

Under s.1 Children and Young Persons Act 1933, there is criminal liability for cruelty to persons under 16 which includes assault, neglect, ill-treatment, abandonment, and exposure of the child to unnecessary suffering or injury to health.

Parental consent and medical treatment of their children

Parental refusal of consent and the child of an HIV positive mother

Re C (HIV test) (2000)

The case arose when the baby's physician became aware not only that the mother (who had tested positive in 1990) was breastfeeding the child (despite the risk of transmission of HIV), but that the parents refused even to have their daughter tested for the virus, placing their faith in their healthy lifestyle as the optimal treatment even if the child tested HIV-positive. At the age of almost five months, it was considered that the baby had already been exposed to a 20 to 25 per cent risk of having contracted the HIV virus, breastfeeding having contributed to this level of risk.

The local authority, supported by the official Solicitor acting as the baby's guardian ad litem applied for a specific issue order under the Children Act 1989 that the four-month-old baby born to this HIV positive mother be tested for HIV. Both parents objected. The order was granted by Wilson, J., who declared that testing should take place, ruling that:

  i) The arguments for overriding the wishes of the parents and testing the baby were overwhelming.

ii) If the test was conducted and was positive, firm professional advice could be given to which afflicted baby was entitled.

iii) If the parents rejected that advice, the court might well order monitoring including further testing and, if the baby went into decline, combination therapy.

iv) If the test was negative, the urgent question would then arise of whether breastfeeding should cease. His Lordship said that as good parents they owed it to the baby radically to reconsider their stance on breastfeedings if any test proved negative. However, the court would not order the mother to stop breastfeeding. 'The law could not come between the baby and the breast.'

The parents appealed, contending that the judge should not have criticised their views as to the inadequacy of the orthodox approach to treatment for HIV without evaluating those views and also evaluating the impact upon the parents and the baby, of any imposed decision.

The English Court of Appeal had to consider the reasonableness or otherwise of parental refusal to agree to the medical testing of their child. It subsequently refused the application, and held: The question whether the child should or should not be tested was a matter relating to the welfare of the child, not to the rights of the parents; and it was clearly not in the child's best interests for either the parents or the health professionals to remain ignorant of the child's state of health.

Re C (HIV Test) illustrates that parental wishes are not usually determinative of a case involving medical treatment of a child.

It contrasts with *Re T* (1997) (the liver transplant case) (see below) where, in a break with precedent, the Court of Appeal placed considerable weight on parental wishes rather than clinical factors in connection with the issue of authorisation of a liver transplant for a toddler.

Section 8 orders under the Children Act 1989

These orders were introduced by the Children Act 1989 in October 1991 and include the following: Residence order; Contact order; Prohibited Steps order; Specific Issue order. The restriction on making such orders is contained in s.1(5) to the Children Act 1989. In matters involving certain aspects of the child's medical treatment, a prohibited steps order may be applied for, depending on the circumstances, in order to either prevent a specific procedure to be carried out on the child except with the court's permission; or a specific issue order may be applied for to request the court to give certain directions in order to resolve any dispute over proposed medical treatment for the child.

CHILDREN'S RIGHTS

Determining the 'best interests of the child'

Who usually decides what is in the best interests of the child? When the child is very young, it is usually the child's family. In the event of a dispute which goes to court, it will be the courts' decision, disagreements often occurring either between parents or between the parents and a third party such as a doctor or some other professional who has been looking after some aspect of the child's life such as a teacher or educational specialist or if there is uncertainty over the scope of the court's jurisdiction. If a wardship application is made, then as long as the wardship order is in force, no major decision can be made with regard to the child's welfare and upbringing without court approval or until a court hearing has taken place or until 21 days has elapsed from the date of the order, whichever is the earlier.

Jurisdictions which consider children cases
(i) Wardship and inherent jurisdiction

The English courts may consider children cases under their wardship jurisdiction or under their inherent jurisdiction. The court's inherent jurisdiction includes the court's wardship powers. The key difference under the Children Act 1989 (effective since October 14, 1991) is that local authorities can no longer apply for a wardship order for a child as a matter of course or as a means of appeal if they have had an application for another order refused. Under s.100 to the Children Act 1989 they have to show why they are invoking the court's inherent jurisdiction, and must establish that they cannot achieve what they are trying to achieve for the child by using any other available order. Under s.100 to the Children Act 1989, leave (court permission) is required before a local authority may be granted a wardship application. The best interests of the child 'test', as perceived and interpreted by the cour, will be applied in every case.

(ii) Under the Children Act 1989
s.8 orders

(a) 'prohibited steps order': an order that no step which could be taken by a parent in meeting his parental responsibility for a child, and which is of a kind specified in the order, shall be taken by any person without the consent of the court.

(b) 'specific issue order': an order giving directions for the purpose of determining a specific question which has arisen, or which may arise, in connection with any aspect of parental responsibility.

Examples of acting in the 'best interests of the child'

English courts frequently state that they are acting 'in the best interests of the child' but does this slogan have any core content? By necessity, it is a concept of variable content and indeterminate until formulated and crystallised by a court Some possible examples of the variable content of this slogan are as follows:

i) To have the child's welfare and well-being promoted/protected

e.g. *Re S (A Minor) (Medical Treatment)* [1993] where the court ruled that 'the test must remain the welfare of the child as the paramount consideration.'

ii) The application of the 'principle' tends to be governed by the specific facts
Generally, if the child's life is being threatened by non-treatment: the courts usually authorise treatment in the face of the parental refusal. Cases involving anorexic children are *Re W* (1992) and *Re C (Detention: Medical Treatment)* (1997). For psychotically disturbed children, see: *Re R* [1992]. For children receiving psychiatric care, see: *South Glamorgan v W and B* and *Re K, W and F* [1993]. Yet children who refuse treatment (supported by their

parents) on religious grounds sometimes have their refusal of treatment overridden 'in their best interests': *Re E (A Minor) (Wardship: Medical Treatment)* [1993] (15-year-old leukaemia patient) ; *Re S (A Minor: Medical Treatment)* [1994].

iii) relieving suffering is seen as part of their 'welfare'
This refers to cases involving severely disabled newborn children. Here, the sanctity of life principle might sometimes be followed but not always. Cases in this category are: *R. v Arthur; Re C; Re J; Re A (conjoined twins)* but not *Re T* (the liver transplant case).

iv) protecting children from a pregnancy
This might be through sterilisation as in *Re B* (the Jeanette case) (1987) (House of Lords). One of the objections to sterilisation is that it cannot protect the child from rape or sexual exploitation; it merely removes the visible signs of these abuses to him.

THE GILLICK CASE AND CHILDREN'S RIGHTS

Gillick's case had been seen by some writers as the dawn of a new era of children's rights (see e.g Eekelaar 'The emergence of children's rights' (1986) 6 OJLS 161) and as we have seen, several statutory 'rights' are now contained in the Children Act 1989. However, the mere statement of rights, even in a statute, does not mean that children will suddenly acquire a range of new rights enforceable in a court of law, particularly when English common law and the Children Act 1989 allows scope for interpretation of the law in a given situation. As we have seen, post-Gillick, it has been possible for a court to say that a child does not have the right to refuse certain medical treatment, if the result of following the child's wishes, is serious physical or mental injury to the child concerned, or even the possibility of death. The English courts have said that their decision to ignore the child's stated wishes in various cases, was done in that child's best interests; or that the child was not of sufficient age or understanding to make a legally valid choice, in other words, was not *Gillick* competent; or that although the child might have been *Gillick* competent from time to time, 'true' *Gillick* competence was achieved once and for all. In fact, all these cases represent judicial (and sometimes medical) paternalism because the courts pay considerable deference to the views o: the doctors in this context, and in most cases, the medical op-nion usually determines the court's decision. This continuing cefer- ence, reflected in the usual application of the *Bolam* prin-iple, militates against any right of true choice on the part of chiEdren, particularly those that have not yet achieved *Gillick* compe-ence and in life-threatening situations, even if they have achievend it. If abiding by a child's decision means there is a strong ikeli- hood of that child's death, the courts will simply not grar-t any right to refuse treatment because, irrespective of which criteria one uses, they believe that they are acting in the best interests of that child.

International perspectives

The UN Convention on the rights of the child

The 1989 United Nations Convention on the Rights of the Child (the Convention) creates in international law a duty upon states to accord children rights on a par with adults. A child is defined as 'every human being up to the age of 18 years' but the wording of the Convention does not address the starting point of childhood i.e. when does childhood begin? So the question remains: is it at conception, birth or even somewhere in between? Children's rights are limited especially in their right to vote but in international law the Convention is binding or states that ratify it as the UK did in December 1991. Howeve-, it is important to realise that ratification does not make the Convention part of the domestic law-the British government would need to enact the relevant legislation, as it has done wi-h The Human Rights Act 1998 which incorporated most of the Euro- pean Convention on Human Rights on October 2, 2000.

THE MEDICAL TREATMENT OF SEVERELY DISABLED BABIES

Ethical perspectives

In the tradition of ethical codes which date back to several centuries and in accordance with the modern practice o- medi- cine, doctors have a prima facie commitment to respect and preserve life. Nowhere has this been more evident than at birth and in the early weeks of post-natal life. In historical terms, it is only relatively recently that the salvaging of all infan-s born

alive has been seen as a desirable social goal (Silverman
'Mismatched attitudes about neonatal death' Hastings Centre
Report 12 (1981)).

Sanctity of human life v quality of life

This area brings into conflict several ethical principles, namely
the notion of the sanctity of human life (preservation of life in all
circumstances) against the quality of life. Further, the distinction
between 'killing and letting die or allowing to die' is raised as
well as the principle of 'double effect' whereby an action that is
intended to do good may be justifiable even though its foreseen
or unforeseen result is harmful. These difficult situations have
been canvassed in several English cases such as *R. v Arthur*
(1981) and a host of cases dealing with severely disabled
newborns who were born with varying degrees of mental and
physical disabilities and deformities.

   Difficult decisions have to be faced by doctors in treating
these infants. Campbell (1989) asks: 'Can it ever be right to
withhold or withdraw treatment in the knowledge that death
will result? Should death be hastened to avoid pain or distress
when further treatment seems futile?' Should parents have the
final decision on the medical treatment of their children? The
question that has sometimes arisen in the English courts has
been the extent to which the wishes of the parents of the child
should be taken into account by the court in reaching its
decision. By and large, English law has said that this should be
considered but is not determinative. However, the case of *Re T*
(1997) appeared to suggest that in certain circumstances, parental opinion might or should be given considerable weight
when the court performs the balancing exercise required in
reaching their decisions in these very difficult cases. Decisions
about the severely disabled and dying are problematic and have
been the subject of continuing debate for many years, especially
in the late 1990s over the non-approval by the Court of Appeal
in *Re T* (1997) (above) (see discussion, below) of a liver transplant for an eighteen-month-old boy because his parents felt he
had already been through too much and that they were unable
to give him the commitment which he might need in after-care
should he have the transplant, even though the chances of a
successful transplant were very good. It should be noted that
this was not the classic case of a severely disabled newborn
infant but involved a toddler, but the prominence given to

parental wishes and certain statements from the Court of Appeal have cast some doubt on the law relating to the medical treatment of seriously disabled children.

What is in the child's best interests?

Should parents have the ultimate right to decide on what medical treatment is best for their disabled or seriously ill babies? In the case of very severely handicapped newborns, should parents have the right to decide whether their child lives or dies in certain circumstances?

The judicial approach to severely disabled newborn children

There has been a cluster of cases where the child has been a newborn with severe disabilities. They have been instructive when the courts have to decide on:

(i) Down's syndrome children with varying degrees of disability: *Arthur's case; Re B* (1981)

In *Arthur's case*, Dr Arthur was charged with murder when he prescribed 'nursing care only for a newborn Down's syndrome child who had been rejected by its parents. Large doses of dihydocodein were also prescribed for sedative purposes and the child later died. The consultant's charge was later reduced to attempted murder when it was found that the child had internal physical complications and would have died anyway. Various healthcare professionals testified that the words 'nursing care only' meant different things to different health authorities. In some regions, it meant providing only fluids and basic care, in others, it meant doing everything possible to ensure the baby's survival, from resuscitation techniques to life support machines. Hence there was no uniform medical practice applicable to the term 'nursing care only' in all health authorities.

Dr. Arthur was acquitted. The court stated that as long as the doctor was following a standard medical practice, which was supported by 'a responsible body of medical opinion' (my emphasis) (In other words the *Bolam* test), he was not negligent and the court would be very slow in concluding that the doctor was breaking the law.

Bolam applies even where only one medical opinion supports the practice in question

Thus, as the law has operated, the Bolam test is satisfied provided there is one medical opinion which supports the

practice in question, regardless of whether there are variations
across the country and there may be other health authorities
which do not support the particular procedure or practice. The
Bolitho decision by the House of Lords suggests that the
procedure should also be 'logical' and presumably supportable
in terms of current practice to justify its operation. There was no
suggestion in the Arthur case that the wishes of the parents
would be determinative of the court's decision.

Just before the Arthur case was decided, the *Baby Alexandra
Case(Re B)* had been decided in the Court of Appeal yet the
court was not referred to it and there is no reference to it in the
Arthur judgment.

The 'demonstrably awful' test

Re B (1981) *(The Baby Alexandra Case) Re B (A Minor) (Wardship:
Medical Treatment)* (Court of Appeal)

The baby suffering from Down's Syndrome had an intestinal
blockage which would have proved fatal in a few days without
an operation. The parents opposed the operation, believing that
it was in the best interests of the child not to have the operation
and to be allowed to die rather than to live as a physically and
mentally disabled person. The child's life expectancy was estimated at between 20-30 years. When one surgeon decided that
the wishes of the parents should be respected, the local authority sought an order authorising other surgeons to perform the
operation. The Court overruled the parents' decision and
authorised the operation. Templeman, LJ declared that the
prognosis must be that the child's life must 'demonstrably be so
awful' that it would not be in its best interests to have the
operation.

Faced with this choice, the Court of Appeal felt it their duty to
decide that 'the child must live.'

Indeed, the Court indicated that the question for the court
was whether the proposed treatment was in the child's best
interests, not whether the wishes of the parents should be
respected.

The operation went ahead and the child survived for six
years.

(ii) Child born with severe impairments and already dying:
Re C (1989)

Re C (1989); *Re C (a minor) (wardship:medical treatment)* [1989]

C was born prematurely and hydrocephalic, with her brain structure irreparably damaged at birth with no possibility of brain function being restored. She was dying. The question was: *what treatment, if any, should be given to the baby?* The court authorised an operation to relieve pressure on her brain. Mr Justice Ward made an order that the hospital authorities be given permission that the child be 'treated to die' but to die with the greatest dignity and the least pain, suffering and distress. The Official Solicitor appealed to the Court of Appeal which held that the child was to be treated in a manner appropriate to its condition; she had no hope of a happy life; her condition had been terminal even before her birth. The court, in considering as paramount the welfare and best interests of the child was entitled to approve recommendations designed to ease the baby's suffering rather than prolong its life. The court explained that a baby would be regarded as *'irreparably damaged'* if it was *'permanently unable to interact mentally, socially and physically'*. The court's view was to leave it to the pediatric team to decide how to treat the baby. There was a clear consensus about the prognosis and C was certain to die even if this could be delayed for a short time.

(iii) Newborn severely disabled babies who are not in fact dying but whose quality of life is extremely poor: *Re J* (1990); *Re J* (1992)

Re J (1990) (Re J (a minor) (wardship: medical treatment,

The Appeal Court was faced with Baby J, born 13 weeks prematurely and weighing two and a half pounds at birth, suffering severe brain damage, quadraplegic and on a ventilator; he suffered from fits, was diagnosed as blind, probably deaf, paralysed and was unlikely ever to learn to speak or to comprehend what was going on around him. But the child could feel pain. So the child's quality of life was seen as very poor. Yet this child was not in fact dying nor on the point of death and it was estimated that he would probably not survive his late adolescence. A wardship hearing sought to resolve the conflicting views on the child's best interest and Mr Justice Baker held that if the baby fell ill again, doctors would be entitled not to carry out life-saving treatment. The doctors all agreed that the child should not be put back on a ventilator because this might cause even greater brain damage and might not improve his chances of survival.

On appeal, Lord Donaldson observed that to prolong life is not the sole objective of the court and to require it at the expense of other considerations may not be in the child's best interests. The court held that it would be in this severely handicapped child's best interests for non-resuscitation to be authorised if he fell critically ill again, in view of the hazardous nature of reventilation and risk of further deterioration. Baby J could be kept alive indefinitely, but having assessed his quality of life if kept alive, the court opined that the task of determining what was in a child's best interests was a balancing exercise.

Principle in Re J-baby's quality of life significant

Where a ward of court suffered from physical disabilities so grave that his life would from his point of view be so intolerable if he were to continue living that he would choose to die if he were in a position to make a sound judgment, the court could direct that treatment without which death would ensue from natural causes need not be given to the ward to prolong his life, even though he was not on the point of death or dying. However, the court could never sanction positive steps to terminate the life of a person. The crucial point is that although this child had severe brain damage, was quadraplegic and on a ventilator, he was not actually in danger of imminent death and could be expected to survive into his teens. However, his 'quality of life' was seen as very poor, and he could feel pain. Thus, the Court of Appeal applied the 'quality of life principle' and even mentioned a 'substituted judgment' approach in treating severely handicapped babies.

Re J (1992)　In a later *Re J*, medical staff did not think it appropriate to attempt to save the life of a 16-month-old brain damaged child with invasive intensive care if he suffered a life-threatening condition. His mother obtained an order that treatment should be given to prolong his life. The court immediately suspended the order which was later upheld on appeal. The medical profession will therefore not be required to carry out treatment against their clinical judgment, irrespective of parental demands; parental consent is required but there is no right to demand treatment, in these cases.

(iv) In addition the courts have sometimes had to decide on very young children whose parents object to their receiv-ing potentially life-saving transplants because they believe these children have already endured enough medical treatment and should not be made to endure any further treatment.

Re T (1997); *Re T (Wardship: Medical Treatment)* (the liver transplant case)   The baby, T, was born in April 1995 suffering from biliary atresia, a life-threatening liver defect and an operation when he was three and a half weeks old was unsuccessful. Without transplantation he would not live beyond the age of two to two and a half. The unanimous medical opinion was that prospects of success of a transplant were good (apparently an 80-90 per cent success rate) and it was in the baby's best interests to undergo the operation when a donor became available. The parents were both health care professionals, experienced in the care of sick children and had jobs in a distant Commonwealth country. They did not wish T to undergo transplant surgery and refused their consent to an operation should a liver become available. The surgeons did not accept the mother's reasons for refusing consent and were prepared to proceed with the operation without the mother's consent if the court gave its consent. The doctors therefore referred the matter to the relevant local authority of the mother's area which applied to the High Court to exercise its inherent jurisdiction with respect to the child under s.100(3) to the Children Act 1989. The application was granted by the lower court and the mother appealed.

The Court of Appeal granted the appeal, saying that while parental wishes were merely one consideration, the fact that the mother here said she could not offer the commitment to the toddler which he warranted, because they were abroad, was an important consideration. *The reasonableness or otherwise of the mother was not crucial.*

The prospect of forcing the 'devoted mother' of this young baby (by then a toddler) to the consequences of this invasive surgery led her to the conclusion, that 'it is not in the best interests of the child' to give consent to the operation and require him to return to England for the purpose of undergoing liver transplantation. She believed that the best interests of the child required that his future treatment be left in the hands of his devoted parents.

The Court of Appeal (Butler-Sloss, Waite and Roche, L.JJ.) held that when an application was made to the court under its inherent jurisdiction the welfare of the child was the paramount consideration, and although a parent's consent or refusal of consent was an important consideration to weigh in the balancing exercise, it was for the court to decide the matter and in so doing it might overrule the decision of a reasonable parent.

Her Ladyship placed great weight upon 'the close attachment between the mother and baby' emphasising that 'the welfare of the child depends upon his mother.' The case of an intestinal obstruction of the Down's syndrome baby (such as *Re B* (1981)) which could be cured by a simple operation, was distinguished from the present case which required complicated surgery and many years of special care from the mother. Even greater significance was placed on the evidence of the consultant which expressed the view that 'the decision of a loving, caring mother should be respected.'

The mother's appeal was allowed.

In *Re T*, the Court of Appeal:

(i) decided not to follow well-established precedent dating back to 1981 (Re B);

(ii) placed a highly unusual amount of emphasis on parental /mother's opinion rather than heed unanimous medical opinion which estimated 80-90 per cent success rate for the operation;

(iii) confirmed that the sanctity of human life is not an absolute principle .

Thus, even if the child might survive an operation, the force of parental opposition might sometimes carry so much weight that it would override what many might see as being in the child's best interests. In the past, the courts have consistently overruled parental opposition (see: *Re S (A Minor) (Consent to Medical Treatment)* [1994], *Re E (A Minor)* (1992), *Re S (A Minor) (Medical Treatment)* [1993], *Re R (A Minor) (Blood Transfusion)* (1993)).

Was the appeal court really justified in not giving greater weight to the unanimous medical prognosis that the transplant would save this child and that its chances of success were very high indeed?

Post-Re T: Clinical factors again determinative? Parental opposition not decisive factor Re C (1998); Re C (Medical Treatment) (1998)

A case decided after *Re T* is *Re C*, where despite parental opposition, the court authorised the withdrawal of ventilation from a severely disabled 16-month-old baby suffering from spinal muscular dystrophy, who was dying. The doctors treating her were of the opinion that her condition fell into the 'no chance' situation and wished to withdraw ventilator support and allow her to die with palliative care in the event of cardiac arrest. Her Orthodox Jew parents felt unable to consent to this course of action and insisted that she be reventilated should she suffer respiratory relapse. Her doctors refused to accede to the parents' wishes, maintaining that further treatment would cause her increasing distress, possible further medical complications and was futile as her life expectancy was unlikely to extend beyond 18 months. The hospital authority applied for a High Court declaration approving their care management plan.

The court held that : (1) C's condition was a 'no chance' situation as defined in the RCP guidelines since she suffered from 'such severe disease that life-sustaining treatment simply delays death without significant alleviation of suffering'. (2) They would give permission to treat C, as advised by her doctors, to ease her suffering and permit her life to end peacefully and with dignity, such treatment being in C's best interests. (3) They would not make an order which would, directly or indirectly, require a doctor to treat a child in a manner contrary to his clinical judgment, following *Re J* (1990).

This case appeared to follow the previous line of authority in that parental opposition was not a determinative factor and the fact that the child's parents were Orthodox Jews whose religion forbade them to sanction any action shortening life was not determinative. The child's parents were adopting the sanctity of life approach rather than any 'best interests' principle and wanted their daughter to carry on living regardless of her quality of life. The court here did, however, consider predominantly clinical factors (as in *Re C (HIV Test)* [1999] (see above)). Post-*Re T*, therefore, the *Re B* (1981) line of precedent (where parents' views are not determinative) has been preferred but as ever, in this field, the particular circumstances of a case will determine the eventual decision and courts will distinguish precedents where they believe this will be in the child's best interests.

The David Glass case

R. v Portsmouth NHS Trust ex parte Glass [1999]

David Glass was born prematurely with hydrocephalus where fluid accumulates on the brain. He also had cerebral palsy and epilepsy. Against all medical expectations, the child survived. When he was 12, David had a tonsillectomy and suffered from various infections. Eventually, he was placed on a life support machine and the doctors believed the child was dying. The medical team therefore wanted to give him diamorphine and allow him to die, but his mother refused. His mother, Carol Glass (the applicant), went to court to establish the right to an assurance that, should David be re-admitted, he would not be given diamorphine. Having been hospitalised several times, the child's mother was told it was not in David's interest to keep him alive, and they wished to let him die without distress or pain. She applied for judicial review, making complaints as to the legality of the Trust's treatment of David.

The lower court judge dismissed the application, holding that the instant case was not susceptible to judicial review. The applicant's appeal to the Court of Appeal was refused on the basis that (i) judicial review was always regarded as a procedure of last resort; (ii) Several orders in the Family Division could be made which dealt specifically with these sorts of situations: A specific issue order could be made under s.8 to the Children Act 1989, or a declaration in the best interests of the child; or the child could be made a ward of court; (iii) the important concern of the court was to ensure that what was determined was in the best interests of the child.

This case eventually reached the European Court of Human Rights which unanimously upheld the parents' appeal and held that the NHS *did* breach the right to respect for private life, as guaranteed by Art 8 of the European Convention on Human Rights. This breach took place when the hospital authorities decided to over-ride the mother's objection to the treatment proposed for her severely disabled son in the absence of authorisation by a court.

Allocation of scarce resources

The treatment of severely disabled newborns has also given rise to debates about whether it is economically defensible, in an environment of scarce resources, to maintain babies whose chances of life are exceedingly poor rather than using resources to treat persons needing renal dialysis, for example.

The use of QALYs—quality-adjusted life years—has been suggested to assist in decision-making over the allocation of health care resources. The principle of using QALYs is based on the assumption that "if a rational individual was given the choice, that person would prefer to live a shorter life with a minimum amount of suffering and disability as opposed to living for a longer period of time, but with severe disability and suffering." QALYs appear to be useful in making decisions about which choice of treatments will be the most beneficial to an individual, but QALYs do not provide a means of deciding which patients to treat and not to treat.

TREATING DISABLED INFANTS IN THE 21st CENTURY

The European Convention for the Protection of Human Rights and Fundamental Freedoms

With the coming into force of the Human Rights Act 1998 (the 1998 Act) thus incorporating the European Convention for the Protection of Human Rights and Fundamental Freedoms (The European Convention) into English law on October 2, 2000, it is relevant to pose the question of whether any decision to withdraw or withhold medical treatment from disabled new-born children would be in breach of certain Articles of the 1998 Act (such as art.2—the right to life; and art.3-the right not to be subjected to inhuman and degrading treatment including the right to die with dignity). Indeed, would allowing a child to die be against the 1998 Act? *A National Health Service Trust v D (Baby D) (2000)* The Times, July 19, suggests that it would not.

Parental opposition to non-treatment not decisive-best interests test only criterion

Baby D (2000)

In July 2000, in *A National Health Service Trust v D* (2000) the Family Division of the High Court ruled that doctors should not automatically or necessarily prolong the life of a 19-month-old boy, suffering from irreversible lung disease, heart failure and renal dysfunction, in the event of respiratory or cardiac failure, rejecting a plea from the child's parents who were opposed to the non-treatment of their baby. Cazalet, J. noted that the applicants, the NHS Trust, were supported by a very strong body of medical opinion, and maintained that in view of the baby's extremely poor health and the poor prognosis, it was not in his best interests to undergo resuscitation. Furthermore, palliative drug treatment had resolved that condition. On the other hand, the child's "very loving and committed parents", whose care of him was exemplary, strongly opposed the application as being premature.

The High Court stressed the paramountcy of the child's welfare and its high respect for the sanctity of human life; indeed, following *Re J (Wardship: medical Treatment)* (1991) "[t]here was no question of approving, even in the case of the most horrendous disability, a course aimed at terminating life or accelerating death". It was concerned only with the circumstances in which steps should be taken to prolong life. On the basis of applying the best interests test and allowing the child to die with dignity, there was no breach of art.2 (the right to life) or art.3 (the right not to be subjected to inhuman or degrading treatment, including the right to die with dignity) of the European Convention for the Protection of Human Rights and Fundamental Freedoms (the European Human Rights Convention). A declaration was granted, subject to a direction that there should be permission to continue to treat the baby without artificial ventilation, unless such a course seemed inappropriate to the doctor in charge of the child.

Portsmouth NHS Trust v Wyatt (2004) (*The Baby Wyatt Case*)

In October 2004, the High Court was faced with another case of a severely disabled baby, Charlotte, who was born prematurely, at 26 weeks gestation and weighing 1 lb and 5 ins long. She had chronic respiratory and kidney problems coupled with profound brain damage that left her blind, deaf and incapable of voluntary movement or response. She was placed in an incubator and the doctors unanimously believed that she was most unlikely to leave the hospital. However, 11 months after she was born, she was still alive and doctors caring for the child were asking for court permission that they should not be bound to ventilate her the next time she stopped breathing but this was opposed by the child's parents, who were devout Christians and believed that she should be given further chances to survive. She had already stopped breathing three times.

Mr Justice Hedley ruled that the child should be allowed to die and that in the event of her stopping breathing again, and the parents disagreed with the doctors on the course of treatment, the doctors should not be obliged to send the child for artificial ventilation or similar aggressive treatment. He also ruled that she should be given as much comfort as possible and have as much contact with her parents as possible.

Postscript: On August 23, 2005, Baby Wyatt, was aged 22 months years old, weighed fifteen pounds and has made far more improvement than the medical experts predicted. A day earlier, Hedley, J reversed his earlier ruling at a review of the baby's condition. Non-ventilation would have to be justified as being in the child's best interests.

Conjoined twins

Disabled newborns is certainly a description that would fit conjoined ('Siamese') twins who are born connected at the head or abdomen.

Separating conjoined twins in the year 2000-Court can override parental wishes

Central Manchester Healthcare Trust v (1) Mr and Mrs A ; and (2) A child (by the Official Solicitor, her guardian ad litem) ; (Re A) (Children) (Conjoined twins: medical treatment) (2000)

In Britain, conjoined twins, given the false names Jodie (J) and Mary, (M) were born at St. Mary's Hospital, Manchester on August 8, 2000 joined at their lower abdomens. One twin, J, was alert, with a heart and lungs, the other, M, did not possess these organs, and was reliant on the other for life. Their parents are devout Roman Catholics from abroad (Gozo in Malta), who came to Britain seeking medical advice and treatment, with the help of the two governments. They maintained that separating them is "not God's will" and wanted nature to take its course, even if that meant the loss of both children.

In a unique legal action, the English courts were asked to decide whether to sanction an operation to separate the month-old twins, which could save Jodie but mean the killing of Mary. Medical experts at Manchester said that a failure to operate would mean that both children were likely to die within three to six months. Separation of the twins would, according to the medical experts, mean that one twin would die immediately but the other might survive, although her medical condition would need careful monitoring.

At the High Court in August 2000, Mr Justice Johnson gave surgeons authorisation to separate the girls. Five days later, the parents appealed on the grounds that Johnson, J. erred in holding the operation was (i) in M's best interests, (ii) in J's best interests, and (iii) in any event, lawful.

The Court of Appeal considered this desperately difficult case and among the questions raised was: would separation of the twins amount to the murder of one of them (assuming the medical prognosis was correct), if separation resulted in the imminent death of one of them?

On September 22, 2000, the Court of Appeal confirmed the earlier lower court ruling which was to authorise the separation of the twins, who were then six weeks old. The court's opinions are contained in a 130-page judgment.

The Court of Appeal Ruling-Some Key Points

* On the medical aspects of the case, Johnson, J. was correct in concluding that this was an appropriate case in which to override the objections of the parents. M was not receiving treatment (or any substantial treatment) at the time of the application or appeal. This focused on the active invasion of M's body for the purposes of the separation. That would not prolong her life, rather it would terminate it. The question was not: was it in M's best interests that the hospital should continue to provide her with treatment which will prolong her life? The case was not about providing that kind of treatment. What was proposed raised the question: was it in M's best interests that an operation be performed to separate her from J when the certain consequence of that operation was that she would die? There was only one answer to that question: that it was not in her best interests.

* The Court of Appeal had to make its own assessment of the respective best interests of J and M. As to that, there was no doubt that the scales came down heavily in J's favour. The best interests of the twins was to give the chance of life to the child whose actual bodily condition was capable of accepting the chance to her advantage, even if that had to be at the cost of the sacrifice of the life which was so unnaturally supported. The least detrimental choice, balancing the interests of M against J and J against M, was to permit the operation to be performed.

* The crucial question was whether or not the operation could be lawfully performed under the criminal law. The reality was that M was killing J [by draining her blood

supply which would eventually prove fatal]. That provided the legal justification for the doctors coming to J's
defence and removing the threat of fetal harm to her
presented by M. The availability of such a plea of quasi-
self defence, modified to meet the quite exceptional circumstances nature had inflicted on the twins, made
intervention by the doctors lawful.

- The feelings of the parents were entitled to great re-pect,
especially so far as they were based on religious convictions. But the court could not escape the responsibility of
deciding the matter to the best of its judgment as to the
twins' best interests.

- Continued life, whether long or short, would hold
nothing for M except possible pain and discomort, if
indeed she could feel anything at all. The proposed
operation would therefore be in the best interests of each
of the twins. The decision did not require the court to
value one life above another. The proposed operation
would not be unlawful. It would involve the positive act
of invasive surgery and M's death would be foreseen as
an inevitable consequence of an operation which was
intended, and was necessary, to save J's life. But M's
death would not be the purpose or intention of the
surgery and she would die because tragically her body,
on its own, was not and never had been viable.

The appeal was dismissed. The babies' parents did not appeal to
the House of Lords against the decision. The operation to
separate the twins was carried out and the prognosis for the
surviving twin appears to be good, although her condition
continues to be monitored. Despite the tragic circumstances of
the case, if the operation ultimately had not proceeded it would
not have saved a life where without judicial or medical intervention, two lives would certainly have been lost.

3. MEDICAL CONFIDENTIALITY

INTRODUCTION

Healthcare professionals such as doctors and nurses are generally expected to preserve the confidences of their patients. There is a well-established tradition of confidentiality among healthcare professionals which has been an integral part of a code for many centuries and may be said to be the cornerstone of medical practice. This requires a duty of secrecy with regard to information about patients. For doctors it is contained in the Hippocratic Oath which dates from around 500BC from the Greek philosopher/medic Hippocrates. That part of the Hippocratic Oath states:

> All that may come to my knowledge in the exercise of my profession or not in connection with it, or in daily commerce with men, which ought not to be spoken abroad, I will not divulge abroad and will never reveal.

The International Code of Medical Ethics also states: A doctor shall preserve absolute secrecy on all he knows about his patients because of the confidence entrusted in him.

Similarly, the Declaration of Geneva declares: I will respect the secrets that have been confided in me, even after the patient has died.

The undertaking to preserve confidentiality continues even after death. Early into the 21st century, many questions relating to preserving the confidentiality of patients or indeed of doctors can no longer be resolved by simply referring to these codes but require careful, rational consideration appropriate to a rapidly changing working environment. There is now a network of doctors, nurses and other healthcare professionals involved in care and there is a need for patient records to which many people must have access, as part of the care 'team' and the need to communicate information to insurance companies or new employers and the computerisation of records.

The British Medical Association (BMA) has declared that the volume of queries on confidentiality and disclosure forms the bulk of inquiries that it receives from BMA members. Hence, while doctors and other healthcare professionals are well aware of their traditional duty of confidence and the need to protect confidentiality, increasingly complex dilemmas now arise which are not easily dealt with by simply citing or relying upon a code. Confidentiality also remains an important part of the GMC's Blue Book and the UKCC's Code of Conduct.

In order properly to advise a patient, the doctor may well be given confidential information that the patient does not wish to be disclosed to a third party. These facts might have different implications and their relative importance and sensitivity will vary across different branches of medicine. The duty is certainly not absolute and there are several exceptions which are discussed below. However, there are often conflicting moral or legal considerations which override a duty of confidentiality. For instance, can a private interest in maintaining confidentiality be outweighed by a public interest in safety, for example, where certain doctors are HIV positive but their patients have not been informed of this in a clinical situation where they may be in danger of contracting the disease? If a doctor or healthcare professional breaches the confidence there could well be censure from his professional body, which in the case of doctors, will be the GMC.

BMA definition of confidentiality

The BMA defines confidentiality as:

> The principle of keeping secure and secret from others, information given by or about an individual in the course of a professional relationship.

But general guidance cannot supply definitive solutions to all problems or all situations that might arise in the course of a doctor-patient relationship. Rules on confidentiality need to keep abreast of current developments, and the rapidity of technological change. Interpretations may often change as a sign of the times and changing values and situations. Genetic testing and new communications technology present fresh challenges to the duty of confidentiality.

Some examples of where a duty arises

Examples are: between doctor and patient; priest and penitent; solicitor and client, and banker and customer. Two main issues have tended to arise within the healthcare professional/patient relationship:

(i) Disclosure to third parties, including other doctors, nurses, clerical staff, relatives, the employer, police, and the media.

(ii) Subject access: the right of the individual to obtain access to their own records/information. (see the Data Protection Act 1998)

GUIDANCE IN PROFESSIONAL CODES

The BMA guidance

The BMA has no disciplinary authority but operates as a trade union for doctors. Consequently, its advice provides a background to the GMC's instructions. In essence, the BMA guidance is a comprehensive survey of the general principles and exceptions.

The GMC Guidance

The GMC does have the authority both to lay down rules of professional conduct and to discipline those who breach them as it is the governing and licensing body for doctors. The power to discipline and ultimately even to have the doctor's name erased from the register is now contained in Pt.V of the Medical Act 1983 (as amended).

General Medical Council (GMC) guidance: confidentiality: protecting and providing information (2000)

Subject to eight exceptions, the GMC imposes a strict duty on registered medical practitioners to refrain from disclosing voluntarily to any third party information about a patient which he has learnt directly or indirectly in his professional capacity. This Guidance is not legally binding but non-compliance could incur censure, suspension or even being 'struck off' the medical register for serious misconduct (under the Medical Act 1983). The exceptions mentioned in the Guidance where the doctor may properly breach confidentiality are: (i) Disclosure within medical teams where it might sometimes be essential to pass confidential information between members of the team; emergencies where it is not possible to obtain a patient's consent; but a patient's request not to share certain information with other team members must be respected. (ii) Disclosure to employers and insurance companies. (iii) Disclosure where the patient or his/her legal advisor gives consent. (iv) Disclosure where it is impossible to obtain the patient's consent but which is 'in the patient's medical interest' so that information may be given to a close relative-cases where the patient is incapable of giving consent to treatment because of immaturity, illness or mental incapacity. (v) When, in the doctor's opinion, disclosure to someone other than a relative would be in the best interests of the patient, the doctor must make every effort to get the patient's consent, but if this is not obtained and he believes that disclosure is in the patient's best interests, then he may go ahead and disclose; e.g. where there is suspicion that the patient is a victim of neglect, physical or sexual abuse, information should be given to an appropriate responsible person or statutory agency, in order to prevent further harm to the patient; this may also, unusually, require disclosure of the patient's condition to a close relative (e.g. if it is terminal) and not to a patient because the doctor thinks the patient might be seriously harmed by the information. (vi) Disclosure in the interests of others in accordance with specific statutory requirements; e.g. of a notifiable disease such as cholera, smallpox or typhus; notification of a termination of pregnancy must be sent within seven days of the abortion to the Chief Medical Officer; information that must be disclosed under s.172 of the Road Traffic Act 1988; disclosure to the medical adviser of the Driver and Vehicle Licensing Agency, of relevant medical details of a driver who is continuing to drive against medical advice (see *Hunter v Mann*, discussed, below); disclosure under The Terrorism Act 2000; (vii) Disclosure after a patient's death; the general rule is non-disclosure even after death but the extent of disclosure will depend on the circumstances such as whether the information is already public knowledge, and how long it has been since the patient died. (viii) Disclosure of information necessary for the purposes of a medical research project approved by a recognised ethical committee.

Appeals from decisions to 'strike off' may be made under s.40 of the Medical Act 1983, to the Privy Council.

The Nursing and Midwifery Council Code of Professional Conduct

The responsible governing and licensing body for doctors is the General Medical Council. For nurses, it is now the Nursing and Midwifery Council. With self-regulatory organisations, there is a long tradition of enunciating rules and regulations for the professions.

The NMC Code states, inter alia, that nurses and midwives 'must treat information about patients and clients as confidential and use it only for the purpose for which it was given.' (para.5.1)

And further under para. 5.1: 'You must guard against breaches of confidentiality by protecting information from improper disclosure at all times.'

Exceptions to the duty are similar to those that apply to all healthcare professionals including doctors, i.e. the consent of the patient, (para. 5.3) where it is in the interests of the patient (eg sharing the information with another healthcare professional), court orders, under statute, and where it is in the public interest to do so, to protect the public. Para. 5.4 states that where there is an issue of child protection, they must act at all times in accordance with national and local policies. The Department of Health has also issued an NHS Confidentiality Code of Practice which covers similar areas and a wider confidentiality communications strategy is being developed by the DH and the NHS Information Authority.

JUSTIFICATIONS FOR CONFIDENTIALITY

Johnson in *Pathways to Medical Ethics* (1990) identifies three justifications: first, the patient's autonomy-that is, the right of the patient to have his confidences respected by the doctor so that any information he divulges to the doctor in order for a diagnosis to be made is given on the basis of confidentiality; second, the doctor's integrity, which is the fact that the doctor's undertaking to the patient about what use will be made of the information that has been obtained so this promise is then broken if the information is divulged to a third party without the patient's permission; and thirdly, the consequences for the future relationship: if confidences are broken, the patient might not pass on vital information to the doctor and this might result in a misdiagnosis or the wrong treatment being given to the patient which could have potentially damaging or even fatal results.

Ethical justifications

Two main ethical theories can be formulated in support of confidentiality: (i) the 'consequentialist' one which would equate an improvement in people's health and general well-being and happiness resulting from a doctors being fully informed of their patients' condition and circumstances so as to be able to treat them as effectively as possible; (ii) the Utilitarian argument which is that a duty of confidence cannot be absolute and can be breached in certain circumstances. The reasons for disclosure would have to outweigh those for maintaining secrecy. The common law would only allow disclosure if the patient consented or it would in the public interest to breach the patient's confidence.

As Stauch et al. put it, 'the utilitarian view is particularly appropriate to confidentiality as it will readily admit that the duty is not absolute and can be breached in certain circumstances' (Stauch et al. *Sourcebook on Medical Law* (2002)).

AG v Guardian Newspapers (No.2) [1990] illustrates the utilitarian approach wherein Lord Goff said that "although there is a public interest in preserving confidences which should be preserved and protected by the law, nevertheless that public interest may be outweighed by some other countervailing public interest which favours disclosure".

Upholding Autonomy and Respect for a person's privacy

Preserving confidentiality can also be justified by invoking the moral principles of autonomy and respect for a person's privacy (used by the deontologists who use the language of duty and morality).

The duty of confidentiality is to be maintained even after a patient's death but it is not entirely clear as to whether there is a strict legal obligation to keep confidences after the death of a patient if the relevant information is in the death certificate which is a public document, since this information is generally accessible. In addition, it should be noted that doctors do not enjoy a privilege equivalent to legal professional privilege.

Confidentiality for people under 16

The legal position with regard to healthcare for persons under 16 is considered in detail in the chapter on Children and Healthcare (see ch. 2) and is also considered in the chapter on Consent (see ch. 1). Suffice to say for present purposes that according to the Guidance issued jointly by the BMA, GMSC, HEA, Brook Advisory Centres, FPA and RCGP:

- the duty of confidentiality owed to a person under 16 is as great as that owed to any other person. Regardless of whether or not the requested treatment is given, the confidentiality of the consultation should still be

respected, unless there are convincing reasons to the
contrary.

● Any competent young person, regardless of age, can
independently seek medical advice and give valid consent
to medical treatment.

● Competency is understood in terms of the patient's ability
to understand the choices and their consequences, including the nature, purpose, and possible risk of any treatment (or non-treatment)

This has to be read with reference to the leading House of
Lords' ruling in the *Gillick* case (*Gillick v Wisbech and W. Norfolk
AHA* [1985] 3 All ER 402). This case establishes that people
under 16 who are able fully to understand the treatment
proposed and its implications, are competent to consent to
medical treatment regardless of age.

The GMC Guidance reiterates that people under 16 are legally
able to consent on their own behalf to any surgical, medical or
dental procedure or treatment if, in the doctor's opinion, they
are capable of understanding the nature and possible consequences of the procedure. Clearly, the more serious the
medical procedure proposed, a correspondingly better grasp of
the implications is required. Doctors should particularly consider what are in essence the Lord Fraser guidelines when
consulted by people under 16 for contraceptive services. (see ch.
2)

Under the heading 'Immature Patients', the Guidance states:

'The General Medical Council advises that disclosure without
consent may be justified where the patient does not have sufficient
understanding to appreciate what the advice or treatment being
sought may involve, cannot be persuaded to involve an appropriate person in the consultation, and where it would, in the doctor's
belief, be essential to the best medical interests of the patient. Thus
it is clear that the doctor is not entitled to breach confidentiality
unless all these conditions are met. Therefore, even when the
doctor considers the young person is too immature to consent to
the treatment requested, confidentiality should still be respected
concerning the consultation, unless there are very convincing
reasons to the contrary'.

Under 'Exceptional circumstances', it states:

Although respect for confidentiality is an essential element of
doctor-patient relationships, no patient, adult or minor, has an
absolute right to complete confidentiality in all circumstances.

Confidentiality must be balanced against society's interests in protecting vulnerable people from serious harm. Thus, in rare cases, for example, a breach of confidentiality may be justified if the patient's silence puts others at risk and the doctor cannot persuade the patient to make a voluntary disclosure.

In exceptional circumstances, the doctor may believe that the young person seeking medical advice on sexual matters is being exploited or abused. The doctor should provide counselling with a view to preparing the patient to agree, when ready, to confidentiality being relaxed. This task assumes greater urgency if the patient, siblings or other minors continue to be in a situation of risk so that in some cases, the doctor will have to tell the patient that confidentiality cannot be preserved. Disclosure should not be made without first discussing it with the patient whose co-operation is sought. To breach confidentiality without informing the patient and in contradiction of patient refusal may irreparably damage the trust between doctor and patient and may result in denial by the young person that abuse has taken place.

Legal bases for confidentiality

Sources of the legal obligation of confidence

There is some uncertainty as to the legal foundation of the duty of confidentiality or why there is a legal obligation of confidence (Law Commission, Breach of Confidence (Law Com.No.110, 1981. Cmnd 8388). Seven grounds were identified by Wacks (1977) as to the basis of a legal obligation including contract (implied or express), the general duty of care in negligence (in the law of tort) and a special obligation in equity, where equity here refers to the special jurisdiction which grew up as a subdivision of judge-made law and the corpus of law that has accumulated within it. Contract, equity and property or a mixture of these have at different times provided the basis on which the courts have granted relief. The lack of clarity prompted a Law Commission inquiry which reported in 1981 (see Law Commission No.110, above) but despite making several recommendations, including a new statutory tort of breach of confidence, so far, nothing has actually been turned into statute.

BREACH OF CONFIDENCE

Elements of the action for breach of confidence

Lord Goff (*AG v Guardian Newspapers (No.2)* (1990), outlined the three elements which give rise to an action for breach of confidence: (a) when confidential information comes to the knowledge of a person; (b) in circumstances where he has notice, or is held to have agreed, that the information is confidential; and (c) with the effect that it would be just in all the circumstances that he should be precluded from disclosing the information to others.

He then added three limiting principles:

- the principle of confidence only applies to information to the extent that it is confidential (ie that it is private); once it enters the public domain, it is generally accessible to the public and then, as a general rule, the principle of confidentiality can have no application to it.
- it does not apply to useless information or to trivia.
- the public interest in preserving confidences may be outweighed by some other countervailing public interest which favours disclosure.

Justifications for breaching confidentiality

As we have seen from the GMC Guidance, there are several justifications for breaching confidentiality, ranging from statutory to public interest reasons. Some of the more common exceptions will now be considered under the following headings:

  (i) Disclosure with Patient's Consent
 (ii) Statutorily Permissible Breaches of Confidentiality
    (a) Road Traffic Act
    (b) Terrorism Act 2000
    (c) Healthcare Statutes
(iii) Disclosure in the Public Interest on the basis of
    (a) Protecting the public generally
    (b) Protecting the public from crime
    (c) Protecting third parties

There are also cases where the courts have upheld the duty of confidentiality and therefore maintained a prohibition on disclosure to third parties by the doctor, for example in relation to a patient's sexual conduct.

Disclosure with patient's consent

The patient may certainly give his or her express consent to pass confidential information on to a third party either orally or in writing and this will justify a breach of confidence. On the other hand, the patient may be taken to give implied consent when a patient makes no objection to, for example, the sharing of information. The typical situation is where there is a healthcare team providing care to the patient.

Disclosure allowed by statute

Obligations under the Road Traffic Act 1988 in relation to a doctor's confidentiality, came under judicial scrutiny in *Hunter v Mann* (1974). A car, taken without the owner's consent, was involved in an accident. After the accident both the driver and passenger left the scene and could not be traced. Later that day, a doctor treated a man and a woman for injuries. The woman said they had been involved in a car accident. The police later approached the doctor and asked for the names of those who had been treated. Section 168 (3), (now s.172) provided that:

"Where the driver of a vehicle is alleged to be guilty of an offence to which this section applies.
  (b) any other person shall be required as aforesaid give any information which is in his power to give and which may lead to the identification of the driver."

The issue for the Court was whether a doctor who failed to comply with the provision under s.168, in respect of information brought to his knowledge in the course of his professional relationship with a patient, was guilty of an offence under s.168(3). The doctor argued that the relevant words should be given a restricted meaning, so as to exclude confidential information, and those in a special position of confidence such as doctors.

Boreham, J. stated that the doctor is under a duty not to voluntarily disclose, without the consent of the patient, information which he, the doctor, has gained in his professional capacity. It was important to bear in mind the distinction between *privilege* which is to be claimed in legal proceedings and a *contractual duty* not to disclose. Privilege refers to a right to withhold from a court or a tribunal exercising judicial function, materials which would otherwise be available in evidence. The contractual duty of confidence exists between banker and customer, doctor and patient and accountant and client. *Such a duty is subject to, and overridden by, the duty of any party to that contract to comply with the law of the land...* In the present case, he saw no ground for saying that a restricted meaning should be given to the words of the statute. Hence, the doctor remains liable under the statute. The doctor is expected to provide the patient's name and address but not the clinical details relating to the patient.

There is no general obligation to volunteer information to the police unless a specific statute creates such a duty. It is not usually a crime to stay silent except in the context of anti-terrorist legislation.

Terrorism Act 2000 (previously covered by s.18 Prevention of Terrorism Act 1989)

Section 18 of the Prevention of Terrorism Act 1989 made it an offence for any person having information which he believed could be of material assistance in preventing terrorism or apprehending terrorists to fail without reasonable excuse to give that information to the police. The duty of confidence between doctor and patient was not seen as a reasonable excuse for failing to go to the police. The 1989 Act was replaced by the Terrorism Act 2000 which no longer requires healthcare professional to inform the police if there is any reasonable suspicion of a person being involved in terrorist activities. There is only a duty on everyone, including doctors, to inform the police if they believe or suspect certain offences concerning *funding* of terrorist activity have been committed: ss.19, 20: Terrorism Act 2000.

Healthcare statutes

AIDS is not a notifiable disease under the Public Health (Control of Diseases) Act 1984 but under the AIDS (Control) Act 1987, health authorities must provide reports to the responsible minister. The minister (the Secretary of State for health) can also order hospitalisation and, if necessary, detention of sufferers under the Public Health (Infectious Diseases) Regulations 1985, SI 1985/434.

Health Act 1999, s.23(2)

The Health Act has created the Commission for Health Improvement (CHI) which can be authorised to inspect NHS premises and take copies of documents, includes authorisation of patient records. Under s.23(2) The general rule is that the statute and regulations cannot identify an individual without that person's consent (unless they cannot be traced after taking reasonable steps to do so) but this rule does not apply if there is an investigation by CHI into the management, provision or quality of care. Hence an individual can be identified to CHI provided it is not practicable to anonymise the information or the Commission considers there is a serious risk to the health or safety of patients arising from the matters under investigation and that the Commission considers that the information should be disclosed without that individual's consent.

Health and Social Care Act 2001

This Act has created the power to make regulations to permit the use of patient information to improve patient care or in pursuit of the public interest. Again the power can only be used if it is not practicable to anonymise the information or to obtain the patient's consent.

Police and Criminal Evidence Act 1984

Police may obtain a warrant when investigating a serious offence, to obtain material which would assist them in their inquiries. However, s.9 of the 1984 Act deals with 'excluded material' which would include a patent's medical records, samples of tissue, and fluids. An application would have to be made to a circuit judge if the police wishes to examine these.

Disclosure in the public interest

Apart from the traditional duty of secrecy incorporated into the professional codes of health workers, there is a strong public interest in maintaining confidentiality so that individuals will be encouraged to seek appropriate treatment and share information relevant to it.

A balance needs to be struck between upholding public and private interests. For example, there is a public interest in freedom of speech and also a private interest in maintaining the privacy of an individual's communications or activities. There is also a public interest in maintaining the secrets of the security service against foreign powers as there is in the disclosure of alleged wrongdoing.

What is the 'public interest'?

The concept of the 'public interest' is a well-known exceptional situation where the right of an individual to confidentiality as contemplated by statute, case law and professional guidance may be overruled by society's interest in disclosure. It has always been in the nature of an overriding supervening public interest but there is no universal definition of what it means. It has been discussed in cases such as *AG v Guardian Newspapers* (1990) (the Spycatcher case) and *W v Egdell* (1990). In other words, as with many such cases in medical law, and by virtue of the generality of the concept, each case has to be considered on its own merits, so that precedent plays a smaller part than in other areas of law.

(a) Protecting the Public Generally: *X v Y; H v N*

Two contrasting types of cases illustrate the English courts' approach to the issue of breaching confidence in the interests of protecting the public generally. In *X v Y* (1988)(the HIV doctors), a national newspaper acquired and published, in breach of confidence from a health authority employee, details regarding two general practitioners (GPs) who had developed AIDS but were continuing to practise. The Health Authority sought an injunction to stop further publication of the doctors' and patients' names. The newspaper argued that the public at large, and the doctors' patients, in particular, had an interest in knowing that doctors were HIV positive.

Rose, J. considered the evidence regarding transmission of HIV from doctor to patient where the doctor had received proper counselling about safe practice. He concluded that the risk to patients was negligible and there were greater risks from the possibility that if they could not rely on confidential treatment, people with AIDS, or who feared they might have AIDS, would not seek medical help. In granting the injunction, the learned judge remarked that:

> 'preservation of confidentiality is the only way of securing public health; otherwise doctors will be discredited as a source of education, for future individual patients will not come forward if doctors are going to squeal on them. Consequently, confidentiality is vital to secure public as well as private health, for unless those infected come forward they cannot be counselled and self-treatment does not provide the best care . . .'.

Hence, the Court prohibited the tabloid newspaper from identifying the two HIV positive doctors.

More recently, in *H v N (a Health Authority)*; *H v Associated Newspapers Ltd* (2002), the Court of Appeal upheld a ban on the identification of an HIV positive NHS dentist, where the dentist had applied for an injunction restraining a health authority from revealing his identity to the newspapers. The dentist had disclosed (in confidence) to the health authority the fact that he was HIV positive. He had, however, ceased to treat his patients. The newspaper wished to reveal the identity of the health authority but this was also prohibited by the court because such identification would lead to the deductive identification of the dentist. The health authority had a legitimate interest in protecting the information they had obtained in confidence from one of their workers which, on balance, outweighed the right of the press to inform the public of the dentist's identity.

In *Egdell*, the second type of case, the Court of Appeal took a different view.

(b) Protecting the Public from crime

In *W v Egdell* (1990) the patient, W, was a prisoner sentenced to indefinite detention in a secure hospital, following conviction for the manslaughter of five people and the wounding of two others. He could be released only by order of the Home Secretary if he were found to be no longer a danger to public safety. He applied, unsuccessfully, to a mental health review tribunal to be transferred to another unit which would be a step towards his discharge. He then applied for a conditional discharge. His legal advisers sought the advice of Dr Egdell, an independent psychiatrist to support his application but the latter's opinion was that the patient was still dangerous, had a psychopathic personality, no real insight into his condition and a morbid interest in explosives. The application for discharge was withdrawn but the adverse report was not passed to the tribunal or the hospital where W was detained. Dr Egdell asked that a copy of his report be placed in W's hospital file but W's solicitors refused as the report has been commissioned confidentially. Realising that his report would not be included in his notes, Dr Egdell sent a copy of the report to the medical director of W's hospital and to the Home Office.

W's solicitors obtained an injunction to restrain Dr Egdell from disclosing the contents of the report at the hearing but unknown to them, disclosure had already taken place. W sued Dr Egdell for breach of confidence, but both the lower court and Court of Appeal upheld the breach on the grounds of the public interest, i.e. the protection of the public from dangerous criminal acts.

The Appeal Court confirmed that Dr Egdell did owe W a duty of confidence but Bingham, L.J. opined that:

'The breach of such a duty is . . . in any case, dependent on the circumstances . . . The decided cases establish that (1) that the law recognises an important public interest in maintaining professional duties of confidence but (2) that the law treats such duties not as absolute but as liable to be overridden where there is held to be a stronger public interest in disclosure.'

Bingham, L.J. observed that 'the critical question was how the balance should be struck between the public interest in maintaining professional confidences and the public interest in protecting the public against possible violence'. On the evidence, he said that:

'There is one consideration which . . . weighs the balance of public interest decisively in favour of disclosure . . . Where a man has committed multiple killings under the disability of serious mental illness, decisions which may lead directly or indirectly to his release from hospital should not be made unless a responsible authority is properly able to make an informed judgment that the risk of repetition is so small as to be acceptable . . . Dr Egdell did . . . act in accordance with the law and his conduct was . . . necessary in the interests of public safety and the prevention of crime.'

The implication, therefore, was that in the exceptional circumstances, with the potential danger to the public still present, the duty could be breached.

Brazier in *Medicine, Patients and the Law* (1992) submits 'that *X v Y* and *Egdell* do not mean that a doctor may never disclose that a patient has AIDS, or that he may always disclose findings about a patient's health'. As she points out, 'In each case, the powerful interest in maintaining confidentiality must be balanced against the danger ensuing if confidentiality is not breached. Only where there is clear and significant risk of the patient causing harm to others which cannot be abated by any other means may confidence be breached . . . For disclosure to be lawful there must be an overwhelming public interest in disclosure'.

R. v Crozier (1990) Court of Appeal

In *R. v. Crozier*, *W v Egdell* was considered (and analogies drawn between the psychiatrists in each case), where the public interest defence of the prevention of a crime was also upheld by the Court of Appeal. There, a psychiatrist, instructed by the defendant in an attempted murder case, disclosed his report to the prosecution (which concluded that the defendant was suffering from a psychopathic disorder) when he realised that the defence had not produced it in court, where a sentence of imprisonment of nine years had been passed. As a result, the Crown informed the judge of the contents of the report, and the judge quashed the sentence of imprisonment, making a hospital order instead. The Appeal Court thought there was a stronger case for disclosure in the public interest than in maintaining the duty of confidentiality.

The notion of the 'public interest' remains open to interpretation and the cases suggest that the particular situation that comes before the courts would have to be sufficiently serious in terms of the danger posed before the breach of confidence would be justifiable. The perceived potential danger would have to be proven and physical harm to a third party would probably need to be the greatest risk. Hence, for example, there does not appear to be any 'right' to disclosure in any spouse (of the other spouse's condition).

(c) Disclosure to Protect Third Parties

Tarasoff-a leading American case

The duty of confidence is not absolute and respecting confidences at all costs can have dire consequences, as the well-known American case of *Tarasoff* (1976) illustrates. In August 1969, the patient, P, was a voluntary outpatient receiving therapy at a Hospital in the University of California at Berkeley. The plaintiff's case was that P informed his therapist that he was going to kill an unnamed girl, his former girlfriend, who was readily identifiable as Tatiana Tarasoff when she returned home from spending the summer in Brazil. The therapist contacted the police who briefly detained the patient but released him when he appeared to be rational and he promised not to harm the woman. The therapist's superior directed that no further action be taken to detain P. Thus, no one warned the victim about the threat. In October 1969, shortly after her return from Brazil, P went to see her at her home and killed her there. Her parents sued the psychologist/therapist, his superior and the university.

The court held that there is a duty of care owed by the therapist to the woman murdered by the therapist's patient. It accepted that there was a balance to be drawn between the public interest in effective treatment of mental illness and the consequent requirement of protecting confidentiality, and the public interest in safety from violent assault. 'The protective privilege ends where the public peril begins'.

Protecting third parties even if no potential crime is threatened

In *Re C (A Minor) (Evidence: Confidential Information)* (1991) a breach of confidence was necessary to protect third parties but not to prevent a crime. The facts were that there was a proposed adoption of a one year old baby. The mother withdrew her consent a day before the adoption hearing. At an adjourned hearing, the adopting parents' solicitor produced an affidavit sworn voluntarily by the mother's GP, containing evidence of her mental condition and fitness to bring up a child. The mother objected to the admissibility of the evidence as it was a breach of medical confidentiality. She was unsuccessful in the lower court and appealed.

Sir Stephen Brown regarded this case as unusual with no previous authority directly in point; all the cases which had been cited to them were referring to very different situations. Since it involved the adoption of a little child, it was a very serious matter for the child, and a serious decision for the court to have to make when the mother was withholding her consent. The court needed to have all relevant and significant information before it to assist it in making a right decision.

The case turned on its own special facts and the court had considerable hesitation in concluding that any breach of confidence had taken place. The learned judge declared 'In this case the doctor was justified in making available her evidence . . . I believe that a judge, if carrying out some balancing exercise, would be fully justified in coming down clearly in favour of admitting this evidence. It should also be recognised that the disclosure of the material contained in this affidavit was the subject of a restricted disclosure. It was being made available only to the judge who had to decide the application, and to those who were also bound by the confidentiality of the hearing in chambers'. Accordingly, he concluded that the judge was correct to rule that this evidence was admissible and that it should be admitted.

Prohibiting disclosure to third parties

In *Wyatt v Wilson* (1820) an action was taken against George III's physician to stop him publishing his diary which contained information about the King's health and mental instability. The action was upheld.

Information relating to sexual conduct could be subject to legally enforceable duty of confidentiality

In *Stephens v Avery* (1988), the plaintiff and first defendant were close friends who freely discussed matters of a personal and private nature on the express basis that what the plaintiff told the first defendant was secret and disclosed in confidence. The first defendant passed on to the second and third defendants, who were the editor and publishers of a newspaper, details of the plaintiff's sexual conduct, including details of the plaintiff's lesbian relationship with a woman who had been killed by her husband. The plaintiff sued the defendants, claiming damages on the grounds that the information was confidential and was knowingly published by the newspaper in breach of the duty of confidence owed by the defendant to the plaintiff. The defendants applied to strike out the claim as disclosing no reasonable cause of action but their application was refused.

On appeal, the Court held that information relating to sexual conduct (in that case, a lesbian relationship) could be the subject of a legally enforceable duty of confidentiality, if it would be unconscionable for a person who had received information on the express basis that it was confidential subsequently to reveal that information to another.

On the basis of *Stephens v Avery*, information concerning the sexual conduct of a patient, if imparted to a doctor in circumstances of confidentiality, will be protected even though it is not strictly medical information as such. In *A v B plc* (2001) reported on November 2, 2001 in *The Times*, the High Court appears to have confirmed that the law of confidentiality applies irrespective of the absence of the sexual partners' agreement to disclosure of such information.

In *R. v Wilson* (1996), in the Court of Appeal, the defendant appealed against his conviction for actual bodily harm under s.47 of the Offences against the Person Act 1861. He had been charged as a result of marking his wife's buttocks with his initials by the use of a hot knife. This was done with her consent, and it appears from the case reports, at her request. The implications from the case appears to be that there was a potential breach of confidentiality here if the police were informed by the doctor who became aware of the marks when he was examining her in the course of a medical examination. The fact that the information was not strictly medical would not entitle the doctor to assert the duty of confidentiality because, first, on the basis of *Stephens v Avery* (above), it has the necessary basis of confidence and secondly, it was imparted in the circumstances of a medical consultation. The information had to be kept confidential.

Remedy for improper disclosure: an action for defamation

The action of defamation may also be available if a doctor's disclosure does take place which causes responsible persons to shun the patient do he or she becomes open to ridicule, hatred or contempt. Clearly, diagnoses of AIDS, venereal disease, alcoholism and indeed allegations of child abuse would all be possibly defamatory if they were disclosed to a third party and were subsequently proved to be untrue. Of course, if what the doctor said is true, this would be a complete defence. Another defence would be qualified privilege if the doctor reasonably believed his statements to be true and he communicated them to a person with a legitimate interest in relevant information such as the police.

HOSPITAL REPORTS AND CONFIDENTIALITY

Reports prepared in contemplation of litigation are covered by legal privilege

Reports will usually be prepared by hospitals after an incident. If these are merely routine, then they are not prima facie, covered by legal privilege. However, if such reports are prepared in contemplation of litigation, they might be covered by legal privilege and cannot usually be disclosed.

In *Lee v South West Thames RHA* (1985), an infant suffered brain damage due to treatment in one of two hospitals. The first was under the control of Hillingdon AHA and the second was under the control of North East Thames AHA. Disclosure of reports compiled by the ambulance crew of SW Thames RHA for the purpose of Hillingdon obtaining legal advice was refused. The court held that they were covered by legal professional privilege. The rationale for this decision seems to be that a defendant should be able to obtain evidence without having to disclose the findings of the other party.

In *Re HIV Haemophiliac Litigation* (1990) a large number of haemophiliacs received transfusions of blood infected with HIV. They sought to bring an action against the Department of Health on the grounds that the Department was negligen in failing to ensure that there was enough blood available for donation in the UK, which necessitated having to obtain blood from the USA. The government refused disclosure of certain documents on the ground that the law did not permit such disclosure. These documents contained briefings for ministers as to whether a policy for self-sufficiency in blood products should be established and what measures should be required for such a policy, planning decisions relating to the Blood Products Laboratory and the decision whether and how to organise the Blood Transfusion Service.

The Court of Appeal held that discovery of the documents was necessary in order for the plaintiffs to make a thorough presentation of their case. However, reports prepared as part of the organisation's normal administrative routine, would not be included and therefore subject to disclosure.

Confidentiality, informants and public policy

Identity of informant can remain confidential for 'public policy' reasons

Another reason for maintaining confidentiality has been the notion of 'public policy'. The English courts have been prepared to exclude confidential personal information if its exclusion is based on public policy reasons for instance in issues of vital importance to the State: see *Duncan v Cammell Laird* (1942). The courts have also used public-policy grounds to justify the exclusion of evidence relating to police sources of information in order to facilitate the investigation of crime. However, the issue of whether information could be kept confidential purely because it was confidential was examined by the House of Lords in *D v NSPCC* (1977), where the National Society for the Prevention of Cruelty to Children, a national charity which has the power to bring care proceedings, received a complaint that a child was being maltreated. The Society sent one of its inspectors to investigate the complaint and visited the mother at her home; the complaint was found to be false, as the child had been well treated. The mother of the child she had allegedly abused, brought proceedings in negligence against the NSPCC, following the illness she had suffered (allegedly from shock) from the society inspector's visit. She alleged that the society had failed properly to investigate the complaint made against her and applied for an order that the NSPCC should disclose to her all the documents in its possession relating to the identity of the person who had made the false allegation against her.

The society denied negligence and applied for an order that there should be no discovery of documents which might reveal the identity of the complainant/informant. They argued that without guaranteed confidentiality of sources, individuals might be discouraged from coming forward. The House of Lords rejected the mother's disclosure application and held that in the interests of the proper functioning of a body such as the NSPCC, charged with the duty of protecting children against ill-treatment, they should have immunity from disclosure, analogous to the guaranteed anonymity of police informers. Several further points were made by the Law Lords:

(i) There was no public interest in safeguarding confidentiality per se in the law of evidence.
(ii) However, confidential information may be protected if there is a sufficiently strong public interest in doing so. Lord Hailsham held that there was a public interest that the party able to bring care proceedings should receive information under a cloak of confidentiality. Whether it was the police or the local authority or the NSPCC, they were all entitled to claim protection for the confidentiality of their sources.

Lord Diplock's comment is particularly instructive, when he said:

> "The private promise of confidentiality must yield to the general public interest that in the administration of justice, truth will out unless by reason of the character of the information or the relationship of the recipient of the information to the informant a more important public interest is served by protecting the information or the identity of the informant in a court of law".

Hence, the case also confirmed the principle of disclosure in the interests of the administration of justice.

Access to medical records

The implementation of data protection legislation in early 2000 changed patients' statutory rights of access to their health records. This is by virtue of the Data Protection Act 1998. Here are the main points of the legal requirements on doctors as holders of health records: (see: BMA Guidance and relevant statutes)

- All manual and computerised health records about living people are accessible under the Data Protection Act 1998. The data controller is obliged to comply only where he can be sure of the identity of the person requesting the information: s.7(3) Data Protection Act 1998 (DPA).
- Access must be given equally to all records regardless of when they were made.
- Competent patients may apply for access to their own records, or may authorise a third party, such as their lawyer, to do so on their behalf.
- Parents have access to their child's records if it is in the child's best interests and not contrary to a competent child's wishes (a competent child would be a '*Gillick* competent' child: (see Ch. 2).
- People appointed by a court to manage the affairs of mentally incapacitated adults may have access to information necessary to fulfil their function.

Exemptions
The main exemptions are that information must not be disclosed if it is:

- likely to cause serious physical or mental harm to the patient or another person; this only applies where the information relates to the physical or mental health of the patient or condition of the patient: Art.3(1): Data Protection (Subject Access Modification) (Health) Order 2000 (DPO); or if the data controller is the health professional currently or most recently responsible for the patient, or after the data controller has consulted such a professional: Art.5(2) DPO 2000;
- relates to a third party who has not given consent for disclosure (where the third party is not a health professional who has cared for the patient); disclosure is permitted where the third party does give consent to disclosure or it is reasonable to comply without the third party's consent: s.7(4) DPA.

Copies of the records

Patients are entitled to a copy of their records, i.e. a photocopy of paper records or print out of computerised records.

Applications for access to records

There is no legal requirement that prevents doctors from informally showing patients their records or, bearing in mind duties of confidentiality, discussing relevant health issues with carers. The fees charged will depend on the type of record and whether the patient wants copies of the records or just to see them.

Patient has no absolute right to medical records

In *R. v Mid-Glamorgan FHSA ex p. Martin* (1995) the Court of Appeal has held that a health authority has the right to deny a patient access to his medical records if it was deemed to be in the patient's best interests to do so.

Access to records of deceased patients

The Data Protection Act 1998 only covers the records of living patients. If a person has a claim arising from the death of an individual, he or she has a right of access to information in the deceased's records necessary to fulfil that claim. The patient's personal representative also has the right to apply for such access: see s.3: Access to Health Records 1990. The provisions and fees are slightly different from those in the Data Protection Act.

Statutory right of access to employment or insurance medical records

An individual has the statutory right to access to any medical report relating to the individual which is to be, or has been, supplied by a medical practitioner for employment or insurance purposes under the Access to Medical Reports Act 1988. Under s.5 thereof, the patient also has the right to correct any inaccuracies in such records and the record holder has the option of whether to make the amendments or note the alleged inaccuracies. The record holder has the right to refuse access to such records if it is believed that disclosure would 'be likely to cause serious harm to the physical or mental health of the individual or others'. The patient's consent must be obtained before such records can be disclosed and the patient must also be informed of the right of access, and the right to consent and to amend the records.

Supreme Court Act 1981

Sections 33 and 34 of the Supreme Court Act 1981 permit disclosure of documents, both prior to commencement of proceedings, and during the course of those legal proceedings. This is an exception to the principle of confidentiality. The provisions of the Act permit disclosure to the applicant's legal and medical advisers only. Given that doctors are now permitted to show patients their records on an informal basis, there appears to be no legal obstacle to prevent the advisers showing the applicant his medical notes.

CONFIDENTIALITY, HIV and AIDS

Ethical perspectives

Although AIDs carries with it a damaging stigma because of its implied sexual connotations and its serious association with drug addiction, it does not automatically follow that disclosure of HIV-seropositivity should be disclosed by a doctor to a third party. The delicate problem here is whether relaxation of the confidentiality rule would lead to a failure to seek advice and treatment and thus to the spread of the disease, or whether the imposition of absolute secrecy would deny others the opportunity to avoid the risk of exposure to infection. Should a sexual partner be informed of the risk if the patient declines to inform him or her? There is arguably a potentially dangerous situation if the person known to be affected is employed in an environment where he might expose others to the virus. The public dimension also enters the equation so it is not just a case of balancing conflicting private interests. Since AIDS is not a notifiable disease, at least its exemption helps to maintain confidentiality. Arguably, mandatory notifiability would inhibit people from undergoing testing and in any event, HIV is transmitted in very rare circumstances, if at all (see Mason and McCall Smith (2002)).

The GMC has advised doctors that patients should be persuaded of the need for their GPs to be informed of the diagnosis of HIV seropositivity but states that the patient's wishes should be respected if consent to disclosure is refused. The exception will be where the doctor believes that a failure to pass on this information exposes other health staff to serious risk. In any event, the doctor must be prepared to justify such action.

GMC guidance

The General Medical Council (GMC) has issued specific guidance on serious communicable diseases.

Informing other health care professionals

If you diagnose a patient as having a serious communicable disease, you should explain to the patient:

- the nature of the disease and its medical, social and occupational implications, as appropriate;
- ways of protecting others from infection;
- the importance of giving the professionals who will be providing care information which they need to know about the patient's disease or condition. In particular, you must make sure the patient understands that general practitioners cannot provide adequate clinical management and care without knowledge of their patients' conditions.
- If patients still refuse to allow other healthcare workers to be informed, you must respect the patients' wishes except where you judge that failure to disclose the information would put a healthcare worker or other patient at serious risk of death or serious harm. Such situations may arise, for example, when dealing with violent patients with severe mental illness or disability. If you are in doubt about whether disclosure is appropriate, you should seek advice from an experienced colleague. You should inform patients before disclosing information. Such occasions are likely to arise rarely and you must be prepared to justify a decision to disclose information against a patient's wishes.

Disclosures to others

You must disclose information about serious communicable diseases in accordance with the law. For example, the appropriate authority must be informed where a notifiable disease is diagnosed. Where a communicable disease has contributed to the cause of death, this must be recorded on the death certificate. You should also pass information about serious communicable diseases to the relevant authorities for the purpose of disease control and surveillance.

A patient's death does not, of itself, release a doctor from the obligation to maintain confidentiality. But in some circumstances disclosures can be justified because they protect other people from serious harm or because they are required by law.

Giving information to close contacts

You may disclose information about a patient, whether living or dead, in order to protect a person from risk of death or serious harm. For example, you may disclose information as to a known sexual contact of a patient with HIV where you have reason to think that the patient has not informed that person, and cannot be persuaded to do so. In such circumstances, you should tell the patient before you make the disclosure, and you must be prepared to justify a decision to disclose information.

You must not disclose information to others, for example, relatives, who have not been, and are not, at risk of infection.

This Guidance, which does not have the force of law, suggests that if there is a serious and identifiable risk to a specific individual, and this might include a spouse or sexual partner, then disclosure appears to be permitted. *Re C (A Minor (Evidence: Confidential Information)* (1991) provides some authority for arguing that in the case of the spouse or partner who is also a patient of the doctor, they may be given confidential information by the doctor without committing a breach of the duty (see above).

If a sexual partner intentionally infects his partner without disclosing that he has AIDS, he may be liable to criminal prosecution and imprisonment: see *R v Dica* (2004)

On the litigation front, it is perhaps arguable that a patient would have a prima facie cause of action against a doctor who warned his or her spouse or other sexual partner of their potential risk. Mason and McCall Smith (2002) believe it is unlikely that a court would award damages to such a plaintiff, and the argument that disclosure was necessary to protect others from a possibly fatal risk will certainly carry a great deal of weight and may well counterbalance the two private interests.

As far as prisons are concerned, we have an environment which many might consider highly susceptible to the spread of the condition and the consequences of disclosure of a positive status could be disastrous for the individual concerned. Consequently, while a policy of confidentiality is the norm, it is difficult, if not impossible to maintain so long as positivity is seen to be synonymous with segregation, the provision of separate utensils and similar 'safety' measures, and there has therefore been some limited breaching of confidentiality in accordance with a 'need to know' policy on the part of staff (see Groves *"Prison Policies on HIV under review"*) (1991) BMJ). However, the possibility of disclosure discourages voluntary testing and counselling and also prohibits effective public health measures.

INTERNATIONAL PROTECTION OF PRIVACY RIGHTS?

It is possible to argue that the principle of confidentiality would come under the broader notion of privacy that operates in jurisdictions like the USA. However, English law does not recognise any explicit right to privacy. Nevertheless, Art.8 of the European Convention of Human Rights (ECHR) has been interpreted by the European Court of Human Rights as affording protection to individual privacy (see *Malone v UK Applications*, No. 8691/79 (1984) which might be useful for future UK applicants. Art.8 of the ECHR provides:

1. Everyone has the right to respect for his private and family life, his home and correspondence.
2. There shall be no interference by a public authority with the exercise of this right except in accordance with the law and is necessary in a democratic society in the interests of national security, public safety or the economic well being of the country, for the prevention of disorder or crime, for the protection of health or morals, or for the protection of the rights and freedom of others.

For the leading case on Art.8 and medical confidentiality see *Z v Finland* (1998).

From October 2, 2000, the European Convention became part of English law by virtue of the Human Rights Act 1998 which entered into force on that day. Thus Art.8 (ECHR) can now be invoked in the English domestic courts to support the right to confidentiality.

4. MEDICAL NEGLIGENCE

INTRODUCTION

The main principles in English law which determine medical negligence, are, in essence, the same principles as the general principles which operate under the English tort of negligence. In the context of medical practice, however, there are certain aspects of the basic law on negligence which require special attention, such as causation and the relevance of standard medical procedure, as recognised and accepted by a responsible body of medical opinion, known as the Bolam test.

NEGLIGENCE IN ENGLISH LAW

Negligence in English law may be described as any conduct that falls short of the standard expected of a person where a duty of care is owed and which causes foreseeable damage to another person. Hence, in order to establish negligence (in the medical context or otherwise): (i) the plaintiff must prove that *the defendant owed the plaintiff a duty of care* in the particular situation; (ii) If so, *that the defendant breached this duty* in the sense that he failed to confirm to the standard of care required by the law? (iii) that *the plaintiff suffered injury or loss (damage) as a result of the defendant's actions*, either directly or as part of a transaction (although causation requirements would have be established) (see *Lochgelly Iron and Coal Co. v M'Mullan* [1934] and *Burton v Islington* [1992], per Dillon, L.J: "it is now elementary that the tort of negligence involves three factors: a duty of care, breach of that duty and consequent damage").

Duty of care between doctor and patient

The conventional view in English law is that a duty of care does exist between a healthcare professional and her patient. This is usually the case where patients are in hospital, where the staff are responsible for their care, and in general practice, where doctors have a duty of care to those on their lists.

GENERAL PRINCIPLES

Health professionals may be held accountable if there is a complaint to their professional body, that is, the General Medical Council, or United Kingdom Central Council for Nursing, Midwifery and Health Visiting. There is also a complaints procedure available to a patient, to a hospital, or FHSA, or health service ombudsman. They could also be liable under the criminal law but an intention to kill or cause grievous bodily harm would have to be proved; an intention to relieve pain through prescribing painkilling drugs which is known would shorten life, would not constitute an intention to murder: _R. v Adams_ (1957). Under the civil law, healthcare professionals may also face a malpractice suit. Another general principle is that no civil liability normally arises from a mere omission if it makes no difference to the outcome (see _Barnett v Chelsea_ [1968]).

No contract between doctor and patient treated by the NHS

In English common law, the tort (civil wrong) of negligence is a well-established cause of action and together with the law of battery, plays a major part in the arena of Medical law. This is because as a general principle, there is no contractual relationship between doctor and patient (see _Pfizer Corp. v Ministry of Health_ (1965)) except where the patient seeks treatment privately. Even where patients have entered into contracts with their doctors, the courts have decided to impose on the doctor only those obligations which are imposed in tort; in other words, provided a duty of care is established between doctor and patient, then the usual requirements for proving negligence would apply. Thus, the doctor's duty to his National Health Service (NHS) patient, which applies to both acts and omissions, is in tort and not contract. Hence, if such a doctor is negligent, such medical negligence forms part of the law of tort. In _Kent v Griffiths & the London Ambulance Service_ (2000), the Court of Appeal held that once an ambulance (999) call has been accepted by a hospital, a duty of care is owed and the defendant becomes liable for failing to respond in time, for example, to prevent the claimant suffering respiratory arrest and a miscarriage.

On the other hand, if the doctor treating a private pa ient falls below the standard required of him by the law, that pa ient may sue him for breach of contract.

Who should be sued?

An action in negligence is normally brought against the health authority as being vicariously liable for the doctor or other health professional's negligence. Direct action against the hospital for the failure of the hospital to provide a competent medical practitioner has not yet been established in English law.

The plaintiff may sue the doctor directly (i.e. the General Practitioner (GP)) if negligence is alleged against the GP. The GP in the UK is solely responsible for the treatment of her patients and the health authority will not be responsible unless it has intervened in the GP's treatment of the patient. All partners in a practice may be liable for the actions of one of their members. The GP will normally be a member of a medical defence society or union to which he will refer any claim made against him and the society will then advise him and will undertake the defence or settlement of the claim. A GP will be vicariously liable for the negligence of staff employed by him such as nurses, but he will not be responsible for the acts of a locum or deputising doctor.

But if the GP has referred the case to some other health service employee, the patient may sue that individual or the health authority (HA) or both in a joint action. In practice, the Health Authority (rather than an individual employee) is usually sued on the grounds of convenience and on the basis of (i) the duty of the hospital to care for its patients; and (ii) the vicarious liability of a Health Authority for the negligence of its employees. The GP will not be covered by the NHS indemnity which applies to hospital doctors unless a claim arises in respect of work undertaken under a health authority contract.

NHS indemnity-arrangements for negligence claims in the NHS, October 1996

There is an NHS indemnity if the health care professional (i) was working under a contract of employment and the negligence occurred in the course of that employment; or (ii) was not working under a contract of employment but was contracted by an NHS body to provide services to persons to whom that NHS body owes a duty of care; or (iii) neither of these but where the NHS owed a duty of care to the persons injured.

This does not apply to family health service practitioners working under contracts for services, for example, GPs, general dental practitioners, family dentists, pharmacists or optometrists; or other self-employed health care professionals e.g. independent midwives; employees of FHS practices; employees of private hospitals, local education authorities or voluntary agencies.

The basic elements to prove for an action in medical negligence

(i) A duty of care was owed to the patient in question;
(ii) there was a breach of that duty by the defendant; and
(iii) injury or harm was caused to the patient as a result of that breach (which was not too remote);
[or the question may be asked: Did the conduct of the defendant (doctor) amount to a breach of a duty of care which he owed to the injured plaintiff/claimant (patient)?]

Are these elements any different from an 'ordinary' action in negligence?

No, but there are particular features in a medical negligence claim:

(i) one of the most difficult tasks is proving causation; i.e. that (assuming it was primarily one doctor) the doctor's 'negligence' (i.e. conduct which fell below that of a reasonably competent/skilful doctor in that position) actually caused the plaintiff's injury;
(ii) there is the other problem of there being a group who were all possibly responsible parties—GP, consultant, other hospital doctors, nursing staff etc. (i.e. the medical team);
(iii) the general approach of judges has been not to readily find doctors/healthcare professionals liable or guilty in negligence, applying the Bolam test as the general standard: see *Bolam v Friern Hospital Management Committee* (1957). In other words, in the vast majority of cases, provided the healthcare professional complied with the current standard procedure which would be supported by at least one responsible body of professional opinion, it would be very difficult to prove negligence.

Vicarious liability

An employer is liable for the torts of an employee committed 'within the course of employment' but not for the negligent acts of an independent contractor. A consultant surgeon might be liable according to the comments made by Denning L.J. in *Roe v Minister of Health* (1954).

Tort of false imprisonment

The tort of false imprisonment is also relevant as far as the detention of mentally disordered patients are concerned since such patient's detention must be justifiable under the common law or the Mental Health Act 1983, or will constitute the tort of false imprisonment. (see *Bournewood Community and Mental Health NHS Trust, ex parte L* [1998])

Standard of care expected from a doctor

The standard of care expected from a doctor toward his or her NHS patient is that of the reasonably skilled and experienced doctor who has the same expertise in that speciality, with no concessions being made for inexperience (see *Nettleship v Weston* [1971]; *Wilsher v Essex AHA* [1986]).

Trainee doctors working long hours

The long hours worked by the trainee doctors has also been a long-standing matter for debate and even litigation, as in *Johnstone v Bloomsbury HA* (1991) (see below).

Deviation from 'usual practice' not necessarily negligence

In *Hunter v Hanley* (1955) SC 22, a Scottish case, which preceded *Bolam* by two years, the so-called 'customs test'-whereby a defendant's conduct is tested against the normal usage of his profession or calling-was endorsed. It was said that: "there is a heavy onus on the pursuer (plaintiff) to establish three facts, and without all three his case will fail. First, it must be proved that there is a usual and normal practice; secondly, it must be proved that the defender has not adopted that practice; and thirdly (and this is of crucial importance) it must be established that the course the doctor adopted is one which no professional man of ordinary skill would have taken if he had been acting with ordinary care." Mere deviation from ordinary professional practice would not necessarily be evidence of negligence. It would depend on the particular circumstances.

Inexperience no defence–Junior and inexperienced doctors

In *Jones v Manchester Corporation* [1952], the court said that errors due to inexperience are no defence. In *Wilsher v Essex AHA* [1987] the Court of Appeal (per Glidewell, L.J.) stated that 'the law requires the trainee or learner to be judged by the same standard as his more experienced colleagues. If it did not, inexperience would frequently be urged as a defence to an action for professional negligence.' This case later went to the House of Lords.

In *Johnstone v Bloomsbury* [1991] the Court of Appeal recognised the scope for young, overworked doctors bringing actions against health authorities in respect of injury to their health caused by excessive working hours.

Keeping abreast of current developments

In *Crawford v Board of Governors of Charing Cross Hospital* (1953) Times, December 8, the lower court found that there had been no breach of duty when an operative procedure was performed resulting in paralysis, which six months previously had been the subject of a report in *The Lancet* suggesting that the procedure was likely to produce such paralysis. However, the Court of Appeal rejected the claim, declaring that doctors cannot be expected to read every article in the medical press. Failure to read a single article, it was said, may be excusable but disregard of a series of warnings in the medical press could well be evidence of negligence. In the light of the volume and rapidity of development of medical knowledge, technology and techniques, it is unreasonable to expect doctors to be aware of every possible new development. However, in the light of the 'general competence' of a practitioner, he would be expected to be reasonably up to date and aware of major developments in his field or which would be known by someone in his position.

The Bolam test

What is the standard of care required by the law? According to the leading case of *Bolam v Friern Hospital Management Committee* [1957] McNair, J. said:

"The test is the standard of the ordinary skilled man exercising and professing to have that special skill. A man need not possess the highest expert skill; it is well-established law that it is sufficient if he exercises the ordinary skill of an ordinary competent man exercising that particular art."

However, there may be accidents where English law decides that no one will be held liable (see *Roe v Ministry of Health* [1954]). A crucial and much-quoted phrase in the *Bolam* case deals with the ascertainment of breach and McNair, J. declared that a doctor would not be liable in negligence if he acted:

". . . in accordance with *a practice accepted as proper by a responsible body of medical men skilled in that particular area* . . . a man is not negligent merely because there is a body of opinion who would take a contrary view." (italics added)

The italicised phrase has become the touchstone for ascertaining whether or not a particular healthcare professional acted negligently in a given situation, thus so long as it was possible to point to 'a body of medical men' (but not merely one medical practitioner) whose practice supported the defendant's professional conduct in the situation under litigation, this satisfies the *Bolam* test, even though there could well be other medical groups who would not have followed the same practice as the defendant's. Thus, the standard of care is that which is set by at least one 'responsible' group of medical practitioners.

Yet, there is a line of authority in English law in cases such as *Hucks v Cole*, decided in 1968, that laid down that even if there had been compliance with accepted practice, this did not necessarily preclude a finding of negligence. These two divergent lines of authority seem to go back over a century. Yet the 'classic' statement from McNair, J. although uttered in a lower court judgment in 1957 appears to have been regarded even by the highest English courts as 'the law' on this area since the 1980s up until, and including the 1997 House of Lords decision in *Bolitho*, which referred to *Hucks v Cole* with approval.

The 'Bolamisation' of medical law

The so-called *Bolam* test has led to the 'Bolamisation' of Medical Law (as stated by Keown in "The Rise and Rise of the 'Bolam Test' " [1995] *Singapore Jo. Legal Studies* 342) as its more general interpretation has been applied fairly consistently since about the 1980s.

The Bolam Case [1957] 1 WLR 582 (High Court)

The plaintiff, Mr. Bolam, was a manic-depressive who was given electro-convulsive therapy. There were dangers associated with this treatment, such as seizures which would cause fractures of the patient's bones but measures such as restraint and the provision of relaxant drugs would reduce those dangers. However, Mr Bolam was not given any of these measures nor any routine warning about the danger of fracture or the availability of relaxants or restraints so that he could choose to have them utilised to reduce the risk of any personal injury he might suffer. Being unaware of these dangers, he did not ask about them and in the course of his therapy, he suffered very severe fractures of his pelvis. He therefore sued the hospital and following the judge's direction to the jury, judgment was given for the defendant hospital.

Mr Justice McNair said:

> "[Where] you get a situation which involves the use of some special skill or competence, then the test as to whether there has been negligence or not is not the test of the man on the Clapham omnibus, because he has not got this special skill. The test is the standard of the ordinary skilled man exercising and professing to have that special skill."

McNair, J. continued, "A man need not possess the highest expert skill" and that "it is well established law that it is sufficient if he exercises the ordinary skill of an ordinary competent man exercising that particular art." He also makes the now famous statement about a doctor not being guilty of negligence if he has acted "in accordance with a practice accepted as proper by a responsible body of medical men skilled in that particular art." He then declares "Putting it the other way round, a man is not negligent if he is acting in accordance with such a practice, merely because there is a body of opinion who would take a contrary view."

The Privy Council in a Malaysian appeal also applied the *Bolam* test in *Chin Keow v Government of Malaysia* [1967]. A year later, *Hucks v Cole* was decided but this case was not reported until 1993.

In the leading House of Lords' case of *Sidaway v Board of Governors of the Bethlem Royal Hospital and the Maudsley Hospital* [1984], the test received a powerful endorsement from Lord Diplock, who praised its ability to bring up to date an ancient common law principle, that it was comprehensive and applied to every aspect of the duty of care owed by a doctor to his patients in the exercise of his healing duties (per Lord Diplock in *Sidaway* (1984)). The *Bolam* test has also been approved in other common law jurisdictions and approved by the Privy Council (see *Chin Keow* (above)) although it has not had the virtually universal acceptance it has enjoyed in English courts until the 1980s. The 'test' was applied to 'treatment' in *Whitehouse v Jordan* [1981] and then to 'diagnosis' in cases like *Maynard v West Midlands RHA* [1981].

Should it matter if the doctor is a specialist?

In *Hunter v Hanley* (1955) SC 200 Lord Bridge makes it clear that a specialist will be judged by the 'standard of the specialist of ordinary skill'. This is also indicated in Sidaway's case (per Lord Bridge).

Can an error of clinical judgment ever amount to negligence?

In *Whitehouse v Jordan* [1981], the defendant was in charge of the plaintiff's delivery. It was a high risk pregnancy, and the plaintiff was born with severe and irreparable brain damage, allegedly as a result of the defendant obstetrician's negligence. After the mother had been in labour for 22 hours, the latter had made six attempts at normal delivery using forceps before realising this was impossible. The plaintiff, suing by his mother, argued that (i) the defendant had been negligent in pulling too hard and too long; and (ii) the defendant should have moved more quickly to utilise delivery by Caesarean section. The trial judge held that although the decision to perform a trial of forceps was a reasonable one, the defendant had in fact pulled too hard and was therefore negligent. The Court of Appeal reversed this-Lord Denning said that an error of clinical judgment was not negligent. The case reached the House of Lords where Lord Denning's views were rejected. The Law Lords ruled that an error of clinical judgment could be negligence if it is an error which would not have been made by a reasonably competent professional man acting with ordinary care.

Lord Edmund Davies declared:

"To say that a surgeon committed an error of clinical judgment is wholly ambiguous, for, some whole errors may be completely consistent with the due exercise of professional skill, other acts or omissions in the course of exercising 'clinical judgment' may be so glaringly below proper standards as to make a finding of negligence inevitable . . . [d]octors and surgeons fall into no special category . . . If a surgeon fails to measure up to that standard in any respect ('clinical judgment' or otherwise) he has been negligent and should be so adjudged."

Lord Fraser also declared:

"The true position is that an error of judgment may, or may not, be negligent; it depends on the nature of the error. If it is one that would not have been made by a reasonably competent professional man professing to have the standard and type of skill that the defendant holds himself out as having, and acting with ordinary care, then it is negligent. If, on the other hand, it is an error that such a man, acting with ordinary care, might have made, then it is not negligence."

In *Whitehouse*, the Law Lords held that the defendant had not been negligent because there had not been sufficient evidence to justify the trial judge's finding of negligence.

Interpretations of the Bolam test

The *Bolam* test may be interpreted in different ways: should it be up to the courts or the doctor to set the standard of reasonable care? Many cases dealing with this issue post-*Bolam* appear to have favoured the latter interpretation. The House of Lords were certainly in favour of this interpretation in the mid-1980s in cases such as *Sidaway* and *Maynard v West Midlands RHA* [1984].

In *Maynard* (1984), the doctors were uncertain whether the plaintiff's condition was either tuberculosis or Hodgkin's disease. Since the latter condition would be fatal without treatment, they decided that rather than wait for some weeks for the results of a sputum test to confirm tuberculosis, they would perform a diagnostic procedure to test for Hodgkin's disease. This procedure involved a risk of damage to the recurrent laryngeal nerve and even though the procedure was performed competently, the risk materialised. The plaintiff alleged that it was negligent of the doctors to perform the procedure rather than await the results of the sputum test, which would have confirmed tuberculosis. The trial judge found for the plaintiff on the basis of preferring the evidence of the expert witness for the plaintiff rather than that of the defendant's expert witness and this decision was eventually affirmed by the House of Lords. Lord Scarman's interpretation of the *Bolam* test was that:

"It is not enough to show that there is a body of competent professional opinion which considers that their[s] was a w ong decision, if there also exists a body of professional opinion, equally competent, which supports the decision as reasonable in the circumstances."

Lord Scarman observed that a judge's mere 'preference' for one body of distinguished opinion over another was not sufficient to establish negligence in a doctor whose action had received the 'seal of approval' of those whose opinions the judge did not prefer.

In *De Freitas v O'Brien* [1993] deference to the medical profession was again preferred. Here, the plaintiff underwent an operation on her spine. The procedure was one which only a very small number of neurosurgeons (four or five or out two hundred and fifty countrywide) would consider safe. But the neurosurgeons considered that they had a very high degree of expertise. The surgeon was held to be not negligent, even though the exploratory surgery which had been undertaken carried an unavoidable risk of infection. The only concession the judge was prepared to make here was that the view of a body of medical opinion could be scrutinised by the court.

The Sidaway case [1985] House of Lords

The plaintiff suffered from persistent pain in her neck and shoulders, and was advised by a surgeon employed by the defendant hospital governors to have an operation on her spinal column to relieve the pain. The surgeon warned the plaintiff of the possibility of disturbing a nerve root and the possible consequences of doing so but did not mention the possibility of damage to the spinal cord even though he would be operating within three millimetres of it. The risk of damage to the spinal cord was very small (less than 1 per cent) but if the risk materialised the resulting injury could range from the mild to the very severe. The plaintiff consented to the operation, which was carried out by the surgeon with due care and skill. However, in the course of the operation the plaintiff suffered injury to her spinal cord which resulted in her being severely disabled.

She brought an action against the hospital governor and the surgeon's estate (the surgeon having died five years before the trial began) for personal injury. Being unable to sustain a claim based on negligent performance of the operation, the plaintiff instead argued that the surgeon had been in breach of a duty owed to her to warn her of all possible risks inherent in the operation with the result that she had not been in a position to give an 'informed consent' to the operation.

The House of Lords held:

(1) (per Lord Diplock, Lord Keith and Lord Bridge, Lord Scarman dissenting) The test of liability in respect of a doctor's duty to warn his patient of risks inherent in treatment recommended by him was the same as the test applicable to diagnosis and treatment, namely that the doctor was required to act in accordance with a practice accepted at the time as proper by a responsible body of medical opinion. Accordingly, English law did not recognise the doctrine of informed consent. However (per Lord Keith and Lord Bridge), although a decision on what risks should be disclosed for the particular patient to make a rational choice whether to undergo the particular treatment recommended by a doctor was primarily a matter of clinical judgment, the disclosure of a particular risk of serious adverse consequences might be so obviously necessary for the patient to make an informed choice that no reasonably prudent doctor would fail to disclose that risk. (*Bolam* applied)

(2) (per Lord Templeman) When advising a patient about a proposed or recommended treatment a doctor was under a duty to provide the patient with the information necessary to enable the patient to make a balanced judgment in deciding whether to submit to that treatment, and that included a requirement to warn the patient of any dangers which were special in kind or magnitude or special to the patient. That duty was subject to the doctor's overriding duty to have regard to the best interests of the patient. Accordingly, it was for the doctor to decide what information should be given to the patient and the terms in which that information should be couched.

(3) Since (per Lord Diplock, Lord Keith and Lord Bridge) the surgeon's non-disclosure of the risk of damage to the plaintiff's spinal cord accorded with a practice accepted as proper by a responsible body of neuro-surgical opinion and since (per Lord Scarman and Lord Templeman) the plaintiff had not proved on the evidence that the surgeon had been in breach of duty by failing to warn her of that risk the defendants were not liable to the plaintiff.

The appeal was dismissed and the Appeal Court decision was affirmed.

In *Sidaway*, Lord Scarman again enunciated the *Bolam* test thus:

> "The Bolam principle may be formulated as a rule that a doctor is
> not negligent if he acts in accordance with a practice accepted at
> the time as proper by a responsible body of medical opinion even
> though other doctors adopt a different practice. In short, the law
> imposes the duty of care, but the standard of care is a matter of
> medical judgment."

Sidaway reveals that the majority favoured the *Bolam* test so the
yardstick for the standard of care is reasonable professional
practice.

Lord Scarman, (dissenting) adopted the 'prudent patient'
standard and rejected the *Bolam* test in relation to the duty to
inform. He declared that whether the doctor was in breach of
his duty to inform was to be determined not exclusively by
reference to the current state of responsible professional opinion
and practice, though both were relevant considerations, but by
the *court's* view of whether the doctor gave the consideration
which the law required him to give to the right of the patient to
make up his own mind in the light of relevant information
whether or not to accept the treatment proposed.

His Lordship's comments on the prudent patient are worth
noting:

i) The law can require the court to ask: what would a
reasonably prudent patient think was significant if in the
situation of this patient?
ii) The 'prudent patient' test calls for medical evidence; the
two critically important medical factors are: the degree of
probability of the risk materialising and the seriousness of
possible injury if it does; and the character of the risk.

Applying the test to the facts of the case, his Lordship concluded that the risk of damage to the spinal cord was not
material. Lord Scarman also stated:

> "English law must recognise a duty of the doctor to warn his
> patient of risk inherent in the treatment which he is proposing . . .
> The critical limitation is that the duty is confined to material risk.
> The test of materiality is whether in the circumstances . . . the court
> is satisfied that a reasonable person in the patient's position would
> be likely to attach significance to the risk."

How much information should be given to the patient?

English law only requires the doctor to give the broad nature of the treatment to the patient in order for that patient to make a valid decision on whether to consent but once the patient is informed in such terms, any complaint that the information given was inadequate, would be a negligence claim (see *Chatterton v Gerson* [1981]). In other words, the patient's only cause of action would lie in an action for negligence. The question in every case will be: was *sufficient information* given to the patient so that she could make an informed choice and the question will always arise as to what was 'sufficient' in the circumstances of the case?

Material risks must be disclosed

The implications of *Sidaway*, as far as the extent of disclosure to a patient is concerned, are:

- Material risks of a procedure must be disclosed, subject only to 'therapeutic privilege' (see below) which a doctor might be required to justify; according to *Canterbury v Spence*, a risk can be defined as material if a reasonable person in the patient's position, if warned of the risk, would be likely to attach significance to it. It would also be material if the medical practitioner is, or should reasonably, be aware that the particular plaintiff, if warned of the risk, would be likely to attach significance to it;
- If the patient asks further questions about the proposed treatment, the doctor is bound to respond to those questions unless he has grounds for withholding some information because of 'therapeutic privilege', for instance if it is thought .that giving the patient the information would be detrimental to the health of the patient; thus, it may be thought that disclosure would be more harmful to the patient than not giving the information in view of the patient's particular emotional or mental state or medical history. Lord Scarman suggested that there would have to be a serious threat of psychological damage to the patient.

Gold v Haringey-The test for disclosure of information revisited

The test for disclosure of information laid down in Sidaway was examined by the Court of Appeal in *Gold v Haringey* [1987]. Mrs

Gold decided that she wished to have no further children. Her consultant obstetrician suggested that she be sterilised. The operation went ahead, with Mrs Gold's consent, but was not successful. She subsequently became pregnant again. The plaintiff had been properly informed about the operation that it was not guaranteed to succeed. However, Mrs Gold alleged that the consultant had been negligent in failing to discuss the treatment properly because: first, the doctor had failed to explain the risk of failure; and secondly, he had not discussed any alternative method by which steps could be taken to avoid Mrs Gold becoming pregnant by her husband undergoing a vasectomy. All the medical witnesses called said they would have warned Mrs Gold of the risk of failure, but that a sizeable proportion of doctors (estimated at 50 per cent) would not have done so at the time when she had the operation (and this would have satisfied the *Bolam* test). However, the lower court judge decided that the existence of this substantial body of medical opinion did not resolve the matter, because *Sidaway* only applied to therapeutic procedures, not to non-therapeutic procedures for contraceptive reasons. Mrs Gold was therefore awarded £19,000 damages and the Health Authority appealed.

The Court of Appeal allowed the appeal, saying the *Bolam* test *applied to non-disclosure even in relation to a non-therapeutic procedure*, such as the plaintiff's contraceptive sterilisation. The plaintiff therefore lost her action.

Blyth v Bloomsbury (1993)

In *Blyth v Bloomsbury HA* [1993], the plaintiff, a nurse, claimed that she had asked her doctor about the side-effects of the contraceptive drug Depo-Provera. At the time, it was generally accepted medical opinion that Depo-Provera was well-tolerated, and no significant side-effects had been reported. However, the doctor who treated her was aware there might be a problem with irregular bleeding; and that another doctor in the hospital had carried out research (which was contained in the hospital files) which indicated that there may be other side effects. The patient subsequently experienced menstrual irregularity and bleeding. She brought an action for damages, alleging that as she had expressly inquired of the risks inherent in the contraceptive she should have been told of all the risks known to the hospital at the time.

The plaintiff eventually lost her case in the Court of Appeal on the facts, as it found that she had not in fact requested that *particular* information.

Does Blyth takes the Bolam test further?

Blyth appears to take the *Bolam* test to the stage where it will not matter what a doctor tells a patient in response to a general inquiry any more than what he tells her in response to a specific inquiry (per Kerr, L.J.). All that the doctor has to prove is he complied with the medical practice or procedure required in the same way that some other group of doctors would have done. In contrast to patients in the USA and Canada, who have the right to be informed about material risks before deciding whether to consent to treatment, UK patients have no such right under the application of the *Bolam* test or *Sidaway*.

CAUSATION

The plaintiff must also usually establish that the defendant's negligence caused the harm in question-namely, that the defendant's act or omission was the actual cause of the damage. The claim will fail unless this can be proven. In these private law cases, causation must be proved on a balance of probabilities, which means that it has to be shown that it is more probable than not that the negligence caused the injury or damage which is the subject of the complaint.

Evidential and causative factors involved in trying to establish medical negligence-the 'but for' test

The plaintiff has to prove the defendant caused the injury in fact and law and the injury must not be too remote. In seeking to prove as a matter of fact that the defendant caused the claimant's loss or injury, the 'but for' test is used. The courts ask: would the claimant have suffered the injury but for the defendant's negligence? If the answer is negative, then the defendant is liable since he must have caused the harm (see *Barnett v Chelsea Hospital* (1969)).

Proving the negligence caused the plaintiff's injury could be even more problematic because the patient might have been treated by a team of healthcare professionals, so there could be several possible defendants or there might have been several possible reasons for the patient's particular mishap which he suffered while in hospital under the doctor's care.

Extending the 'but for' test where there is negligent failure to warn of risks?

Chester v Afshar (2004) Principle: A neurosurgeon who failed to warn a patient of the small risk of injury inherent in surgery, even if properly carried out, could be liable to the patient when that risk materialised, even though the risk was not increased by the failure to warn and the patient had not shown that she would never have had the operation carrying the same risk.

In *Chester v Afshar* (2004), the House of Lords extended the 'but for' principle in causation in the specific context of a failure to warn patients of the side effects of treatment. The patient suffered from severe back pain and was referred to the defendant, an eminent neurosurgeon, who advised her to have surgery. The operation was properly performed with the patient's consent but it left the patient partially paralysed. Such damage was known to be an inherent risk of the operation, in the region of 1% to 2%. The patient sued in negligence alleging that the surgeon had failed to advise her of that risk and that the breach of duty entitled her to damages. The judge found that the surgeon had indeed not informed the patient of the risk before the operation, that he had been negligent in not doing so and that if the patient had known of the risk, she would not have consented to the operation at that time. She would have consulted a second or third medical opinion before deciding what to do. He concluded that the patient had established a causal link between the breach of duty and the injury. The Court of Appeal and the House of Lords (3:2) affirmed the lower court decision.

The House of Lords held that:

- a patient should have a remedy in damages if the doctor breached that patient's right to make a fully informed decision before consenting to treatment.
- Hence, to recover damages, a claimant will no longer have to prove that but for the failure to warn, he would never have consented to the same treatment or operation at any time.

In other words, exceptionally, the patient did not have to prove, for the purposes of causation, that she would never have had the operation at any time if properly warned, only that if properly warned, she would not have consented to the operation which was in fact performed and which resulted in the injury.

COMMENT

The *Chester* ruling goes against the well-established principle whereby the claimant would only succeed if causation could be established, i.e. that the failure to warn either caused or increased the injury risk. Yet none of the established authorities were overruled by the Law Lords in *Chester* which applied the *Fairchild* case (2002) which allows the rules of causation to be modified in exceptional circumstances. In *Taylor v White* (2004), decided in November 2004, the Court of Appeal clarified the position of *Chester* and *Fairchild*, by stating that *Chester* was merely applying *Fairchild* because there were policy grounds for doing so in that case and because of the exceptional import-ance of the issue of informed consent to medical treatment and the negligent failure to warn a patient of the side effects of treatment. *Chester* appears to have been a decision based on public policy grounds and *Taylor v White* confirms that it is by no means certain whether it would necessarily be followed in different circumstances. It also appears to bring the require-ments for informed consent in battery and negligence closer.

For the moment, *the basic principle in causation remains* that a tortfeasor is not usually liable for harm when his wrongful conduct does not cause that harm.

Differences of medical opinion

Medical opinion may be divided on whether the defendant's conduct accorded with medical procedure as was illustrated in *Maynard v West Midlands RHA* [1984] and *Ashcroft v Mersey RHA* [1983]. The judge must resolve such differences and decide which he prefers, giving reasons (*Sewell v Electrolux* (1997)).

Judge must resolve differences in medical opinion-Sewell

What if the experts who are called by either side of the case (for the claimant and defendant) radically disagree with each other on crucial points which have a significant bearing on issues of causation in a medical case? In *Sewell v Electrolux Ltd* (1997) The Times, November 7, the Court of Appeal decided that a judge hearing a claim for damages for personal injury involving conflicting expert medical opinion, had to address and resolve that conflict. The claim arose from an accident at work where the sole issue turned on conflicting expert medical opinion. He could not decide the case without making findings of fact or giving proper reasons but by relying on the burden of proo . In the case itself, whose facts are not relevant to our present discussion, Lord Justice Hutchison opined that "There was a clear cut and irreconcilable difference of opinion between the two consultant surgeons which it had been for the recorder to resolve." This approach was followed in the subsequent House of Lords' case of *Bolitho v City of Hackney* (1997) decided a month later.

Causation and multiple causes

There may be cases where the injury might have been the result of multiple causes. Here the court would have to ask: was the defendant's breach of duty a necessary element in the chain of causation? For example, did the defendant's conduct expose the plaintiff to an added risk of harm?

In *McGhee v National Coal Board* [1972], an employee of the defendant brought an action alleging that his dermatitis had come about because of the coal board's failure to provide him with proper washing facilities. This meant that he had to cycle home with the brick dust, to which his work unavoidably exposed him, still caked to his skin. There was no doubt that brick dust caused the plaintiff's injury. The difficulty was to determine whether the 'guilty' dust, which continued to stick to the plaintiff on his journey home, had played any causative role. The House of Lords held that if the defendant's conduct materially contributed to the harm suffered, the court could find that negligence has been proved.

McGhee was approved in *Clark v MacLennan* [1983] which held that where there was a precaution which could have been taken to avoid the precise injury which occurred, the defendant then had to prove that his failure to take his precaution did not cause the plaintiff's injury.

In *Wilsher v Essex AHA* [1988], there were five possible causes for the condition with which the plaintiff was afflicted. In this case, the plaintiff baby was born prematurely, and found to be suffering from a condition which rendered him virtually blind, following treatment in the defendant's post-natal unit. Owing to a breach of duty by hospital staff, the baby had been over-saturated with oxygen in the first weeks of his life. While the child was in the baby unit, an inexperienced junior doctor undertook to monitor the oxygen level in the baby's bloodstream. In doing so, he inserted a catheter into a vein rather than an artery by mistake. The senior registrar failed to notice the junior doctor's mistake and several hours later, when replacing the catheter, made the same mistake himself. However, whilst this might have caused or contributed to the blindness, there were four other natural conditions, all of which had afflicted the baby, and which equally might have had the same effect. There was a low probability that the baby would survive.

The majority of the Court of Appeal found for the plaintiff on causation on the basis of Lord Wilberforce's speech in *McGhee*. The defendant appealed and the House of Lords found for the defendant as the plaintiff was unable to show that the blindness was caused by the lack of oxygen to the extent that the defendant's breach of duty had played a causative role in his injury, since it was only one of five possible causes.

The Fairchild Case (2002) —where impossible to identify which of several defendants were responsible for claimant's injury, all or any of those defendants could be held jointly or independently liable

In *Fairchild v Glenhaven*, the House of Lords appeared to put a gloss on the *Wilsher* case. The claimants had been negligently exposed to asbestos by more than one of their employers which caused them to develop a lung tumour caused by exposure to asbestos. However it was not possible to show which of the exposures caused the tumour. The House of Lords held that so long as it had been proved that the claimants had been negligently exposed to a risk of harm by the defendants and that harm materialised, then all or any of the defendants could be held liable. Liability could therefore be found even though it was impossible to prove which of the exposures had caused the harm.

Lord Hoffman laid down five requirements for a material contribution to the risk of harm to be sufficient proof of causation:

(i) that there is a particular duty to protect against the risk;
(ii) the duty is 'intended to create a civil right to compensation';
(iii) the greater the exposure, the greater the risk;
(iv) medical science cannot establish which of the different exposures was responsible; and

(v) the harm materialises.

Res ipsa loquitur and the establishment of negligence

In some cases, the doctrine, rule or maxim of res ipsa loquitur ("the thing speaks for itself") has been applied. This doctrine applies in cases where the only inference on the evidence before the court was that there was no other possible explanation for the plaintiff's injury or loss except through the negligence of the defendant, (see, for example, *Clark v MacLennan* [1983]). An example is where the plaintiff went into hospital to be cured of two stiff fingers and emerged with four stiff fingers, with no plausible explanation being made, as in Cassidy v Ministry of Health [1951]. Again, if there are multiple possible causes of an injury, for example, the plaintiff could plead res ipsa loquitur-alleging that the injury could not have happened but for negligence and therefore places the onus on the doctor to prove otherwise.

The doctrine has been appropriately invoked if the facts of the case strongly suggest that there is at least an inference of negligence on the defendant's part. The essentials of the doctrine are:

(i) there is no evidence as to how the accident occurred
(ii) the injury has to be of a kind that does not normally happen in the circumstances unless there was negligence.
(iii) The defendant is proven to have been in control of or linked to the situation either personally or vicariously.

Defendant takes his victim as he finds him (the 'thin skull' rule)

If the claimant suffers from a particular condition and suffers more harm than a normal person, the defendant would still be entitled to claim for all of that harm under the 'thin skull' rule whereby 'you take your victim as you find him'. This is intended to protect unusually sensitive claimants (see *Smith v. Leech Brain* (1961)). The defendant is still liable even though that additional harm is not foreseeable.

Burden of proving negligence on plaintiff

The burden of proving the negligence remains throughout on the plaintiff and the doctrine may not usually apply in medical negligence cases because of the uncertainties of medical treatment and the judge still has to decide, on a balance of probabilities, in a civil case, whether the defendant was negligent and whether his negligence caused the plaintiff's injury. An illustrative situation is where a patient is admitted to hospital for treatment of an injured ankle and leaves with an amputated leg and the plaintiff is unable to explain what had happened and neither can the defendant doctor and the plaintiff has identified the doctor whose negligence must have caused the injury (see *MacDonald v York County Hospital Corporation* [1972] (Canadian case). *Fryer v Pearson* (2000) indicates that certain judges might not like the use of the Latin label in cases where the doctrine might be appropriate.

Fryer v Pearson -Res ipsa loquitur in the 21st century

In *Fryer v Pearson and Anor* (2000) The Times, April 4, the Court of Appeal decided that 'people should stop using maxims or doctrines dressed up in Latin, such as *"res ipsa loquitur"* which are not readily comprehensible to those for whose benefit they are supposed to exist (per Lord Justice May). The claimant was a gas fitter, who was injured while working at the defendant's house by a sewing needle concealed in the carpet which broke off in his knee, rendering him no longer able to work. The trial judge held that the doctrine res ipsa loquitur did not apply in the circumstances and gave judgment for the defendant. Lord Justice Waller, said that negligence could be established against the defendants if the only proper inference to be drawn from the evidence was that they had permitted the needle to remain in the carpet, knowing it to be there. On the facts, no such inference could be drawn and the trial judge correctly ascribed the plaintiff's injury to "an unfortunate but freak accident." The plaintiff's appeal was therefore unanimously dismissed.

What if a surgical needle is left in a patient's stomach which could only have got there by being left there in the course of a medical operation or procedure? There seems little doubt that a court, provided the facts were admitted, would conclude that res ipsa loquitur applied, as the Court of Appeal held in *Mahon v Osborne* (1939) where, two months after his abdominal operation, a swab was found in a claimant's body which caused his death. After *Fryer*, perhaps the only difference will be that there will be less usage of the term but not of the principle.

Breaking the chain of causation

The chain of causation or sequence of events leading to the injury can be broken by an intervening act (*novus actus interveniens*) which would then mean the defendant was no longer liable as in *Rance v Mid-Downs* (1991).

CONTRIBUTORY NEGLIGENCE

If the defendant can prove that the claimant was, to a greater or lesser degree, partly to blame for the injury or loss, the Law Reform (Contributory Negligence) Act 1945 allows the compensation payable to be reduced to the extent the court believes it to be just and equitable: s.1(1). The court should assess the total damages and then make the reduction: s.1(2).

The *Bolitho* case-the 'new' *Bolam* or merely a modern 'gloss'?

Some doubt has been cast on the dominance of the so-called *Bolam* test by the House of Lords decision of *Bolitho (administratrix of the estate of Bolitho (deceased) v City and Hackney Health Authority* [1998]). In December 1983, the plaintiff, Patrick Bolitho, then aged 2, underwent an operation to correct a blockage of the arteries. In January, 1984 he was admitted to hospital suffering from acute breathing difficulties. The doctor was summoned on two occasions but failed to attend on both those occasions. Patrick recovered briefly but later collapsed, his respiratory system failed and he suffered a cardiac arrest resulting in severe brain damage. Patrick subsequently died and his mother sued for medical negligence. The issue was whether the defendant was responsible for the brain damage caused by the cardiac arrest. The hospital admitted negligence in the Registrar failing to attend Patrick or arrange for a suitable deputy to examine the child. It was common ground that intubation so as to provide an airway for oxygen would have ensured that respiratory failure did not lead to cardiac arrest.

But the hospital denied liability on the ground that, even if she had attended Patrick, the registrar would not have intubated him. To prevent the cardiac arrest which caused his brain damage, Patrick would have to have been intubated prior to the first bout of breathing difficulties.

The trial judge accepted the registrar's evidence that she would not have intubated Patrick before 2.30pm. when he suffered his fatal seizure and found, applying the Bolam test, that if the registrar had attended and not intubated, she would have demonstrated a proper level of skill and competence according to the standard represented by the defendant's expert's views and that it had not been proved that the admitted breach of duty by the defendants had caused the injury which occurred to Patrick.

The Court of Appeal upheld the lower court's judgment and the plaintiff appealed to the House of Lords.

The two issues for the Law Lords were (i) whether the *Bolam* test applied to issues of causation and (ii) whether it required a judge to accept the views of one truthful body of expert professionals?

On causation, the House of Lords opined that this involved the determination of two questions, namely: (1) 'what would the doctors have done if they had attended?' and (2) 'if the doctor(s) would not have intubated, would that have been negligent?' The Law Lords' view was that the *Bolam* test has no part to play in the first question-on causation-because the factual inquiry is in the realms of hypothesis and the question 'what would have happened?' does not answer the first question of causation. However, the *Bolam* test is central to the second question-'what would the competent doctor have done?' To prove her case, the plaintiff would have had to prove that the continuing exercise of proper care would have resulted in intubation.

On the second question, the Court rejected the view that it is not bound to hold that a defendant doctor escapes liability for negligent treatment or diagnosis just because he leads evidence from a body of experts who are genuinely of the opinion that the defendant's treatment or diagnosis accorded with sound medical practice. Referring to *Bolam*, he said that there it was stated that the practice had to be endorsed as proper by a 'responsible body of medical men' and had to be a standard of practice recognised as proper by a 'competent reasonable body of opinion'. Lord Scarman had also referred to a 'respectable' body of professional opinion (in *Sidaway*). He continued : "The use of these adjectives—responsible, reasonable and respectable—all show that the court has to be satisfied that the exponents of the body of opinion relied on can demonstrate that such opinion has a logical basis." His Lordship referred to *Hucks v Cole* and the *Edward Wong* case in support.

In *Hucks v Cole* (1968), the Court of Appeal found the defendant to have been negligent, stressing that the fact that other practitioners might have done the same thing as the defendant practitioner is a very weighty matter but not conclusive. In *Edward Wong Finance Co Ltd v Johnson Stokes & Master (a firm)* [1984] which was not a medical case, the Privy Council held that the body of professional opinion, 'though almost universally held, was not reasonable or respectable'.

Lord Browne-Wilkinson pointed out that these decisions demonstrated that in some cases of diagnosis and treatment, despite a body of professional opinion sanctioning the defendant's conduct, the defendant can properly be liable in negligence. However, in the 'vast majority of cases', the fact that distinguished experts hold a particular opinion will demonstrate the reasonableness of that opinion. However, he added "if in a rare case, it can be demonstrated that the professional opinion is not capable of withstanding logical analysis, the judge is entitled to hold that the body of opinion is not reasonable or responsible."

Lord Browne-Wilkinson declared:

> ". . . it will very seldom be right for a judge to reach the conclusion that views genuinely held by a competent medical expert are unreasonable . . . It is only where a judge can be satisfied that the body of expert opinion cannot be logically supported at all that such opinion will not provide the bench mark by reference to which the defendant's conduct falls to be assessed."

The facts of *Bolitho* did not fit one of those rare cases and there was no basis for dismissing the defendant's expert evidence as illogical. Intubation was not a routine, risk-free procedure and would be particularly difficult for children who would remove the tube unless sedated.

The House of Lords upheld the previous decisions in the case, holding that, despite the doctor's negligence in not attending or arranging for a suitable deputy to attend, the claim failed for want of causation. The plaintiff's appeal was dismissed.

Has Bolitho overtaken Bolam?

In *Joyce v Merton* [1996] the Court of Appeal stated that they had the authority to scrutinise expert evidence to determine whether that evidence represented a responsible judgment of good practice. But neither this case nor *Hucks v Cole* (possibly because it was not reported at the time although its existence was known) led to a change in the approach to medical malpractice litigation. In *Marriott v West Midlands HA* [1999], the Court of Appeal appeared to follow *Bolitho* and the judges concluded that the expert opinion advanced in the doctor's favour was not defensible and that it could be subject to analysis to test its reasonableness. However, it is probably premature, in the absence of more post-*Bolitho* case law, to assess its longer-term impact.

Fuller disclosure required -the influence of Bolitho?

After *Bolitho*, the courts have given some indication of moving somewhat away from the *Bolam* approach towards insisting that doctors give fuller consideration to the autonomy of the patient. This seemed to be the approach in the *Pearce* case (1999), the first case to consider the effect of Bolitho on information cases.

The Pearce case (Pearce v United Bristol Healthcare NHS Trust) [1999]

Mrs Pearce, the mother of five children, became pregnant. On November 27, when the baby was 14 days overdue, she requested that it be induced or delivered by caesarean section. Her consultant explained the risk of inducing labour and that the recovery from a caesarean section was slower.

He advised her that she should proceed to a natural delivery and she accepted his advice. On December 4, Mrs Pearce was admitted to hospital and gave birth to a stillborn baby. Mrs Pearce and her husband sued the defendant for damages in negligence. The trial judge dismissed their claim. On appeal, the plaintiffs argued that the consultant should have advised Mrs Pearce of the increased risk of the baby being stillborn if delivery was delayed beyond November 27, and that had she known of the risk she would have insisted on delivery by caesarean section.

The Court of Appeal dismissed the appeal and held:

(1) In determining what information to provide a patient, a doctor has to have regard to all the relevant circumstances, including the patient's ability to comprehend the information and the physical and emotional state of the patient. Normally, it is a doctor's legal duty to advise a patient of any significant risks which may affect the judgment of a reasonable patient in making a treatment decision (*Sidaway* [1985] and *Bolitho* [1997]).

(2) The evidence established that the increased risk of still-birth in delaying delivery of the baby after November 27 was very small, something like 1 to 2 in 1,000.

(3) The experts who gave evidence did not consider this risk to be a significant one. Particularly having regard to the first plaintiff's distressed state, this was not a proper case for the court to interfere with the clinical opinion of the expert medical man responsible for treating the patient.

(4) Even if the first plaintiff had been advised of the risk, the inference from the evidence was that she would still have agreed to a natural delivery.

Lord Woolf, MR declared that if a patient asks about a risk, it is the doctor's legal duty to give an honest answer. On the standard of disclosure, he said:

"If there is a significant risk which would affect the judgment of a reasonable patient, then in the normal course it is the responsibility of a doctor to inform the patient of the significant risk, if the information is needed so that the patient can determine for him or herself as to what course he or she should adopt."

Basing their judgments on a synthesis of both House of Lords' decisions (*Sidaway* and *Bolitho*) the Court of Appeal now appears to recognise that the medical profession do not have the prerogative to set the standard of disclosure.

Pearce retains the 'reasonable doctor' test for breach of duty and appears to have put a gloss on *Bolam* and shifted the weight of responsibility to the *courts* to decide the standard of disclosure, but the clinical judgment of the doctor as to the extent of the disclosure will not be easily overturned except in the most obvious case.

Carver's case (2000)

After *Pearce*, *Carver v Hammersmith & Queen Charlotte's Special HA* (February 2000), held the health authority liable in negligence for the failure of the doctor to explain that 'Bart's test' for Down's syndrome was not a diagnostic test, unlike amniocentesis, but was only a screening test which could not detect one-in-three Down's syndrome foetuses.

Standard of care and negligence in cervical smear test

In *Penney & Ors. v East Kent HA* (1999) The Times, November 25, the Court of Appeal (Lord Woolf, MR, May and Hale L.JJ.)

held that a cervical screener who failed to realise that a test contained obvious abnormalities and should be referred for further examination, was negligent. A court had the right to subject expert medical opinion of medical practice to logical analysis. The negligent reading of cervical smears led to the claimants being wrongly told they were free from cancer.

The Court of Appeal held that the standard to be applied was that of a reasonably competent screener exercising reasonable care at the time when the screening took place and referred to *Bolam, Maynard* and *Hunter v Hanley*. The contrary evidence of the defendants' experts could not stand up to 'logical analysis'. The Bolam test had no application where what the judge was required to do was to make findings of fact, even where those findings of fact were the subject of conflicting expert evidence.

The court dismissed the appeal of the defendant authority and upheld the lower court judgment, finding the defendant liable in respect of the negligent assessment of their cervical smear tests.

Limitation of actions

Actions for personal injuries must be brought within three years from when the cause of action accrued; or three years from the date of the claimant's knowledge of the right of action, whichever if the later : see s.11: Limitation Act 1980.

Medical litigation in the United Kingdom

Since January 1, 1990, the costs of hospital litigation have been borne by the NHS Trusts under the NHS Indemnity Scheme. From 1995, a new Clinical Negligence Scheme for Trusts (CNST) was set up which established standards for the management of risks and claims. Some of these have had a substantive impact on promoting good practice and some seek to mitigate the failure of the common law to set standards. The National Health Service Authority now administers the CNST and administers control over claims to ensure a speedy resolution of indefensible claims and seeks to minimise the cost to the NHS.

The House of Lords case of *Wells v Wells* [1999] 1 AC 345) and *Heil v Rankin* (2000) Lloyd's LR Med 203 suggests that awards of general damages will increase. According to the National Audit Office, in 2001-02, the NHS paid out $446 million for clinical negligence claims and expect to pay around £5.25 billion for estimated future claims.

The question remains as to whether the United Kingdom should introduce a no-fault compensation scheme to which people could subscribe so that problems with proving causation could be eliminated and the need for litigation would be virtually removed.

5. ABORTION AND THE STATUS OF THE FOETUS

INTRODUCTION

Abortion or pregnancy termination remains a controversial issue in contemporary Western society in the early 21st century as much as in the previous century. Abortion as a medical procedure involves the challenging of moral, political, religious, legal, medical and psychological boundaries. It is a problem encountered by societies across the world and the parties involved may, at the time, regard it as the most controversial and problematic situation that a woman may face. Abortion has been practised, however, to a lesser or greater extent, in all societies since prehistoric times. (see Lane Committee Report on the Working of the Abortion Act (1974) Cmd. 5579. Appendix to Section A). It has also been the subject of vigorous debate and controversy in countries like the United States and to a lesser extent, in Britain.

Central dilemma-protecting foetus with legal status v respecting maternal choice

The central dilemma appears to be whether the foetus should be accorded the status of a human being with legal personality so that the law should not allow its destruction or whether the individual woman should have the right to terminate her pregnancy if she wishes.

The number of terminations carried out in England and Wales reached a peak in 1990 when almost 187,000 abortions were performed.

ETHICAL AND PHILOSOPHICAL PRINCIPLES

The main issues in abortion are: whether the foetus merits protection as a 'person' and if so, at which point in the pregnancy; whether it has a right to life and legally protected interests, whether a woman has a right to decide what happens in and to her body, whether there is some ethical link between abortion and infanticide, and whether there is any point after conception where it is possible to draw the line beyond which killing should not be permissible. Key points identified at which point the foetus warrants legal protection are: conception, implantation, 'quickening', the capacity to feel pain, consciousness and viability and of course, birth.

Professor Dworkin in *Life's Dominion* (1993), says that the abortion debate should be about the sacredness of human life rather than about personhood or rights and argues that the deliberate extinction of human life at any stage is an offence against the sanctity of individual life. Dworkin interprets 'sacred' to mean 'inviolable'.

In practical terms, abortion may involve a consideration of whether the mother or father has the ultimate right to decide to terminate a pregnancy, whether the foetus itself has any 'right' to be born, and determining the criterion for deciding when a foetus is capable of being born alive within the meaning of the law. Of course, abortion is not a purely medical issue but one that must also be evaluated by the legal and ethical rules of any given society. Nevertheless, it is the state of medical knowledge that informs and sometimes determines the legal regulation of cases involving an abortion.

Double effect

The doctrine of double effect became well-known in the early part of the 20th century whenever physicians confronted problems involving abortions. The maternal v fetal conflict required impossibly difficult decisions to be made as to whose life to save. The doctrine seemed to require that a physician must intend only the repair of the uterus and not the death of the foetus.

Moral stances on abortion

The British Medical Association has published a detailed guide to the moral, ethical and legal perspectives on abortion. (see *The Law and Ethics of abortion*: BMA views, March 1997, rev. December 1999) According to this guide, there are at least three stances that people have taken of abortion: (i) pro-abortion; (ii) antiabortion; and (iii) that abortion is acceptable in some circumstances.

The BMA's advice on abortion

The BMA's advice to its members is to act within the boundaries of the law and of their own conscience. Patients are, however, entitled to receive objective medical advice regardless of their doctor's personal views for or against abortion. Furthermore, a doctor could be sued for damages if, because of a failure to refer, a delay is caused which results in the woman being unable to obtain a termination.

Foetal pain

The BMA recommends that, when carrying out any surgical procedures (whether an abortion or a therapeutic intervention) on the foetus *in utero*, due consideration must be given to appropriate measures for minimising the risk of pain. This should include an assessment of the most recent evidence available.

Historical perspectives

In 17th century European law, aborting a quickened foetus was not indictable. The English 1803 Act (Lord Ellenborough's Act) made abortion a felony punishable by death. America followed the English common law from the 17th to the 19th centuries, making abortion before quickening only a misdemeanour, or legal for therapeutic reasons if recommended by two physicians. It was only after the Civil War in America that most states made abortion illegal, with stiff penalties and firm cut-off points.

ABORTION LAW IN UK: STATUTES AND CASE LAW

England

Lord Ellenborough's 1803 Act was eventually replaced by the Offences Against the Person Act 1861 (OAPA), in which the fundamental law is still contained, although it has to be read with the Abortion Act 1967 (as amended in 1990) and the Infant Life (Preservation) Act 1929.

Three statutes regulate current abortion law: brief legislative background

The three statutes which regulate abortion law in the UK are the Offences Against the Person Act 1861 (OAPA), the Infant (Life

Preservation) Act 1929 and the Abortion Act 1967 (as amended by the Human Fertilisation and Embryology Act (HFEA) 1990).

The Offences Against the Person Act 1861

Under the Offences Against the Person Act 1861 (OAPA), s.58 thereof makes it an offence to procure or attempt to procure a miscarriage by a third party; self-induced miscarriage or using an instrument to do so. The word 'abortion' only appears in the marginal notes to the sections. The OAPA was passed to protect the mother from any self-help she might undertake since termination of pregnancy was far more hazardous in the mid-1860s than at present.

The Infant Life (Preservation) Act 1929 (the 1929 Act)

This stipulated that if a foetus is 'capable of being born alive' then it cannot be killed in the mother's womb, i.e. *in utero*. This Act therefore created the offence of child destruction-the killing of a child 'capable of being born alive' before it was capable of having an existence independent of its mother.

Section 1 of the 1929 Act states:

> 1 (1) Subject as hereinafter in this section provided, any person who, with the intent to destroy the life of a child capable of being born alive, by a wilful act causes a child to die before it has an existence independent of its mother, shall be guilty of a felony . . .

One criterion of determining whether a child is capable of being born alive is where the baby can breathe for a few hours through its lungs unaided, without deriving any of its living or power of living through the connection to its mother; having independent pulmonary ability, which was confirmed in *C v S* (1987)(see below). The exception is that no person should be convicted of this offence if he acted in good faith for the purpose only of preserving the life of the mother. The 1929 Act was enacted to deal with the gap left by OAPA. The 1929 Act also introduced the legal presumption that a foetus which had achieved 28 weeks' gestation was capable of being born alive. As Mason in 'Abortion and the Law' in *Legal Issues in Human Reproduction* (ed. McLean) (1990) stresses, "it did not imply the converse-that is, that a foetus of less than 28 weeks' gestation was not capable of being born alive". A second purpose o the Act was to legalise the operation of craniotomy-the deliberate crushing of the fetal skull in the mother's pelvis, inevitably causing fetal death. This was widely practised to save the life of the pregnant woman before caesarean section became commonplace.

At common law, there was already some protection offered to doctors as illustrated in the leading case of *R. v Bourne* (1939) where it was declared that: No person ought to be convicted under s.58 OAPA unless the jury are satisfied that the act was not done in good faith for the purpose only of preserving the life of the mother. This case was the impetus to reform the law.

In *Bourne*, the surgeon, a reputable physician, notified the authorities that he intended terminating the pregnancy of a girl of 15, who had been raped by a group of soldiers under particularly unpleasant and violent circumstances. The girl's parents had given their consent to the operation. Bourne was charged under section 58 of the Offences Against the Person Act 1861. He defended himself on grounds of good medical practice, and that the words 'unlawfully' as found in the 1861 Act, did not apply to therapeutic abortions, and asserted that the girl's mental and physical health might have suffered had the pregnancy continued.

Macnaghten, J. linked the 1861 and 1929 statutes and ruled that the burden rested on the Crown to satisfy the jury that the defendant did not procure the miscarriage of the girl for the purpose of preserving her life. He chose to apply the 1929 Act to any termination in good faith by a registered medical practitioner, observing that "the word 'unlawfully' [in s.58 of the 1961 Act], is not a meaningless word. I think it imports the meaning expressed by the proviso in s.1(1) to the Infant Life (Preservation) Act 1929 and that s.58 of the Offences Against the Person Act 1861 must be read as if the words making it an offence to use an instrument with intent to procure a miscarriage were qualified by a similar proviso. In this case, therefore . . . the burden rests on the Crown to satisfy [the jury] beyond reasonable doubt that the defendant did not procure the miscarriage of the girl in good faith for the purpose only of preserving her life."

The judge told the jury to take a broad view of the meaning of 'preserving the life of the mother', and that "[the law] permits the termination of pregnancy for the purpose of preserving the life of the mother . . . those words ought to be construed in a reasonable sense, and, if the doctor is of opinion . . . that the probable consequence of the pregnancy will be to make a woman a physical or mental wreck, the jury are entitled to take the view that the doctor . . . is operating for the purpose of preserving the life of the mother."

Macnaghten, J. accepted Bourne's defence and in view of the circumstances, the doctor was acquitted.

In 1948, in *R. v Bergmann and Ferguson*, the *Bourne* approach was further clarified. The judge held that it was not relevant whether the psychiatrist who had certified the need for termination, held a correct opinion as to the existence of such grounds for termination, as long as it was honestly held. This therapeutic abortion approach was further strengthened in *R. v Newton and Stungo* (1958), where the doctor's defence was that the mental condition of his patient had necessitated termination. The defendant had not further treated or supervised the patient after the termination and she died of renal failure as a result. The defendant was convicted but Ashworth, J's declared: "use of an instrument is unlawful unless the use is made in good faith for the purpose of preserving the life or health of the woman. When I say health I mean not only her physical health but also her mental health. But I must emphasise that the burden of proof that it was not used in good faith is on the crown." Hence, as long as the doctor acted in good faith, therapeutic abortion was legal. Keown in *Abortion, Doctors and the Law* (1988) points out that even before *Bourne*, doctors were performing therapeutic abortions according to criteria established by themselves (such as on the ground of mental disorder, to prevent transmission of hereditary disease or to avert mental breakdown, to preserve the mother's life or to defuse the threat of suicide).

Thus, provided these doctors abided by professional ethics, there was little danger of prosecution. *Bourne* was no exception to this since the doctor there actively encouraged his own prosecution. Terry (1990) observes that (i) the English position has been that abortions (although that specific term seldom has been used) are generally illegal, but criminal sanctions will not lie against certain people in certain situations; and (ii) the exceptions from criminal sanction that have been created depend, *de lege*, upon medical criteria and involve the application of medical discretion.' Terry argues that even in its advanced decriminalised state, the 1967 Act, despite having detailed criteria and regulatory standards, 'permits a physician considerable latitude when 'he is of the opinion, formed in good faith, that the termination is immediately necessary to save the life or to prevent grave permanent injury'. He adds that an important side effect of this 'medicalisation of abortion law is that it has tended to keep abortion issues out of the English courts'.

No absolute right to abortion

The current English legal position provides for the abortion decision to be made by the pregnant woman but as a matter of law, her decision is subject to professional medical discretion and no absolute 'right' to abortion is recognised.

A jurisdictional point on abortion laws in the UK

Although the United Kingdom consists of Great Britain and Northern Ireland, the Abortion Act 1967 does not apply to Northern Ireland. Further, neither the Offences Against the Person Act 1861 nor the Infant Life (Preservation) Ac 1929 applies to Scotland and in the Scottish jurisdiction, many statutes are of very little importance because of the common law in Scotland being different. However, as a result of the implementation of s.37 of the Human Fertilisation and Embryology Act 1990, the law and practice of abortion in Scotland is now the same as in England.

The Abortion Act 1967 (as amended by the HFEA 1990)

The Abortion Act 1967 was amended by the Human Fertilisation and Embryology Act 1990 and the amended 1967 Act (in force April 1, 1991) now provides that no offence will be committed where a pregnancy is terminated by a registered medical practitioner in circumstances where two such practitioners have formed an opinion in good faith that one of the following conditions is in existence:

(a) That the pregnancy has not exceeded 24 weeks and that continuance would involve risk, greater than if the pregnancy were terminated, of injury to the physical or mental health of the pregnant woman or any existing children of her family-s.1(1)(a)

(b) That the termination is deemed to be necessary to prevent grave permanent injury to the physical or mental health of the pregnant woman-s.1(1)(b)

(c) That continuance of the pregnancy would involve risk to the life of the woman, greater than if the pregnancy were terminated-s.1(1)(c)
(d) That there is a substantial risk that the child if born would suffer from such severe physical or mental abnormalities as to be seriously handicapped-s.1(1)(d)

The fourth ground has provoked criticism from various quarters in Britain.

Section 5(1) of the 1967 Act—before its amendment by the 1990 Act provided:

> s.5 (1) Nothing in this Act shall affect the provisions of the Infant Life (Preservation) Act 1929
> (protecting the life of a viable foetus).

A further amendment made to extend lawful termination was subsequently brought about by s.37(4) of the 1990 Act, which amends s.5(1) of the 1967 Act to read:

> No offence under the Infant Life (Preservation) Act 1929 shall be committed by a registered medical practitioner who terminates a pregnancy in accordance with the provisions of this Act.

Hence, this prevents carrying out a lawful abortion being interpreted as the possible offence of child destruction under the 1929 Act so that a registered medical practitioner may now perform a legally compliant abortion within the parameters of the 1967 Act (as amended) without worrying about a possible breach of the 1929 Act.

In 2004, there appeared to be a groundswell of opinion within the British Parliament to review the law on abortion and some political and religious leaders called for lowering the 24 week limit to possibly 22 weeks or even less on the basis of medical advances in monitoring fetal development and the increasing survival rates of premature infants. No legislative changes have been made as of August 2005.

Conscientious objection

Section 4 (1) of the 1967 Act provides that " . . . no person shall be under any duty, whether by contract or by any statutory or other legal requirement, to participate in any treatment author-ised by this Act to which he has a conscientious objection".

Section 4(2) states that 'Nothing in sub.s(1) of this section shall affect any duty to participate in treatment which is necessary to save the life or to prevent grave permanent injury to the physical or mental health of a pregnant woman.

Subsection (2) is aimed at preventing a doctor from relying on s.4(1) if his services are required in an emergency situation. But the question arose: who could rely on it and how far could the phrase 'participate in any treatment' extend to persons who were not directly involved in performing or 'assisting' in the abortion?

In *Janaway v Salford Area Health Authority* (1989), the plaintiff, a Roman Catholic, lost her job working as a secretary/ receptionist for the defendant health authority after refusing to type a letter of referral in respect of an abortion patient. She brought an action for unfair dismissal on the ground that her refusal was protected under s.4(1) of the Abortion Act 1967. The issue was what was the true construction of the words in s.4(1)- on the meaning of 'participate in any treatment authorised by this Act'. The Court of Appeal accepted the appellant's argument that s.1(1) and s.4(1) are co-extensive but decided against her on the ground that her intention in typing a letter of referral would not be to assist in procuring an abortion but merely to carry out the obligations of her employment. The typing of such a letter by the applicant would not be a criminal offence in the absence of s.1(1). Both Nolan and Balcombe, L.JJ. accepted the health authority's argument that the word 'participate' in s.4(1) referred to taking part in treatment administered in a hospital in accordance with s.1(3) for the purpose of terminating a pregnancy. On appeal, the House of Lords agreed with Nolan and Balcombe, L.JJ.s' points of view and gave 'participate in any treatment' its ordinary meaning which was participation in the medical process of abortion so that the plaintiff was not involved in this process and could not therefore invoke the protection of the 1967 Act.

Consent to abortion by a competent adult: Re C (1993

As far as consent to an abortion by the competent adult is concerned, the three-stage requirements in *Re C* (1993) (see *Re C (adult: refusal of treatment)* (1993) as laid down by Thorpe, J. apply. Thus, the patient (1) has to take in and retain treatment information; (2) to believe it and (3) to be able to weigh that information, balancing risks and needs.

Abortion by minors and 'rights' to abort

In the UK, a girl aged between 16 and 18 prima facie has the right to consent to medical treatment under s.8(1) of the Family Law Reform Act 1969 or under the common law in Scotland. Hence no question of parental consent arises for this age group. However, an issue that could arise with regard to a girl aged 16 but under 18 is where there might be some question as to her (legal) capacity.

For girls under 16, the controversial question for the courts in the early 1980s was whether such a girl had the right to seek an abortion without her parents giving their consent beforehand.

Mature minor can decide on contraceptive advice or treatment

The Gillick case (1985) House of Lords

A Roman Catholic mother of five daughters (who were under 16 years old) sought a declaration to the effect that a 1980 DHSS Memorandum which appeared to contravene her parental right to decide whether her under-aged daughters should be allowed to receive contraceptive advice and treatment, (by stating that it was up to the doctor's clinical judgment to decide this), was unlawful; and that no contraceptive or abortion services should be supplied by the national Health Service to her daughters without her consent. Mrs Gillick lost her case in the first instance court, won it by a unanimous decision in the Court of Appeal and then lost it on a majority judgment in the House of Lords (3:2) which held that a girl under 16 did not, for that reason alone, lack legal capacity to consent to medical advice and treatment relating to contraception. It is a question of fact in any given case whether such a person has the capacity to consent. Thus, a doctor who gave contraceptive advice and treatment within the framework of the Guidance (on which Lord Fraser based his set of requirements in *Gillick*-see Chapter 2) intending to act in the best interests of the child would not commit a criminal offence.

Court will override minor's wishes if not 'in her best interests'

Re P (1982) A 13-year-old girl, convicted of theft in 1979, had been committed to the care of the local authority. The following year she gave birth to a child so they were then placed in a 'mother and child unit'. The court spoke of her in complimentary terms but said that 'the tragedy of it is that having put her criminal record behind her she seems unable to stop getting pregnant, and cannot thereby put her current life into proper perspective.' When she was 15 years old, in 1931, she became pregnant again. She was still under age and her father, for religious and moral reasons, refused consent to an abortion, but the girl disagreed with this decision. The court held that, even though the local authority was *in loco parentis* under the current statute, it was appropriate in this case to involve the court through wardship proceedings. The court authorised termination and the fitting of an internal contraceptive device which the girl had also requested.

The courts are thus still prepared to override a girl's parents if they believe that the ultimate decision will be in her best interests. At that time, English authority was clear that parental wishes would usually be considered but were not determinative of any issue before the court. Cases dealing with severely disabled babies had been decided by the English courts, and the Court of Appeal decision in *Re B* (1981) dealing with a Down's syndrome baby is indicative of the English court's typical approach which was to listen to but not regard parental wishes as determinative.

The GMC guidance

The latest GMC guidance stresses that if a doctor considers that a patient is incapable of giving consent because of immaturity, he or she may disclose relevant information to an appropriate person or authority if it is essential to do so in the patient's medical interests. This is subject to that patient being told of the intention to disclose. The Guidance follows Lord Fraser's guidelines in emphasising that the judgment of whether the patient is capable of giving or withholding consent to treatment or disclosure must be based on an assessment of their ability to appreciate what the treatment or advice being sought may involve, and not solely on their age. (GMC Guidance *Confidentiality*, 1995)

Spousal consent

The Abortion Act 1967 (the 1967 Act) is silent on the question of spousal or paternal consent. However, the question was resolved in the *Paton* case (1979) which is discussed below. Male spouses do not have the right to veto their wives' decision to have an abortion.

PREVENTING AN ABORTION

The 1967 Act does not say anything about whether anyone has a right of veto over an intended abortion. For instance, can the father of the unborn child prevent an abortion?

In *Paton v British Pregnancy Advisory Service* (1979), the plaintiff sought an injunction restraining his wife from having an abortion under the 1967 Act. The wife had obtained the required certificates from two doctors that she satisfied one of the statutory grounds but the plaintiff alleged that she was acting in bad faith. The plaintiff needed to establish that he had *locus standi* to bring his action, either in his own right or as 'next friend' of the foetus. In the High Court, Sir George Baker, P. said: "The husband . . . has no legal right enforceable at law or in equity to stop his wife from having this abortion or to stop the doctors from carrying out the abortion." The plaintiff subsequently lost his case before the European Commission on Human Rights when he argued that his right to family life under Article 8 of the European Convention on Human Rights had been infringed. The Commission pointed out that Art.8(2) limits that right in so far as necessary to protect the rights of another person-the pregnant woman. (on the question of the status of the foetus, see other comments in *Paton* and *Re F (in utero)* (below)).

In *C v S* (1988), the plaintiff, an unmarried 23-year-old Oxford male postgraduate and the woman, an unmarried 21-year-old Oxford student, met in Oxford in 1986, and sex took place shortly after their relationship began. She became pregnant, and the couple's relationship eventually deteriorated. A doctor prescribed a pill to her, which was believed to have terminated her pregnancy but which did not. She also took anti-depressant drugs and had two X-rays for a chest infection, one of which was without a protective shield. The fact that she was still pregnant became apparent only after she had a body scan. The woman then obtained medical approval from two doctors to have an abortion and the termination was scheduled.

The plaintiff sought, as first plaintiff, on his own behalf and as father of the second plaintiff, a foetus which was 18 to 21 weeks *en ventre sa mere*, an injunction to restrain the defendant from terminating the pregnancy. At the same time, the plaintiff sought an injunction to restrain the health authority from carrying out the abortion, even though all the relevant conditions of the Abortion Act 1967 had been fulfilled. The application was based on the ground that the foetus was 'a child capable of being born alive' within the meaning of s. (1) of the Infant Life (preservation) Act 1929 (the 1929 Act), as specifically preserved by s.5(1) of the Abortion Act 1967. The relevant provisions created the criminal offence of child destruction. The plaintiff was therefore seeking to enforce the criminal law, in order to prevent the abortion from being carried out. Case-law (such as *R. v Bourne*) also suggested that no distinction should be drawn between a threat to life, and a threat to health.

The central issue was whether the foetus which was between 18 and 21 weeks *en ventre sa mere*, was 'capable of being born alive' within the terms of the 1929 Act. Two further issues were: (i) whether the father had the right to be heard on the application of this nature; and (ii) whether a foetus was a legal person capable of suing its mother, through its father as next friend, in order to prevent its mother from terminating her pregnancy.

Heilbron, J. accepted medical evidence as to the stage of development the foetus would normally be expected to have reached. Expert medical evidence suggested that the cardiac muscle of the foetus would be contracting, that primitive blood circulation and physical movements would be demonstrated by the foetus, but that, if delivered by hysterotomy, such a foetus would never be able to breathe either naturally or with artificial assistance (emphasis added). Consequently, Heilbron, J held, following *Paton*, that the applicant potential father had no legal standing to ask for an injunction and that she was satisfied that a potential offence, under the 1929 Act in respect of child destruction, had not been proved. The application of the potential father was dismissed. On appeal, the Court of Appeal held that a foetus of between 18 to 21 weeks which showed signs of primitive movement and blood circulation, but which, if delivered by hysterotomy, would never be capable of breathing either naturally or artificially, was *not* a 'a child capable of being born alive' within the meaning of s.1(1) of the 1929 Act. The Court of Appeal therefore ruled that abortion of the foetus would not constitute the offence of child destruction under the 1929 Act. Thus, regardless of their *locus standi* (legal standing) the plaintiffs were not entitled to an injunction to prevent an abortion from being carried out. An appeal to the House of Lords was also dismissed.

All appeal stages of this case were completed in approximately 72 hours because the foetus was said to be between 18 to 21 weeks old and the longer the case took to be resolved, the closer it would be to the stage of gestation when a legal abortion could not be performed.

'Capable of being born alive'—Bolam principle applied in C v S?

In the High Court in *C v S*, the affidavits of eminent obstetricians indicated the wide difference in their interpretation of the phrase 'capable of being born alive'. One expert opinion was that if an unborn foetus of 18 weeks were to be delivered, it would be live born. The other expert's view was that such a foetus would be unable to breathe even if placed on a ventilator. Thus the latter's view was that 'born alive' was synonymous with viability or having a chance of survival. Hence, his interpretation of a live child was one that was living and breathing by reason of its unaided breathing through its lungs, without deriving any of its living or power of living through any connection with its mother. Faced with opposing views, Heilbron, J. decided that there was a body of 'eminent medical opinion' that found Mr Norris' view unacceptable, which echoes the *Bolam* principle (see ch.4). 'Capable of being born alive' therefore means being able to breathe *unaided* and independent of its mother, and since this foetus would not have been able to do so, it was not capable of being born alive within the meaning of the statute.

Right to abort: mothers v fathers

The legal principle derived from *Paton* and *C v S* is that all mothers, married or unmarried have the right to decide whether to have an abortion (within the limits of the law or, in some cases, at the courts' discretion) but fathers, married or unmarried, have no corresponding right of veto when it comes to deciding on whether to abort.

Selective reduction of multiple pregnancy

A new s.5(2) of the 1967 Act (as inserted by s.37 of the HFEA 1990) allows for selective reduction providing one of the grounds in s.1(1)(a) to s.1(1)(d) in the Abortion Act are met. Selective reductions can thus take place either on the ground of fetal abnormality or because the multiple pregnancy creates the amount of risk to the mother for s.1(1)(a), (b) or (c) to be satisfied.

Abortion pill

The pill RU486 -mifepristone and mifegyne- impairs the womb's ability to hold on to an egg.

It is lawful to prescribe this if one of the grounds in the Abortion Act is met. This pill has been described as 'a medical advance of the same magnitude as the contraceptive pill' (The Sunday Times magazine, January 6, 1991). Three visits are required to administer RU486. At the first, the drug is given in tablet form and the woman is sent home. Forty-eight hours later, the woman should return to be given a pessary containing prostaglandin to complete the process. Within four to six hours, the woman would then be expected to have a heavy period which expels the fertilised egg. The third visit is a check-up and if the drug has failed, a surgical operation is performed.

PROTECTION FOR THE UNBORN FOETUS

The rights and status of the foetus-a foetus cannot be made a ward of court

The argument that the foetus has a right to be protected was further considered in *Re F (in utero)* (1988), where the local authority claimed that an unborn child should be made a ward of court to protect it from injury, because its 36-year-old nomadic mother had a reputation for somewhat aberrant behaviour and had a history of psychiatric problems. She had absconded from the residential care home in which she lived when she was 38 weeks pregnant.

The Court of Appeal held that the court had no jurisdiction to entertain the application, agreeing with Sir George Baker, P in the *Paton* case. It also agreed with the lower court judge that to accept that wardship jurisdiction existed in this case and yet to apply the principle that it is the interest of the child which is to be predominant 'is bound to create conflict between the existing legal interests of the mother and those of the unborn child, and that it is most undesirable that this should occur.' A foetus could not be made a ward of court.

In *Re D* (or the Berkshire case) (1987) which was decided on pre-1989 Children Act legislation, the House of Lords dealt with the issue of whether it was possible to protect an unborn foetus. Such protection would now be possible under the Children Act 1989: see s.31(2) because of the possible 'significant harm' that might be suffered by the child, but an order would be available only once the child had been born as a foetus cannot be made a ward of court.

Legal status of the unborn child-a common law overview

The basic approach of common law countries as far as unborn children are concerned is not to confer rights upon them as legal 'persons'. In English law, an unborn child is clearly not a 'child' or 'person' in law (*Re F (In Utero)* [1988]) with no legal personality and thus, strictly, does not merit legal protection (but see Chapter 1 under the Caesarean section cases). This is also the strict position in Australia (*AG v (Qld), ex rel. Kerr v T* (1983), Canada (*Tremblay v Daigle* (1989) and *R v Sullivan* [1991]) and the United States: *Roe v Wade* (1973) (US Supreme Court).

English law

Can an unborn foetus be murdered in English law?

AG's Reference No.3 of 1994—Policing pregnancy or protecting the foetus? This case of grievous bodily harm was unusual in that the harm that was caused was to the unborn foetus of the woman who was attacked and it raised questions about whether murder may be committed on an unborn foetus, which has no legal personality in English law.

In *AG's Reference (No.3 of 1994)* (1997), a man stabbed his pregnant girlfriend in the abdomen, causing her to be admitted to hospital with numerous stab wounds, including one to her left abdomen which penetrated her uterus. She was admitted to hospital and a cut to the wall of the uterus was discovered and surgically repaired and the mother was prescribed a course of indomethacin to prevent the onset of premature labour. The doctors believed (mistakenly) that the foetus had not been harmed and discharged her from hospital. Approximately two weeks later she suddenly went into labour and gave birth to a daughter at 26 weeks' gestation. Following the birth, it became evident that the baby was two weeks older than previously thought when the attack occurred and that the knife had, contrary to the earlier diagnosis, penetrated the foetus itself, cutting through the left side of her abdomen. As a result of the prematurity of the child, she was perceived as having a 50 per cent chance of survival and despite intensive neonatal care, including several surgical operations, the baby died after 120 days.

Prior to the birth, the man admitted wounding his girlfriend with intent to cause grievous bodily harm (under s.18: Offences Against the Person Act 1861) and was sentenced to four years' imprisonment. Following the death of his child, he was also charged with the child's murder. The lower court held that there was evidence upon which a reasonable jury could conclude that the causal link between the wounding and the death could be established. Even if the facts and inferences suggested by the Crown were established, they could not result in a conviction for either murder or manslaughter and thus it was directed that the respondent be acquitted. The man was therefore acquitted on this second charge.

Two issues were referred to the Court of Appeal by the Attorney General:

1. Whether the crimes of murder or manslaughter can be committed where unlawful injury is deliberately inflicted on a child *in utero* or to a mother carrying a child *in utero*; and where the child is subsequently born alive, enjoys an existence independent of the mother, thereafter dies and the injuries inflicted while *in utero* either caused or made a substantial contribution to the death.

2. Whether the fact that the death of the child is caused solely as a consequence of direct injury to the mother rather than as a consequence of direct injury to the foetus can negative any liability for murder or manslaughter in those circumstances.

The Court of Appeal considered the two elements of the *actus reus* of murder: the unlawfulness of the act and the necessity of the person killed having to be a person in being. On the first element, the Court held, somewhat unusually, that, legally, the foetus is regarded as part of the mother until it has a separate existence from her; hence, to 'cause injury to the foetus is just as unlawful as any assault upon any other part of the mother.' On the second element, it was necessary to consider the point at which a foetus becomes a person in being. Basing his opinion on several common law decisions, Lord Taylor, C.J. accepted that "to cause the death of a foetus in the womb cannot be murder." Despite the Court's acceptance that "when the respondent stabbed his girlfriend the child was not a person in being", it held that there was "no requirement that the person who dies needs to be a person in being at the time that the act causing the death is perpetrated."

Lord Justice Taylor, C.J. also observed that:

> An intention to cause serious bodily injury to the foetus is an intention to cause serious bodily injury to a part of the mother just as an intention to injure her arm or her leg would be so viewed.

Despite the obvious flaw in the reasoning since a body part like an arm or leg is not able to develop into a human being, this merely indicates the transferred malice idea-an intention to cause serious harm to the foetus (which could be regarded as part of the mother) is deemed an intention to cause serious harm to the mother. The Court of Appeal indicated that the judgment was not intended as a step toward the recognition of a fetal right to life.

On appeal, the House of Lords made it clear that a charge of murder could not be founded on the circumstances of the case, and that the Court of Appeal approach was wholly unfounded in fact. However, the charge of manslaughter could be upheld. Taylor, C.J.'s view that a foetus was an integral part of its mother was rejected by Lord Mustill (with whom the other Law Lords agreed). Lord Mustill emphasised that the maternal-fetal relationship was one of 'bond, not of identity'. The foetus was neither a 'person' nor an adjunct of its mother but was simply a unique organism. Thus: "the foetus was an organism *sui generis* (one of its kind) lacking at this stage the entire range of characteristics both of the mother to which it is physically linked and of the complete human being which it will later become." Thus, the criminal law did not recognise violence to the foetus as an offence against a person, unless it was subsequently born alive, as it was not a person in being. The conviction for unlawful act manslaughter was upheld by the Law Lords, because the act was done intentionally, was unlawful, and was also dangerous in that it was likely to cause harm to somebody and that act caused death. As Lord Hope explained, 'the stabbing of the mother was an unlawful and dangerous act and if the boyfriend had the *mens rea* which was required for him to be convicted of an assault on the child's mother, he also had the *mens rea* for unlawful act manslaughter'.

Lord Hope held that the act which caused the death and the mental state which is required for manslaughter do not need to coincide in time. It was therefore immaterial that the child was not a person already born alive when her mother was stabbed. He rejected submissions that since the foetus was not a living person at the time of the unlawful act, manslaughter could not be committed, and emphasised that the 'dangerous' act was determined by what all sober and reasonable people would recognise was dangerous towards persons who were alive when the danger manifested itself. His Lordship emphasised: "For the foetus . . . it is not sensible to say that it cannot ever be harmed, or that nothing can be done to it which can be dangerous. Once it is born it is exposed, like all other living persons, to the risk of injury. It may also carry with it the effects of things done to it before birth which, after birth, may prove to be harmful. It would seem not to be unreasonable therefore, on public policy grounds, to regard the child in this case, when she became a living person, as within the scope of the *mens rea* which the defendant] had when he stabbed her mother before she was born."

Possible effect of AG's Reference No 3 of 1994

It has been argued that this decision 'opens the door for criminal liability to ensue when the subject of an unlawful act is a foetus. The danger is that, even though the foetus has no theoretical legal personality, this assumption will be, and has been, eroded in the minds of the courts.' (Fovargue and Miola in 'Policing pregnancy: implications of *AG's Reference No.3 of 1994*' (1998) Med LR 265). It could be that despite the clear affirmation by the Court of Appeal in *St George's Case* (or the *Collins* case) (1998) of the fact that, for legal purposes, an unborn child is not a person until born, the fact remains that the English appellate courts have also held that the pregnant woman is not per se entitled to put at risk the healthy viable foetus she is carrying. Fovargue and Miola suggest that it is the future application of the decision which is one of the most worrying aspects of the case, and indicates the courts' willingness to intervene in childbirth decisions to save the life of the foetus. They conclude: 'By further personalising the foetus, the House of Lords in the *AG's Reference case No.3 of 1994* legitimise the ethics of the caesarean section cases and provide an opportunity for the development of judicial policing of pregnancy.'

The English Court of Appeal (per Butler Sloss L.J.) in *Re MB (Caesarean Section)* (1997), has made it clear that "[t]he court does not have the jurisdiction to declare that . . . medical intervention is lawful to protect the interests of the unborn child even at the point of birth."

Continuing dilemma-respecting mother's autonomy v desire to protect foetus

The dilemma continues to lie between respecting the mother's autonomy and freedom to live her own life, and the need or desire to protect the foetus, where circumstances are such that the child protection authorities feel that the foetus clearly needs protection.

THE ORIGINS OF LIFE AND EMBRYO RESEARCH

Introduction

Experimentation on embryos is a contentious issue. Some feminists have argued that embryo research should be opposed because it is an exploitation of procreative activity; destroy women's physical integrity; and undermines women's struggle for control of their own reproduction.

Key issue: when does human life come into existence in a developing embryo?

A key issue in the debate on embryo research is: At what point does human life come into existence? There are various points during the development of the foetus that are considered to be significant- the moment of fertilisation, viability, quickening, development of the primitive streak, and implantation. Another point at which an embryo has been said to become a unique genetic entity is at the stage of development after 8 to 10 weeks after conception when brain activity is detected.

Legally, birth has been regarded as being significant. But the argument is that from the moment of fertilisation, the foetus is at that point, a unique genetic entity.

The appearance of the primitive streak is crucial

It is the appearance of the line known as the primitive streak (at around 14 days) on which the Warnock Committee (see below) focused as the crucial transformation between molecular matter and potential human being. Scientists called this molecular matter the 'pre-embryo'. The formation of the primitive streak marks the stage at which a new individual entity would be identifiable. Until the day 14, cells are pluripotential—i.e. t is not known whether they will develop into an hydatiform mole; into twins; into one embryo, or degenerate into nothing.

The philosophical debate

The philosophical debate has centred on the question: 'is the embryo a human being?' The questions that have been much debated is: how do we go about identifying a human being; is it a matter of criteria or of how we feel it is right to treat such a human entity?

The Warnock committee and Warnock report

The report of the Committee of Inquiry into Human Fertilisation and Embryology (the Warnock Report) was published in 1984. Their remit was "To consider recent and potential developments in medicine and science related to human fertilisation and embryology . . ." They recommended that embryo research should continue but subject to regulation. Many of their recommendations were incorporated into the Human Fertilisation and Embryology Act 1990.

Licence required to carry out research

Embryo research is permitted if a research licence is obtained from the Human Fertilisation and Embryology Authority. The research licence allows for the creation and use of in vitro embryos for certain specified projects. It is a criminal offence punishable for up to two years in prison to bring about the creation of an embryo (outside the human body) or to keep or use an embryo except in pursuance of a licence. Para.3 of sch.2 to the Act sets out the type of projects for which these licences may be granted:

(a) The promotion of advances in the treatment of infertility
(b) Increasing knowledge about the causes of congenital disease
(c) Increasing knowledge about the causes of miscarriage

(d) Developing more effective contraception techniques
(e) Developing methods of detecting the presence or absence
of gene or chromosome abnormalities
before the implantation of an embryo

Section 3 of the Act defines the parameters of activity allowed in relation to embryos. The Authority may not authorise the use or retention of a live human embryo after the appearance of the primitive streak-not later than 14 days after the mixing of the gametes. This does not apply to cases where the embryo has been frozen. The Act also provides a right of conscientious objection in s.38. Certain other activities are prohibited e.g. cloning, placing of a human embryo in an animal and vice versa.

6. ASSISTED REPRODUCTION AND SURROGACY

INTRODUCTION

Modern reproductive techniques or 'reproductive technologies' generally refer to artificial reproductive methods or reproductive methods which intervene in human reproduction. Techniques used include artificial insemination using a husband's sperm, that is, injecting woman with the husband's sperm (AIH); artificial insemination using semen from a donor (AID); ova and sperm mixed together in a drop of fluid and placed back in the fallopian tube (GIFT); in vitro fertilisation-fertilisation effected 'in water' outside the body, where, just before ovulation, an egg is collected from the ovary and placed in a laboratory glass (a petri-dish) and semen is added to it so that if fertilisation occurs, it is returned to the uterus where it may implant and then develop as normal (in vitro-fertilisation-IVF). Embryo donation and surrogacy also come within this umbrella of 'reproductive technologies'.

Surrogacy is a short form for 'surrogate motherhood'. We tend to think of these kinds of practices as being of modern vintage, but there is evidence to suggest that the first recorded

AIH took place in 1866 and the broad practice of surrogacy is frequently cited as dating from Biblical times. In more modern times, the origin of the growing modern public debate, awareness and discussion of these phenomena might be more readily traced to July 1978 when Louise Brown became the world's first test-tube baby, which sparked off a decade of intense speculation and anticipation about reproductive technologies. Louise Brown's birth was seen as the dawn of a new way of making babies, namely through artificial methods and the 'new technology'. Of course, other affluent societies such as the USA and Australia and several Western European countries have also been debating the legal, social, political and moral implications of these so-called 'new technologies'.

LEGAL AND ETHICAL FRAMEWORK

The question of who is a 'parent' in law is of some importance particularly in the modern context of the 'new' reproductive technology. There are different types of parenthood.

Types of parenthood

Biological parenthood would be based on mothers and the mere fact of birth. For a father, biological paternity is not a sufficient condition to exercising legal rights and duties of parenthood.

Social parenthood

This would include adoption and the 'child of the family' formula: creating links between spouse and non-biological children 'treated' by that spouse as children of the family. This has been the case with certain Family Law legislation in the UK such as the Matrimonial Causes Act 1973.

Presumptions based on marriage

Several 'presumptions' were created in English law to enforce the social policies of the time, which base the 'legitimacy' of a child on the fact of the marriage of its parents at the time of its birth or even subsequently. Hence:

- at common law, a child born to a married woman is presumed to be the child of the woman's husband.

- a child may also be legitimated by the subsequent marriage of its parents;
- rebuttal of the presumption by a standard of proof higher than balance of probabilities but lower than the criminal standard of 'beyond reasonable doubt';

Parenthood is the underlying principle for ascertaining who has Parental Responsibility under the Children Act 1989. Parental responsibility is automatic for all mothers, married and unmarried but only automatic for married fathers. Unmarried fathers can now acquire Parental Responsibility if their name appears on the child's Birth Certificate and the birth was jointly registered by the mother and putative father but this rule only applies to births taking place after December 1, 2003. (see Adoption and Children Act 2002). Parenthood is also used to ascribe liability for child support under the Child Support Act 1991.

Assisted reproduction and the Human Fertilisation and Embryology Act 1990

Responding to radical developments in reproductive technology the British Parliament enacted the Human Fertilisation and Embryology Act 1990 (the 1990 Act) which statutorily lays down certain key principles. The 1990 Act was passed, in the words of Morgan and Lee in Human Fertilisation and Embryology Act (1991), as a response to the perceived need for legislation 'to regulate research on embryos, to protect the integrity of reproductive medicine and to protect scientists and clinicians from legal action and sanction.' The 1990 Act was preceded by the setting up of the Warnock Committee in 1982 which was followed by the publication of the Warnock Report (Report of the Committee of Inquiry into Fertilisation and Embryology, subsequently republished with an introduction by Dame Mary Warnock, the chair, as *A Question of Life* (1985)) in 1984. The 1990 Act was described as one of the most significant measures of its kind to be brought before Parliament in the last 20 years. (Kenneth Clarke, speaking in 1990)

The HFEA-Human Fertilisation and Embryology Authority-a licensing authority

One of the 1990 Act's significant innovations was to establish a licensing authority-the Human Fertilisation and Embryology

Authority to monitor and control research and the provision of infertility services. It also intended to ensure that there was substantial lay representation on the Authority. It replaced the former Voluntary (later Interim) Licensing Authority which had operated since the publication of the Warnock Report. Its principal function is to license and monitor, through a licensing system, any research and treatment which involves the creation, keeping and using of human embryos outside the body, or the storage or keeping and using of human embryos outside the body, or the storage or donation of human eggs and sperm.

The Authority also has to maintain a register of information about gamete and embryo donors and children born as a result of such treatment. It provides advice to the Health Secretary on developments concerning infertility services and embryology and the formulation of a Code of Practice which is regularly reviewed and has so far undergone three revisions, the latest in 1996.

Status provisions

The mother

Section 27: Human Fertilisation and Embryology Act 1990: (HFEA)

(1) The mother who is carrying or has carried a child as a result of the placing in her of an embryo or of sperm and eggs, and no other woman, is to be treated as the mother of the child.

This section should be read with s.13(5) HFEA, under which a woman may not be provided with treatment services unless 'account has been taken of the welfare of any child who may be born as a result of the treatment (including the need of that child for a father)'.

The father

Section 28(2): HFEA: a husband whose wife receives donated sperm or an embryo created from donated sperm, shall be treated as the father of any resulting child, unless it is shown that he did not consent. A man who is not married to the mother and is not the genetic father may be regarded as the child's legal father if treatment services were provided for the man and woman together by a person to whom a licence applies: s.28(3) HFEA. This provision does not apply to so-called

DIY treatment, where an officially recognised fertility clinic is not used.

Recognition of the status of 'father' in certain circumstances —amendment to the law

Where a child is conceived using genetic material from a man who has already died, it was provided by s.28(6) that that man would not be recognised in law as the child's father. This has now been amended to read 'subject to. . . [the provisions of the HFE (Deceased Fathers) Act 2003]'. As the law currently stands, the child born would *normally* be regarded as non-marital, unless the mother had remarried in which case s.28(5) of the 1990 Act would apply to legitimate the child. Otherwise such children would remain legally fatherless. However, the law has now been changed so that in certain circumstances, the deceased father's name *may* be inserted on the Birth Register under The Human Fertilisation and Embryology (Deceased Fathers) Act 2003 (which has now received the Royal Assent). (see below).

Reproductive technologies: some terms and procedures

   (i) AID: artificial insemination by donor;-insemination of the woman (usually married) by a donor because the husband has (a) defective semen; (b) a hereditary disease likely to be transmitted to his children; or (c) an abnormal sperm which may cause spontaneous abortion; (d) Where a single woman wants a child but is unwilling to conceive by conventional means.
   (ii) AIH: artificial insemination by husband: using husband's semen to inseminate the wife.

Artificial insemination

Artificial insemination (AI) is a technique whereby a man's semen is mechanically introduced into a woman's vagina with the intention that conception will take place. AIH is the least controversial of the available artificial techniques as there is no ambiguity with the resulting child's legal status and the issue of parenthood is not in question. There are a number of medical centres performing it in the UK and it has become an acceptable practice in Britain.

   (i) IVF: in vitro fertilisation;

This refers to the creation of an embryo outside the human body and the child thus born may be related to both, one or neither of its 'parents' (i.e. the carrying mother and her partner or husband).

(ii) GIFT: gamete intrafallopian transfer

This refers to insertion in the womb of eggs, sperm or both for fertilisation to take place in the womb rather than outside it.

SURROGACY

Surrogacy is another method of 'assisted reproduction' and although not a distinct artificial reproductive technique, is a specialised situation where, unlike its practice in ancient times, artificial reproduction techniques are nowadays frequently applied. They replace conception by natural means and hence a surrogate-produced child may have several genetic links. Although the practice of surrogacy (as the second oldest profession) or surrogate motherhood, dates back several centuries, as a modern phenomenon, it started to be reported sporadically in the late 1970s, with *A v C* being the first reported English case reaching the courts in 1978, but only fully reported in 1985! Hence, this case was not properly reported or publicised at that time. A surrogacy arrangement then suddenly burst into prominence in the 1980s with the Baby Cotton case. The other non-English case which caused a sensation in the United States and indeed, in most of the Western world, was the case of *Baby M (In Re M)* surrogacy case involving Mary Beth Whitehead, who went from villain to victim within the space of two years (see the *Baby M* case, below).

Surrogate motherhood

A surrogate mother is a woman who fulfils the role of another woman by having a child for her. Surrogate motherhood is 'any situation where one mother carries a child for another with the intention that the child should be handed over after birth.' (Warnock Committee, 1984).

Another definition is 'any situation where there is an arranged separation of the genetic, gestational and social components of motherhood.' (Shelley Roberts 'Warnock and surrogate motherhood: sentiment or argument?' in *Rights and Wrongs in Medicine* (ed. Byrne) (1986)).

Two situations have arisen: (i) a woman who is infertile and her husband's sperm is then used to artificially inseminate another woman who will carry the child to term; (ii) a woman who is fertile but cannot carry the child to term so ovum is removed and fertilised in vitro by her husband's sperm.

Full and partial surrogacy

The most common current form of surrogacy is 'partial surrogacy' where the carrying woman is fertilised with the commissioning man's sperm either as a result of sexual intercourse or assisted insemination. Full surrogacy is where the commissioning couple provide both sperm and ovum so that the child is genetically entirely theirs, but is carried to term by another woman. This necessarily involves the technique known as in-vitro fertilisation (IVF). Full surrogacy has been called a form of womb leasing (see Gillian Douglas, *Law, Fertility and Reproduction* (1991)).

The Warnock Report of 1984 rejected all forms of surrogacy by a majority of 16:14. The more recent Brazier Report (1998) adopts a more conciliatory line in some respects but nevertheless recommends tougher controls on surrogacy, a stronger policing of the types of 'reasonable expenses' that surrogates are paid and much clearer guidelines on what expenses should be allowable.

ETHICAL ISSUES IN SURROGACY

Certain characteristics of surrogacy bring into question its morality and ethical turpitude which Mason and McCall Smith in *Law and Medical Ethics* (2002) identify as: First: the inclusion of a third party to procreation; secondly, viewing surrogacy as 'being one way of exploiting women for the benefit of men'; but thirdly, the alternative view is to see the 'outlawing of the practice as outright paternalism which denies a woman a chance to use her body as she pleases.'

LEGAL REGULATION OF SURROGACY

The practice of surrogacy is now regulated by the Human Fertilisation and Embryology Act 1990 and the Surrogacy Arrangements Act 1985. The law prohibits the payment of money for the adoption of a child under s.57 of the Adoption

Act 1976. The cases on surrogacy indicate that the court's decision will be governed by the notion of the 'best interests' of the child and the English courts, at any rate, adopt a theory that it is important to maintain the birth mother's relationship with the child, wherever this is required, in the child's best interests.

Surrogacy arrangement not enforceable in English law

The HFEA has inserted a new section into the Surrogacy Arrangements Act 1985:

> Section 1A: No surrogacy arrangement is enforceable by or against the person making it. This applies irrespective of whether the child was created by sexual intercourse, artificial insemination or IVF.

Legality and enforceability of the surrogacy agreement— the American approach

In the famous American case of Baby M (*Re Baby M* (1988)) a New Jersey court ruled the surrogate arrangement to be valid and appeared to signify American law's approval of such contracts. Judge Sorkow applied the *best interests of the child* principle so that the biological father should have custody of the child and his wife was allowed to adopt the child. The surrogate's parental rights were terminated. On appeal, the New Jersey Supreme Court unanimously held that the surrogate arrangement was void and against public policy. It overturned the lower court's termination of the surrogate mother's parental rights and rescinded the adoption order of the father's wife. The surrogate was given visitation rights.

How many possible parents might a surrogate-produced child have?

Five possible parents: commissioning parents; sperm donor; ovum donor; surrogate mother who bears the child. In this connection, it is instructive to refer to s.30 of the HFEA, as far as married couples are concerned. Their application to be treated as the child's parents will be approved provided one of the spouses is the child's genetic parent and various conditions have been satisfied; hence, the requirements of s.30(2)-(7) must be complied with for example that the child's home has been with the applicant husband and wife. (this is discussed below under English cases on Surrogacy).

Section 30 is of no relevance if a surrogate mother changes her mind and is not willing to hand over the baby. As we have already noted, the law clearly states under s.1A of the Surrogacy Arrangements Act 1985 (as inserted by the HFEA 1990), that a surrogate contract is not enforceable.

What can go wrong with a surrogacy arrangement?

Singer and Wells (in *The Reproduction Revolution* (1984)) suggest at least four possibilities:

1. The surrogate mother might indulge in drug abuse and alcohol abuse;
2. She might attempt to extort payment, or additional payment beyond any agreed fee, from the commissioning couple;
3. She might decide, despite contracting to give the baby away upon birth, not to hand over the child once it has been born;
4. The commissioning couple might decide they do not wish to accept the baby once it has been born because it has been born with a physical or mental handicap or because they believe it is not their genetic child.

The third scenario (3, above) actually occurred in *Re P* (the twins' case) where the court had to decide whether to allow the surrogate mother to keep the baby she had carried and given birth to, although the child had been produced through the sperm of the commissioning father and the surrogate's ovum.

English cases on surrogacy

A v C (1978)

An unmarried couple of which the woman had children from a previous relationship, was unable to have any further children. Her partner, A, had a very strong desire to raise his own biological child. They found a woman, C, who agreed, for £500 to be artificially inseminated using the semen of A. C, the surrogate, changed her mind during pregnancy and wished to keep the child and forego the money. After the birth of the child, the natural (biological) father started wardship proceedings to obtain custody (now called Parental Responsibility) of the child.

Comyn, J. described the contract as 'pernicious' and declared that he held the agreement between the parties to be 'against public policy. None of them can rely on it in any way or enforce the agreement in this way. I need only to give one of many grounds for saying this namely that this was a purported contract for the sale and purchase of a child.' Access (as it was then called) was granted to the father. C, the mother, was given care and control of the child, but the child remained a ward of court until majority or further order. The mother appealed.

Ormrod, L.J. described the contract as a 'quite bizarre and unnatural agreement' as well as calling the arrangement a 'sordid little bargain'. Cumming-Bruce, L.J. called it a 'kind of baby-farming operation of a wholly distasteful and lamentable kind'. The Appeal Court refused to grant access to the father justifying their decision as being 'in the best interests of the child'.

The first reported British commercial surrogacy case of the 1980s: the Baby Cotton saga

Re C (A Minor) (Wardship: Surrogacy) (The Baby Cotton Case) (1985)

In the mid-1980s, Baby C was born in January, 1985, produced by a British mother (Kim Cotton) for a childless American couple, via artificial insemination, using the commissioning father's seminal fluid, as a result of a commercial surrogacy arrangement. The agreement was to pay £13,000 for the 'service' that the surrogate mother performed. This was the fee paid to an American organisation, the National Centre for Surrogate Parenting, (NCSP) £6,500 to be paid over to the mother. The mother agreed to hand over the child at birth. Mr and Mrs A arrived in England for the birth. The child was born in hospital and a few hours after the birth, the mother voluntarily left the child in the care of the hospital until the child could be collected by the plaintiffs. The local authority was granted a place of safety order (under legislation that is now repealed by the Children Act 1989, as of October 14, 1991). But the child was already in a hospital which qualifies as a 'place of safety'. The commissioning father, Mr A, commenced wardship proceedings and asked for care and control of the child for him and his wife. At a private hearing, Mr Justice Latey granted a wardship order and gave the local authority time to make inquiries before the case was restored to the list.

Latey, J declared that at the heart of the wardship jurisdiction was what was in the best interests of the child concerned. The commercial aspects of the ethical, moral and social implications regarding the methods used to produce the child were not relevant to the decision as to what was now best for the child. Mr A was confirmed as the baby's father and he and his wife wanted her but the baby's mother did not. The commissioning couple were both highly qualified professional people, with two residences. Materially they would be able to give the baby a very good upbringing. But, more importantly, the Court felt they were both 'excellently equipped to meet the baby's emotional needs if they felt it needed it.' The learned judge thought that 'looking at the child's well-being, physical and emotional' there was no one better than the commissioning couple to have her care.

The plaintiffs were given permission to take the child out of the jurisdiction. The wardship was continued until further order and there was to be no disclosure or publicity which might lead to the identification of the plaintiffs.

The Surrogacy Arrangements Act 1985

The UK became the first country ever to enact surrogacy legislation when it passed the Surrogacy Arrangements Act 1985 (the 1985 Act) whose main aim is to abolish commercial surrogacy. It applies to arrangements that are being made before a woman becomes pregnant with a view to the child being handed over to be brought up by someone else. The Act does not apply to agreements made after a woman has become pregnant. Where the process of reproduction has been assisted, the relevant time is when the embryos or gametes were placed in the woman's body. Since s.1A of the 1985 Act renders surrogacy contracts legally unenforceable, disputes over the upbringing of children must be resolved according to the general law on status (see discussion under Status Provisions in the opening section of this chapter and cases, below). The 1985 Act makes it an offence to negotiate a surrogate arrangement 'on a commercial basis' or to compile information with a view to doing so. But the Act does not cover cases where the only payment is to, or for the benefit of, the surrogate mother. It also provides that the surrogate mother and the commissioning parents cannot be guilty of the offence. The policy behind this is so that the child's upbringing will not be tainted with illegality but there are potential problems in the context of adoption if money changes hands here for any reason since the law bans payments for the adoption of a child whom it is intended to adopt. However, the English courts have given some guidance on dealing with this situation (see further, *Re Adoption Application* under English cases, below).

It is also an offence to advertise the fact that someone is willing to be a surrogate mother, negotiate a surrogate agreement or is looking for someone to act as one. Both the advertiser and the publisher of the newspaper or other medium will be guilty of the offence. No exception is made in this context for a surrogate mother or commissioning parents.

ADOPTION, SURROGACY AND REASONABLE PAYMENT OF EXPENSES

Re Adoption Application clarified the law on the legality of 'reasonable expenses' and the relationship between moneys handed over as reasonable expenses and monetary payments which were prohibited if made as part of payment for a proposed adoption of a baby.

Clarifying the interpretation of 'reasonable expenses' in a surrogacy and adoption case

Re Adoption Application (Payment for Adoption) (1987)

The applicants, Mr and Mrs A, were a childless couple who applied to adopt a child then aged two years and four months, who was conceived as a result of sexual intercourse between the surrogate mother and Mr A in pursuance of a surrogacy arrangement between the applicants and the surrogate mother. The agreement was entered into because Mrs A, in her mid-30s, was infertile. The applicants had been unsuccessful in their attempts to adopt a child both in Britain and abroad. The surrogate was a happily married woman with two children. The applicants answered the surrogate's magazine advertisement and they entered into a surrogate arrangement. This was no 'love affair' but a 'partial surrogacy' whereby the surrogate mother was also the genetic mother of the child. As Latey, J. said, it was 'physical congress with the sole purpose of procreating a child.' It was agreed that the applicants pay the mother £10,000 to compensate her for her loss of earnings, expenses in connection with the pregnancy and for emotional and physical factors. The surrogate and the Mr A had intercourse on a few occasions but this stopped as soon as conception occurred. The applicants paid the surrogate mother £1,000 a few months later and a further £4,000 when the baby was born. The surrogate refused to take the remaining £5,000, saying she had not entered the agreement for commercial reasons, would have handed the child over anyway and had made financial gains from the sale of a book she had co-written describing her surrogacy experiences.

Two days after the birth, the mother and child spent a week with the applicants before the mother returned to her home, leaving the child with the applicants. The child remained with the applicants for over two years and thrived in their care, and the applicants now applied for an adoption order.

Latey, J. considered: (i) whether, in the circumstances, an adoption order would be legally permissible-specifically, had there been 'payment or reward for adoption' which would prevent the adoption? The Court's view was that it was only *after* the baby was born that any of the parties began to think of adoption. Hence, no payment or reward had been made within the meaning of the legislation (then s.50 of the Adoption Act).
(ii) if so, could the court authorise payments retrospectively? s.50 of the Adoption Act 1958 prohibited payment for adoption but also provided that prohibited payments do not include 'any payment or reward authorised by the court'. Payment had already been made but the Court was prepared to authorise them retrospectively. The Court declared that to penalise every payment, no matter how modest or 'innocently made' would be Draconian and in this case, the court had a discretion whether or not to authorise payments.
(iii) would an adoption order be a correct exercise of the court's discretion?
The Court carefully considered reports from the doctor, the health visitor and the guardian ad litem (GAL) (now called Children's Guardian) which confirmed that the child remained happy and contented while in the care of the applicants and granted the adoption order. Even if the payments had been prohibited, the court was prepared to authorise them and to make an adoption order.

Surrogate mother's right to change her mind under surrogacy arrangement

Re P (Minors) (Wardship: Surrogacy) (1987) (the twins)

The commissioning couple, Mr and Mrs B, had no children of their own. The natural mother, Mrs P offered her services to the couple when she heard they were seeking a surrogate mother to bear Mr B's biological child as Mrs B could not carry a child to term. Payments were supposed to be made to the surrogate in instalments at various stages of the pregnancy and after the birth of the child. The mother's pregnancy was brought about by artificial pregnancy (the father donated sperm which was artificially inseminated into the mother) and she gave birth to twins. Having looked after the babies for five months, the surrogate refused to hand over the twins to the commissioning couple and both parties approached the local authority which warded the babies and requested the court to make orders as to their future.

Sir John Arnold, P. declared that the court's duty in deciding the case was to have the welfare of the child as its paramount consideration. The mother had a stronger case because the twins had now been looked after by their genetic mother for the first five months of their lives, and apart from having given birth to them, the care had clearly been satisfactory and the babies had bonded with their genetic mother. The judge found 'nothing to outweigh the advantages to these children of preserving a link to the mother to whom they are bonded, and who had exercised a satisfactory degree of maternal care.' He found it was not important to rule upon the validity of the agreement and any question of rejecting the agreement as being against public policy was not relevant to the present case. The only significance of this being a surrogate agreement was if the nature of the agreement reflected so adversely on the character and moral outlook of the custodians so as to disqualify them both entirely. The court awarded care and control of the babies to their mother and terminated the wardship proceedings.

Obtaining parental responsibility without adoption: section 30 HFEA 1990

In 1990, the case of *Re W (Minors) (Surrogacy)* led to legislative change, causing Parliament to change its view on whether surrogacy should be discouraged at all costs so that in certain circumstances, a couple could acquire Parental Responsibility without having to go to court to adopt the child.

Re W (Minors) (Surrogacy) (1991)—the first surrogacy case involving baby twins

Twins (aged 17 months at the time of the hearing) were born following a surrogacy arrangement. The genetic mother had no womb but was able to produce eggs which were taken from her medically and fertilised in vitro by sperm from her husband. Two resultant embryos were implanted in the host mother who gave birth to the twins who had lived with the genetic parents since then. There was no dispute about that arrangement. The local authority brought proceedings to establish the legal parentage of the children. It then obtained a wardship order to give the court wide powers to supervise the children's future. An order was made imposing restrictions on the publication of information about the children. Applications were made to vary the terms of that injunction. The host mother and her husband applied for the prohibition on their identification to be lifted which was unopposed.

Scott Baker, J. observed that until recently, when the advance of medical science created the possibility of in vitro fertilisation, it was not envisaged that the genetic mother could be other than one and the same person. The advent of IVF presented the law with a dilemma: whom should the law regard as the mother? In this case, it was accepted that the genetic parents were wholly admirable parents and that they should have the upbringing of the twins. The learned judge thought the imminent enactment of legislation of s.30 would enable the court to approve an agreement by all parties that decide these children's future in a practical manner. If the genetic parents succeeded in their application, the twins would be treated in law as being their children.

The court held:

- the welfare and best interests of the children were the first and paramount considerations. Their future lay with the genetic parents and it was necessary to facilitate any steps that cemented their relationship in that household. The terms of an injunction should be no wider than necessary to protect the wards' welfare;
- the local authority's application for declarations as to the twins' legal parentage stood adjourned generally with liberty to restore, upon the undertaking by the genetic parents to make an application for a parental order under the relevant clauses of the HFEA within 28 days of its becoming law [the law has now been enacted and is in force];
- pending the determination of the court as to the twins' parentage, they would remain wards of court under the care and control of the genetic parents;

- that the prohibition of the publication of the identity of the host mother and her husband be lifted, as this was unlikely to operate to the ward's disadvantage or prejudice their interests; and the existing injunction should continue.

Requirements of section 30 of the 1990 Act

Under s.30 of the Human Fertilisation and Embryology Act 1990, certain couples may apply for a parental order. This has been available since November 1, 1994. This order was created at a late stage in the House of Commons proceedings on the Bill in response to the much-publicised *Re W* (1991) (above) hence, under s.30, qualified people may apply to the court within six months of the child's birth for an order that they shall be t eated as the child's parents despite the application of ss.27, 28 and 29. In order to qualify, the applicants must show that they are over 18, married to each other; at least one must be a genetic parent of the child (even though another woman gave birth), the child is resident with them; those who are otherwise treated by the law as the parents have unconditionally agreed to the making of the order (if they can be found); and that no money has changed hands other than in respect of reasonable expenses unless authorised by the court. Section 30 will *not* be available if the child is not living with the applicants, or the applicants are not married to each other, or if the six-month period within which to apply has expired. Under current English law, a court may grant residence orders to the couple who has used assisted reproduction techniques to have a child, and the parental order will last, in the absence of a further court order, until the child is 16 but it will not remove the rights of the legal parents. To deal with this and add finality to the situation, many couples will prefer to adopt the child so that the parental responsibility of the legal parents can be terminated.

Re Q (Parental Order) (1996) (High Court)

This was the first reported case on s.30. The baby, Q, was born in the summer of 1995 as a result of a total surrogacy arrangement. The unmarried surrogate, who received IVF treatment at a licensed clinic, was paid $8,280 to cover her expense and loss of earnings. The commissioning couple applied for a parental order under s.30.

Johnson, J. was satisfied that the statutory requirements had been complied with but he highlighted three points: First, the consent of the carrying mother. She was overcome with doubt when the time actually came to give her consent but she had now done so, and according to the guardian ad litem's report, 'fully understands the effects of a parental order, understanding she loses all parental responsibility, and wishes the order to be made as soon as possible.'

Second, the court had to consider whether or not it should authorise payments totalling £8,280 which had been made to the surrogate mother by Mr and Mrs B. Here the court held that such authorisation could be given retrospectively following the decision of Latey, J. in *Re Adoption Application (payment for Adoption)* (1987) (see above). The guardian first thought that the payment was rather high but on further inquiry concluded that the sum was made up of payments to cover clothes, daily trips to the doctor for injections, child care provision of her own children during some of these visits and similar related expenses. A further £5,000 was a payment to compensate Miss A for loss of earnings.

The court agreed with the guardian that the payment was reasonable and authorised it.

Thirdly, the consultant who had carried out the medical procedures insisted that he and the hospital believed that Mr B was to be treated as the father of the child. The guardian told the court that this was a frequent misunderstanding of the legislation and it was for this reason that the court was asked to give a formal ruling. The court's interpretation of the Act in this case was that there was no man who was to be 'treated as the father' and whose consent was necessary to the making of the order. The court therefore held that to qualify as a father under s.28 of the HFEA 1990, the man must have an existing relationship with the woman who is receiving treatment, not the commissioning mother.

Comment on Re Q

Although Mr B provided the sperm and had intended to rear the child, his relationship was with the commissioning mother, not the surrogate mother. It also appears that where the sum paid for 'expenses' is not unduly large, a court will find very little difficulty in authorising payment retrospectively to the surrogate under 3.30(7) of the 1990 Act,

Payment retrospectively authorised to enable Parental Order to be made

Re C (Surrogacy: Payments) (2002)

Where the surrogate mother was paid more than could be deemed to be 'reasonable expenses' (£12,000), and an application for a Parental Order was made, the Court was prepared to retrospectively authorise the payment because it was in the child's best interests to be treated as the child of the commissioning parents. Unauthorised payments would normally require prior approval but in the circumstances of this case, retrospective authorisation was granted to enable the Parental Order to be made, following *Re Adoption Application* (1987).

British Medical Association (BMA) policy on surrogacy

Despite expressing disapproval of surrogacy practices in the UK during part of the 1980s, in the 1990s, the British Medical Association (BMA) eventually welcomed the British Government's decision to register and regulate agencies involved in surrogacy.

The way forward?

The way forward would probably not be through statutory criminalisation. There would be difficulties in policing surrogacy and trying to ensure the practice is not driven underground is one of the reasons for not criminalising it *in toto*. Another argument against a total ban would be that this would constitute an invasion of privacy under the Human Rights Act 1998 but if regulation is the solution, the question that the Brazier Report raises is: should this be centralised or decentralised?

POSTHUMOUS REPRODUCTION FROM SPERM TAKEN FROM A DECEASED DONOR

The Diane Blood Case

The orphaned embryo-insemination with an embryo fertilised in vitro: (R. v Human Fertilisation and Embryology Authority, ex p. Blood) [1997]

This case deals with the posthumous insemination of a woman, Diane Blood, with an embryo created with the egg collected from the woman and the sperm of her deceased husband, thereby creating a fatherless child. The husband of a childless couple who were trying to have a baby, had contracted bacterial meningitis and had lapsed into a coma. In vitro fertilisation was used in somewhat controversial circumstances in this case. Sperm was taken by electro-ejaculation from the husband while he was in a coma, while he was unable to give his consent who then died without ever having given his consent to the sperm donation in any form. Mrs Blood was nearly 33 years old and had testified that she and her husband had decided to try for a family towards the end of 1994 and although they had not been successful, had not started a course of treatment together before her husband fell seriously ill. She was sure that had her husband not been unconscious, he would have agreed both to the removal and storage of the sperm and to her being artificially inseminated after his death. Mrs Blood wished to be impregnated with her husband's sperm.

The Human Fertilisation and Embryology Authority is charged by the Human Fertilisation and Embryology Act 1990 (the 1990 Act) with the task of regulating and licensing fertility treatment.

The HFEA refused to license the release of the sperm for the procedure to be carried out in the UK or to exercise its discretion to authorise export of the sperm for treatment abroad. The grounds were that the donor had not given written consent for the storage and that it had been taken without his consent or counselling (as required under Sch.3). The HFEA also refused permission for Mr Blood's sperm to be exported to another EU member State where written permission is not required. Mrs Blood tried to challenge these decisions by means of judicial review. The case eventually went to the Court of Appeal.

The Court of Appeal held:

1. It was necessary to apply the law as an amalgam of domestic and EC law because European law was now part of domestic law at least where it applied directly as it did to the question of Mrs Blood's treatment abroad.

2. The storage of the sperm taken from a comatose man without his consent was technically an offence-a criminal assault, but this was an unexplored legal situation so there could be no criticism of the Infertility Research Trust.

3. Even if the statutory exception in s.4(1)(b) of the 1990 Act provides treatment without written consent for a couple together, the exception did not apply to a corpse.

4. The HFEA had been right to refuse to license the fertilisation of the man's sperm in the UK but in refusing the wife an export licence it had not taken into account her right to cross-border treatment under Art.59 and 60 of the EC Treaty. These provisions created a directly enforceable right to receive medical treatment in another member state.

5. If allowed to export the sperm, Mrs Blood could get lawful treatment in Belgium and an export licence in this case would not create an undesirable precedent.

In February 1997, the Authority allowed Mrs Blood to export the sperm to a Belgian clinic for posthumous insemination. On December 11, 1998, Diane Blood gave birth to a son, Liam, conceived using semen from her dead husband. As matters stood, it was believed that the son would still be regarded as non-marital, and there would be no recognition in law of Diane Blood's parents to be recognised as the child's grandparents. In 2002, the national newspapers carried the news that Mrs Blood had given birth to another child via IVF, using another portion of her dead husband's sperm, having received treatment from the same Belgian clinic that she had used before.

Post-Blood—the review of consent procedures under the HFEA

In 1997, the government commissioned a review (headed by Professor Sheila McLean) of consent procedures under the common law and the Human Fertilisation and Embryology Act 1990 (the 1990 Act). A Report, *Review of the Common Law provisions relating to the Removal of gametes and of the Consent provisions in the Human Fertilisation and Embryology Act 1990* (1998), was published in July 1998. The Report recommends that written consent should continue to be required for treatment under the 1990 Act.

Government announces changes to rules on birth register in 2000

In August 2000, the Department of Health announced that the government intended to change the law relating to Birth Registers so that the biological father's name could be inserted on the child's birth certificate even though the child was conceived after his death. On December 1, 2003, The Human Fertilisation and Embryology (Deceased Fathers) Act 2003 finally came into force, allowing registration of fathers posthumously in certain circumstances. For Diane Blood, registration means her babies would no longer be regarded as non-marital; women who conceived after their partner died would have the right to have their dead partner's name inserted on the baby's birth certificate and Diane Blood's parents would then be officially recognised as her children's grandparents. Diane Blood has now re-registered her children under the 2003 Act.

The Human Fertilisation and Embryology (Deceased Fathers) Act 2003 (the 2003 Act)

This statute allows the father who dies before the birth of the child, to be registered on the birth certificate in certain circumstances. Note that written consent should still be obtained before posthumous use of sperm can be permitted; the 2003 Act now requires the mother to request registration of the man's name and *written consent* to have been obtained from the late father before a deceased man can be recorded as the deceased father of a child born as a result of fertility treatment after his death; the requirement is that he signed the appropriate written consent *before* his death. However, the requirement of written consent does *not* apply to men who died *before* the 2003 Act was passed. The name of the father may be added to the birth certificate along with reference to the date of death at the request of the mother. While the Act allows a deceased man to be recorded as the father on the birth register this does not give rise to any rights of inheritance or other legal rights (e.g. nationality) which would normally flow from such parental recognition.

ACCESS TO IVF SERVICES

Open to all or only to those within certain age limits?

As far as allowing access to IVF treatment in Britain is concerned, the test of the child's welfare or best interests has been used to limit such access. However, although the basic policy has been to declare the welfare of the child to be paramount, the outcome of one of the well-known cases in this area, the *Harriott* Case, has been controversial and ended up in court. This case pre-dated the 1990 Act.

Section 13(5) of the 1990 Act provides:

'A woman shall not be provided with treatment services unless account has been taken of the welfare of any child who may be born as a result of the treatment (including the need of that child for a father), and of any child who may be affected by the birth".

In *Seale* (*R. v Sheffield HA ex p. Seale*), decided in 1994, Mrs Seale, aged 36, had been experiencing difficulties in conceiving and had applied to Sheffield Health Authority for IVF treatment. The authority rejected her application. In a letter to her husband, it was stated that because of competing health priorities, only £200,000 could be allocated to the provision of assisted reproduction services. The applicant applied to the High Court for judicial review of the decision.

The court held that, in view of its limited resources and the lower success rates achieved with older women, the Authority's policy only to treat women below the age of 35 was not irrational.

The authority was not required to provide this sort of service on demand to any individual patient for whom it may work, regardless of financial and other constraints upon the authority. To consider the financial resources available and to decide that the efficiency of the treatment decreased after the woman reached 35, and would not come within the scope of unreasonableness as defined in the *Wednesbury case* (*Associated Provincial Picture House v Wednesbury Corp* [1947]).

In 1996, Mrs Seale, then aged 38, gave birth to a baby boy as a result of IVF treatment paid for privately by an anonymous business benefactor.

Refusal of Treatment on the grounds of applicant's personal history? R. v Ethical Committee of St. Mary's Hospital (Manchester) ex.p Harriott (The Harriott case) [1988]

Mrs Harriott was experiencing difficulties in becoming pregnant and had applied to her local authority's social services department to adopt or foster a child. Her application was turned down because of her past criminal record (which included soliciting for prostitution) and her allegedly poor understanding of the role of a foster-parent. She subsequently applied for IVF under the National Health Service and once again her application was refused. She then sought judicial review of the decision to refuse her treatment alleging that it was reached by the wrong body and that she was not given adequate opportunity to make representation. Schiemann, J. ruled that she *had* been given an opportunity to make representations against the refusal so there was no procedural unfairness. The learned judge was prepared to accept that a blanket policy to refuse treatment to 'anyone who was a Jew or coloured' might be illegal but the hospital's criteria in this case were acceptable and unobjectionable. The plaintiff therefore failed in her application.

Current law on access to treatment

Under the current law, if a heterosexual couple seek treatment with IVF, individual fertility clinics have a discretion who to treat, so long as they act in accordance with the Code of Practice promulgated by the HFE Authority. Where a couple are refused treatment, reasons must be given, pursuant to para. 3.31 of the Code of Practice (4th ed. 2001) as well as 'the factors. . . which might persuade the centre to reverse its decision.' Options available should also be communicated to the couple as well and information regarding provision of counselling. Two main reasons might justify why treatment may be refused: (i) the couple may be medically unsuitable; (ii) they may be deemed socially unsuitable as parents. Here, the decision will be determined by an assessment of the impact on the welfare and best interests of any child born as a result of the treatment.

The 1990 Act does not say that there is an age limit on recipients of IVF treatment. However, age is a factor which may be taken into account by ethics committees when reviewing applications for this treatment. Age limits are included by many clinics and the latest HFEA Code of Practice includes the ages of the parties seeking treatment and this is linked to 'their likely future ability to look after or provide for a child's needs'. (para.3.17 (e) HFEA Code of Practice 2001). The IVF unit of St Mary's Hospital stipulates that they will only treat couples where the female is less than 40 and the male is less than 50. (see also, the *Seale* case, above)

CLONING

In 1996, Dolly, the sheep, the first vertebrate cloned from a cell of an adult animal, generated considerable interest on a worldwide scale. Although hailed as a remarkable scientific breakthrough, concern was raised both nationally and internationally about the future of this technology, especially in the context of the coning of human beings. Dolly was followed by Polly, a transgenic sheep produced by transfer of the nucleus of a cultured fetal fibroblast. She carries a human gene for blood clotting Factor IX, which is used for treatment of haemophilia. The term 'cloning' is Greek for 'twig'. The British Commission Human Genetics Advisory (HGAC) which reports to Ministers on issues arising from new developments in human genetics that can be expected to have wider social, ethical and/or economic implications, are careful to distinguish between at least two main types of cloning:

(i) Reproductive cloning-where an entire animal is produced from a single cell by asexual reproduction. Dolly falls into this category. Human reproductive cloning would involve the creation of a human being who was genetically identical to another.
(ii) Therapeutic cloning-which are scientific and therapeutic applications of nuclear replacement technology, which do not involve the creation of genetically identical individuals.

These applications may include therapy for human mitochondrial disease and research which might lead to the replacement of damaged or diseased tissues or organs without the risk of rejection reactions. One example would be skin tissue to treat burn injuries.

Cloning is not, per se, a new phenomenon. Many plants can clone themselves and fragments of genetic material are routinely 'cloned' by polynurase chain reaction (PCR) and this has become the basis of DNA fingerprinting and other applications in biotechnology. Recently, Professor Jonathan Slack, an embryologist at Bath University, England, engineered a headless frog clone raising the prospect that headless human clones 'could be used to grow organs and tissues for transplant surgery'.

Legal aspects of cloning

There is some doubt as to whether English law at present actually deals with human cloning. Cloning can denote several processes and at present although the Human Fertilisation and Embryology Act 1990 appears to ban cloning, there is sufficient ambiguity in the wording of the relevant provision for one to argue (as Duddington does in 'The legal and ethical aspects of cloning: parts 1 and 2 (1999) Law and Justice 26; 100) that cloning as we now use it, is not covered.

Section 1(1)(a) of the 1990 Act provides that 'embryo' means a live human embryo where fertilisation is complete. Section 1(1) (b) also uses the term fertilisation by stating that reference to an embryo includes an egg in process of fertilisation. As Wood and Korek point out, the problem here is what Wood calls 'the reconstituted cell' which grew into Dolly, was never fertilised. (see, e.g. Wood, "To What Extent can the Law Control Human Cloning?" (1999) *Medicine, Science and Journal of the British Academy of Forensic Sciences*, vol 39, no.1,p.5). There was no fusion of egg and sperm and it was artificially created.

Section 3(3)(d) of the 1990 Act contains a prohibition on cloning by providing that a licence granted by the HFEA cannot authorise 'replacing a nucleus taken from the cell of any person, embryo or subsequent development of an embryo or subsequent development of an embryo'. Again the difficulty is that although those words appear to prohibit nuclear transfer cloning, which is what was used in the case of Dolly, once more what precisely happened in Dolly's case is not covered because of the use of the word 'embryo'. Hence, as Duddington (1999) points out, the 1990 Act uses the terms 'fertilisation' and 'embryo' which do not cover what is now understood by cloning. As explained, the Act allows certain activities under a licence among which is the storing of gametes.

Section 4(2) of the Act provides that 'a licence cannot authorise storing or using gametes in any circumstances in which regulations prohibit their storage or use but, as Korek in 'Following Dolly' (1997) 147 NLJ 428 points out, this may not cover what happened in Dolly's case. A gamete is a sperm or egg cell but only the cell membrane was used to create Dolly and so it could be argued that this is not a gamete. As Wood says, 'to submit otherwise would be analogous to arguing that an egg devoid of its yolk is still an egg'.

Paragraphs 3 and 4 of Sch.2 provide that 'a licence under this paragraph cannot authorise altering the genetic structure of any cell while it forms part of an embryo . . .'. Again, the word 'embryo' is problematical.

Hence, the present legal position, based on the current legislation, is, as Duddington (1999) submits, that the 1990 Act does not cover *human* cloning. Any argument that the 1990 Act does cover cloning would have to interpret the term 'embryo' as having a meaning that it presently does not have. Consequently, as things stand, any decision on whether to grant a licence to permit reproductive cloning rests entirely with a statutory body, which, admittedly, is subject to judicial review. There is no other scrutiny or monitoring of the situation on any systematic or independent basis.

The Bruno case-cloning not covered by HFEA

The Court of Appeal case of Bruno Quintavalle (*R. (On the application of Bruno Quintavalle on behalf of Pro-Life Alliance) v Secretary of State for Health* [2002]) which held that cloning fell outside the HFEA 1990 altogether, prompted parliament to pass the Human Reproductive Cloning Act 2001, a short Act which prohibits the second and decisive step in reproductive cloning, namely placing a Cell Nuclear transfer (known as CNR)-cloned embryo in a woman's uterus. This is a form of cloning in which a nucleus taken from an adult human is introduced into an egg that has not been fertilised. The egg is then stimulated artificially to begin the division and embryo-formation process. The Act does not prevent the creation of cloned embryos by CNR for research purposes (which would be regarded as 'therapeutic' cloning).

s.1 of the 2001 Act reads:

(1) A person who places in a woman a human embryo which has been created otherwise than by fertilisation is guilty of an offence.
(2) A person who is guilty of an offence is liable on conviction on indictment to imprisonment
for a term not exceeding 10 years or a fine or both.
(3) No proceedings for the offence may be instituted —
    (a) in England and Wales, except with the consent of the Director of Public Prosecutions;
    (b) in Northern Ireland, except with the consent of the Director of Public Prosecutions for Northern Ireland.

7. STERILISATION OF PATIENTS LACKING MENTAL CAPACITY

INTRODUCTION

Medico-legal issues arise from the medical procedure of sterilisation when it is performed on mentally incompetent patients, usually female (with some rare exceptions), who might be minors or adults, as an act of medical paternalism: where the operation is claimed by a third party, usually a relative or a healthcare professional, and approved by a court, as being in the 'best interests' of the patient. This chapter examines English law, although reference will be made to the Canadian case of *Re Eve*, in the context of discussing a leading English case (*Re B*), and also discusses contraceptive sterilisation, where the intention is the permanent removal of reproductive capacity again as a means of protection from an 'unwanted' pregnancy with which the incompetent or mentally handicapped patient is perceived as being unable to cope. Consensual sterilisation may be chosen as a voluntary and increasingly popular means of contraception by willing and competent adults.

ETHICAL PRINCIPLES

Competent adults have the right voluntarily to choose to be sterilised, but the circumstances in which it is proposed for persons with a mental incapacity, who are incapable of giving consent, can give rise to ethical issues. For instance, the variable nature and degrees of mental handicap raise certain ethical concerns. The patient's autonomy should, as ever, be respected even though the patient may not be capable of giving legally recognised consent yet medical and judicial paternalism has been known to justify sterilisation. The autonomy v paternalism conflict is highlighted in the controversial sterilisation cases that have come before the English courts. Who should have the right to decide whether it is ever in the best interests of a mentally handicapped person to be sterilised? How should one decide what is 'in the best interests' of such a patient? If such operations are carried out, do they really show respect for persons-all persons, whether capable of deciding for themselves or not?

The fact that a person lacks the capacity to give a proper and informed consent to sex and the inability to understand the connection between sex and pregnancy raises the dangers of unprotected sex which could result in pregnancy and issues arise over the ability of these persons to look after any child that might be produced. But this undesirable outcome should not, in itself, justify sterilisation of such persons. Someone has to protect their autonomy whilst making a difficult decision about whether to safeguard their welfare by enabling them to be protected from an unwanted pregnancy.

In the early 21st century, English law still encounters the challenges posed by this situation.

In England, there has been very little media discussion of sterilisation but the few cases that have hit the headlines in the 1970s and in the 1980s, have aroused moral outrage from interest groups and the media and generally strong criticism from British academics. Before 1960, the BMA apparently advised doctors that sterilisation could only be done lawfully for therapeutic reasons (i.e. to improve health). But by the mid-1960s, the National Health Service (Family Planning) Act 1967 permitted local health authorities to provide family planning services and subsequent amendments to this Act in 1972, and re-organisation of the health service eventually reached the current position which allows all main methods of contraception, including male and female sterilisation, to be available under the National Health Service. The English courts discussed the viability of the therapeutic and non-therapeutic distinction in the mid-1970s and in the late 1980s, when the House of Lords eventually rejected it as a viable test for authorisation of sterilisation for a mentally handicapped child and opting for the 'best interests' and 'welfare' test. The one concrete outcome for legal practitioners in the 1980s has been the issuing of several Practice Directions clarifying the procedure for authorisation of sterilisations, the latest being issued in 2001.

In 1987, the Department of Health released figures which indicated that about 90 sterilisations are performed per year in England, on females under 19. The reality is that there is no hard data on the numbers of mentally disabled persons who undergo sterilisation every year.

Consensual and non-consensual sterilisation

Consensual or voluntary sterilisation has become more popular over the years but controversy has grown over non-consensual sterilisation of persons who are intellectually disabled, in the wake of a few cases in the 1980s where the 'rights' of such patients appeared to be compromised or even ignored.

Mason and McCall Smith, in *Law and Medical Ethics* (2002) still consider the area of non-consensual sterilisation to be 'a minefield of powerful objection'. The root problem of this area, they argue, is the fact that it 'raises starkly the subject of what has been named the basic human right to reproduce'.

Key principles from case law

The key principle that emerges from the case law on non-consensual sterilisation, mainly from *Re D* in 1976 to *Re B* in 1987, is that the approval of a High Court judge is usually required for any such operation where it is proposed on a mentally disabled patient, and any operation that is performed can only be authorised if it is in the best interests of the patient. This 'best interests' or 'welfare test' as it is also called where the 'welfare of the patient is paramount' is the only criterion and is also the yardstick used to validate ex post facto, (i.e. after the event) any medical procedures carried out by healthcare professionals on mentally disabled adults provided they were administered in those patients' best interests. Strictly speaking, mentally incapacitated adults are the only persons legally entitled to decide on their medical treatment, because of the gap in the law left by the legal reforms unwittingly effected by the Mental Health Act 1983. In practical terms, of course, any consent given to medical procedures would have to be proxy consent, given by parents, guardians or other carers.

In current English law, there is no distinction to be drawn between therapeutic and non-therapeutic sterilisation except that therapeutic sterilisation (to cure or alleviate a medical condition) would not require court authorisation. The 'best interests' of the patient or 'welfare test' is the only guiding principle.

STERILISATION OF MENTALLY INCAPACITATED MINORS

Therapeutic and non-therapeutic sterilisation

Key cases

Re D (1976) High Court

In 1976, in *Re D*, (1976) an English High Court judge made a distinction between *therapeutic* and *non-therapeutic* sterilisation in the context of the proposed sterilisation of a girl of 11 with Sotos syndrome, characterised by accelerated growth, generalised clumsiness, epilepsy, aggressive tendencies, and impairment of mental function. However, it was expected that her condition would improve and that she would have the capacity to marry. Her devoted widowed mother was afraid D would be seduced and give birth to a baby for whom she would be unable to take care, and who might be mentally disabled. D was not as seriously mentally impaired as some others with her condition. Nevertheless, her mother applied for D's sterilisation in order to protect her which was supported by D's pediatrician and gynecologist, but the operation was opposed by D's educational psychologist. The matter had to be resolved by the court, which would not authorise the sterilisation. Heilbron, J held that the only sterilisation that would be permissible would be *therapeutic* sterilisation where the operation would be required to cure or alleviate a particular medical condition. The Court ruled that the matter was both of great importance to the child and a matter of principle of considerable importance. Her Ladyship noted the conflict of professional opinion but refused to sanction the operation, declaring it involved the deprivation of a basic *human right*, i.e. the *right of a woman to reproduce*, and therefore, if performed on a woman for therapeutic reasons and without her consent, would be a violation of that right. Since D could not give an informed consent, but there was a strong likelihood she would understand the implications of the operation when she reached the age of 18, the case was one in which the court should exercise its protective powers.

The court continued her wardship. The learned judge agreed with the consulting doctors' opinion that sterilisation for thera-peutic purposes was within a doctor's clinical judgment only where the sterilisation was the treatment of choice for some disease. Heilbron, J stated:

> 'The evidence does not warrant the view, that a decision to carry out an operation of this nature performed for non-therapeutic purposes on a minor can be held to be within the doctor's sole clinical judgment.'

The operation was neither medically indicated nor necessary and would not be in D's interest; accordingly, it would be prevented.

Heilbron, J. further emphasised: (i) the decision to sterilise for non-therapeutic purposes did not lie within a doctor's sole clinical judgment; and (ii) under the court's *parens patriae* jurisdiction, it had the power to throw a protective net over D in this case in the exercise of its wardship jurisdiction.

After *Re D*, no Code of Practice or official guidance in any form appeared until after the next decade, in the wake of the House of Lords' cases of *Re B* in 1987 and *Re F* in 1989. Several Practice Directions have been issued, the latest one in 2001. *Re D*, however, remained the leading English authority for more than ten years and was even approved by the Canadian Supreme Court in *Re Eve*.

Since *Re D*, the English courts have given permission to perform medical operations under the *parens patriae* jurisdiction. In *Re P* (a minor) (1980), local authorities invoked the court's wardship jurisdiction to permit an abortion on a 15-year-old girl who had previously given birth and was already caring for the first child in facilities provided by the authority. The evidence indicated that the girl was taking good care of the first child but could not cope with a second, and that the girl consented to the operation. It should be noted that the girl was not mentally retarded. Butler-Sloss, J. (as she then was) authorised the abortion, despite the girl's father's objection, on the ground that it was in the girl's best interest.

A Canadian parallel: Re Eve: the mentally disabled adult patient

In the ten years before the next seminal English case on sterilisation reached the English courts, the Supreme Court of Canada decided *Re Eve*, which did not involve a mentally disabled child, but the court there had to consider the extent of the *parens patriae* jurisdiction over a mentally disabled adult. The adult female, 'Eve' aged 24, was 'mildly to moderately retarded' and suffered from expressive aphasia. While at a school for retarded adults, she met a male student who was also retarded but not to the same degree as herself. An application by her mother for the permission to consent to the sterilisation of Eve was eventually rejected by the Canadian Supreme Court, which held, inter alia, that the courts should never authorise a non-therapeutic sterilisation of a mentally retarded person under its *parens patriae* jurisdiction.

The Canadian court took seven years to deliberate on this case but they were able to do this because the patient in question was an adult so there was no urgency in coming to a decision that had to be 'against the clock'. The patient in this case was 24, and not 17, as was erroneously reported in pre-publicity about this case; this is in stark contrast to the situation that transpired in the subsequent English case of *Re B*.

Re B—the Jeanette Case (1987) House of Lords

In 1987, in the controversial case of *Re B* (the Jeanette Case) the House of Lords remarked that it was 'not helpful' to make a distinction between therapeutic and non-therapeutic sterilisation because the only test that should apply in any case where court approval for sterilisation was whether it would be in the best interests of the patient concerned. The context was the proposed sterilisation of a 17-year-old girl with the mental age of four or five who, it was alleged, could not understand the connection between sex and pregnancy and could not cope with pregnancy or looking after a child of her own, but who was in danger of becoming pregnant, because although intellectually disabled, was physically attractive and therefore at risk. She had an aversion to needles, and all drugs seemed to have a bad effect on her. The Law Lords held that it no longer matters whether one classifies a proposed sterilisation as therapeutic or non-therapeutic. All that matters is whether, in the opinion of the court, the operation is in the best interests of the person for whom the procedure is proposed.

House of Lords: welfare principle the only criterion

Five Law Lords led by Lord Hailsham, then Lord Chancellor, unanimously rejected the test case appeal by the Official Solicitor acting on behalf of Jeanette, and stressed that the only issue to be decided in this case was whether sterilisation of this young woman in her particular circumstances would promote her welfare and be in her best interests. The only permissible approach in the present wardship proceedings was to apply the welfare principle, which was to regard the welfare of the minor as the 'first and paramount consideration' as laid down at the time in s.1 of the Guardianship of Minors Act 1971 (now repealed and replaced by the Children Act).

The Law Lords stressed that this case had nothing to do with eugenics and involved no general principle of public policy and confirmed that the lower court and the Court of Appeal were correct in their decision to authorise the operation, and that sterilisation was the only practicable alternative. Lord Hailsham added that the ward had been found in a comprising position in a bathroom with a carer, accentuating what he thought to be the 'significant danger of pregnancy'. Lord Bridge stated that it was clear beyond argument that pregnancy for Jeanette in her mental condition would be an 'unmitigated disaster', so that the only question was how she could best be protected against it.

Accordingly, the Law Lords authorised Jeannette's sterilisation.

Re D not followed

The House of Lords decided not to follow either *Re D* or *Re Eve* and seemed to be stating two main guiding principles. First, there is no 'basic human right' as such, of a woman to reproduce, unless that woman is capable of appreciating its significance. Hence, for example, Lord Hailsham speaks of Jeanette's inability to make the choice whether to have a child or not, as determining whether the right to reproduce would be of any value. Secondly, English law will not necessarily accept that the decision whether or not to sterilise a mentally incompetent minor should be governed by whether the treatment is 'therapeutic' or 'non-therapeutic'. Thus, *the welfare principle is the only criterion* (the 'primary and paramount consideration') utilised by a wardship court, after considering all the medical evidence and particular facts of the case, in deciding whether sterilisation of a minor should be authorised.

The jurisdictional question

Did a residual jurisdiction remain in the High Court after a minor attained majority as part of the scope of the *parens patriae* jurisdiction of the High Court? The implication of the subsequent House of Lords' case of *Re F (F v West Berkshire HA* [1989] is that *nobody* can decide on behalf of mentally handicapped adults, but a doctor can lawfully operate on, or give other treatment to mentally incapable adult patient, *provided* the operation or medical procedure is in that patient's best interests.

COMMENT

The mere fact that a person is unable to appreciate the significance of a particular right does not entitle anyone to deprive him of that right. Indeed, a child's right to be maintained, educated and protected by persons *in loco parentis* doe- not derive from that child's appreciation of that right but from the existence of parental duty (and, it might be added, parental responsibility under the Children Act 1989). Equally, Jeanette's basic human rights should exist regardless of her capacity to appreciate them. In their desire not to be faced with a jurisdictional problem once Jeanette reached 18, the English Law Lords took only 28 days to decide the case, but their assumptions about her future conduct may well have led them to discount other possibilities too readily.

Cases in the aftermath of Re B

Following *Re B*, *Re M* (a minor) (wardship: sterilisation) (1988) and *Re P (a minor) (wardship: sterilization)* (1989) were reported. Sterilisation was approved in both without any appeals The crucial point in these two cases is the introduction of the notion of reversibility; medical evidence was given at both hearings to the effect that the proposed operation was reversible in 5# per cent to 75 per cent of the cases, which was the opinion of the gynecologist in *Re M* who said that he regards the operation of sterilisation by occlusion of the Fallopian tubes as more one of contraception than of sterilisation, especially bearing in mind all the emotive feelings that the use of the word 'sterilisation' arouses. This element of reversibility appeared to persuade the judges to authorise the sterilisations because there was no earlier consensus on the weight to be given to the evidence to support the sterilisation.

In *Re P* (1989), the 17-year-old woman was said to have the intellectual development of a six year old, and although her intellectual development would never improve, she would, with care and counselling acquire some 'social skills'; indeed her communication skills were said to be good and improving She had some maternal feelings but her 'attractive demeanour and limited intellect' would make her particularly vulnerable to seduction and the risk of pregnancy. Medical opinion differed on whether she would give a fully informed consent to abortion and her mother was afraid she would not agree to one. At the time of the hearing, the girl was not yet at risk of pregnancy because she regarded intercourse as painful and she might well value the 'right' to reproduce. Nevertheless, Eastham, J. was prepared to authorise the sterilisation despite the fact that the girl appeared to have some of the characteristics usually said to be absent in mentally handicapped persons. The testimony of an eminent specialist that there was a 'very high percentage chance of success' of reversing the operation, appears to have swayed the court.

The oddly named 'ethical' practice which Eastham, J. referred to in Re P (1989), is worth noting. He said: 'The situation today is that the [sterilisation] operation is not irreversible, although it is still the current ethical practice to tell the patient that it is an irreversible operation as part of the information to be given to them when they are giving consent for the operation to be carried out, although if such a patient changes her mind, no doubt it would be explained to her that the more serious reversal operation could be contemplated'.

Then came Re E (a minor) (medical treatment) (1991) which was seen as a case of therapeutic sterilisation (discussed above) since the 17-year-old woman here suffered from a menstrual condition which could only be cured by a hysterectomy. The court held that as it was an operation required for therapeutic reasons, the parents of a minor could give valid consent and the consent of the court was not necessary.

In Re HG (Specific Issue order: Sterilisation) (1993), the girl was nearly 18, severely epileptic and had a chromosomal deficiency which meant that she was an infant in terms of abilities. She lived in a school in circumstances where she was likely to be at risk from sexual relationships leading to pregnancy. There was no dispute that pregnancy, which she would not be capable of understanding, would be disastrous for her, and that the contraceptive pill was not suitable because of her epilepsy. The deputy judge concluded that 'a sufficiently overwhelming case has been established to justify interference with the fundamental right of a woman to bear a child. I am certainly satisfied that it would be cruel to expose T to an unacceptable risk of pregnancy and that that should be obviated by sterilisation in her interests.'

STERILISATION OF THE MENTALLY INCAPACITATED ADULT

English courts have had some difficulty in coping with applications for sterilisation of mentally handicapped adults, if only because the rather bizarre effect of the replacement of the original parens patriae jurisdiction by the 1959 Mental Health Act (now the 1983 Mental Health Act) which does not contain any provision under which consent may be given on behalf of the patient to treatment other than that for their mental disorder. The only situation in which it is lawful to give mental treatment without consent per se, is usually only in cases of urgency or necessity, where there is, for example, an unconscious patient and there is an immediate need for treatment. Of course, 'immediate' does not have to mean that death is necessarily imminent. In *R. v Bourne*, MacNaghten, J. said that "the law does not require the doctor to wait until the unfortunate woman is in peril of immediate death." referring to the fact that if a woman was in need of an abortion to save her life, the sooner the operation was performed, the better. We now consider the main cases in this area.

Key cases

T v T (1988)

In *T v T*, in the Family Division of the High Court, Wood, J. was faced with the problem of dealing with an application to sterilise a mentally disabled adult woman aged 19 who was also epileptic to and perform an abortion on her. There was no prospect of any improvement in her condition.

Despite the care given by her mother, friends and social workers, T was found to be pregnant and her medical advisers recommended the termination of the pregnancy. The grounds for the termination were that T could not understand the concept of pregnancy or cope with the problems that would be associated with that condition and that she would be incapable of bringing up and caring for the child. Looking to the future, the medical advisers recommended that she be sterilised as she needed protection from future pregnancy and that in all the circumstances that was the only method. Since T could not give consent, the medical advisers were unwilling to perform the operation without the protection of the court. The mother of the girl applied for a declaration that the termination of the pregnancy, and the sterilisation of T would not amount to an unlawful act by reason only of the absence of her consent.

The issue for the Court was: on what legal basis could a consent be granted for medical treatment on such an adult where the wardship jurisdiction was not available?

Wood, J. held that in law there was no one able to consent to these operations, not even the court; and he felt obliged to rely on the doctrine of necessity to declare the proposed operations legal. He also made a plea for a restoration of the court's jurisdiction to grant consent in these sorts of cases.

However, about 19 months later, the Law Lords had the opportunity to consider this matter in *Re F*.

Re F (1989) House of Lords

In *F v West Berkshire Health Authority* (1989), the woman was aged 36 and severely mentally impaired. She had the verbal capacity of a child aged two and the general mental capacity of a child aged four or five. Since the age of 14 she had been a voluntary in-patient at a mental hospital controlled by the defendant health authority. She had formed a sexual relationship with a male patient, P. There was medical evidence that, from a psychiatric point of view, it would be disastrous for her to become pregnant and since there were serious objections to all ordinary methods of contraception, either because she would be unable to use them effectively or because of a risk to her physical health, the medical staff in charge of F decided that the best course of action would be for her to be sterilised. Her mother had to act as her next friend because F's disability meant she was incapable of giving a legally valid consent to the operation. F's mother sought a declaration from the Court that the absence of F's consent would not make sterilisation of F an unlawful act.

The High Court held that the court had no power to give consent on behalf of F or to dispense with the need for such consent because the *parens patriae* jurisdiction of the court in respect of persons suffering from mental incapacity no longer existed. However, he granted a declaration that the sterilisation of F would not amount to an unlawful act by reason only of the absence of F's consent. The Official Solicitor's appeal to the Court of Appeal was dismissed and an appeal was made to the House of Lords, who dismissed the appeal and held that:

1. The court had no jurisdiction, either by statute or under the *parens patriae* jurisdiction, to give or withhold consent to a sterilisation operation on an adult woman disabled by mental capacity;
2. The court did have jurisdiction, however, to make a declaration that the proposed operation was lawful on the ground that, in the circumstances, it was in the best interests of the patient;

3. In determining whether the proposed operation was in the best interests of the patient, the court should apply the established test of what would be accepted as appropriate treatment at the time by a reasonable body of medical opinion skilled in that particular form of treatment (*Bolam* [1957] applied).

The House of Lords also stated, *inter alia*, that: At common law a doctor can lawfully operate on or give treatment to adult patients who are incapable of consenting to his doing so, provided that the operation or treatment is in the best interests of such patients. The operation will be in their best interests only of it is carried out in order either to save their lives or to ensure improvement or prevent deterioration in their physical or mental health.

Necessity

The notion of the common law powers of a doctor acting out of necessity in an emergency was commented upon by various Law Lords. Lord Bridge observed that it was 'axiomatic' that 'treatment which is necessary to preserve the life, health or well-being of the patient may lawfully be given without consent. But, if a rigid criterion of necessity were to be applied to determine what is and is not lawful in the treatment of the unconscious and the incompetent, many of those unfortunate enough to be deprived of the capacity to make or communicate rational decisions by accident, illness or unsoundness of mind, might be deprived of treatment which it would be entirely beneficial for them to receive'.

Best interests

All the judges in *Re F* agreed that the test for determining whether the decision to operate was taken in the best interests of the patient should be in accordance with the well-known *Bolam* test, namely that the doctor must act in accordance with a responsible and competent body of opinion, in relation to that particular area of medical practice and procedure.

Court will decide whether sterilisation is in the best interests of a mentally disabled male patient
Re A (2000) -the male patient

In *Re A (Mental patient: Sterilisation)* (2000) *The Times*, March 15, the Court of Appeal had to consider an application to grant a declaration under the court's inherent jurisdiction that it would be lawful to perform a sterilisation operation by way of vasectomy on a 28-year-old male patient (significantly impaired because of Down's syndrome), despite his inability to consent to the operation. He had been cared for from birth by his mother who was now in her early sixties. She had provided him with a high degree of care and supervision but now felt that her age and health highlighted the need to make sensible plans for the future. Her major concern was that if he moved into local authority care, in the absence of an operation to sterilise, he might have a sexual relationship resulting in his fathering a child for whom he was unable to take responsibility. Sumner, J refused to grant a declaration authorising sterilisation and an appeal was lodged.

In the Court of Appeal, Dame Butler Sloss, P. stressed that the House of Lords had made it quite clear in *In re F (Mental Patient: Sterilisation)* (1989) that an operation to sterilise had to be demonstrated to be in the patient's best interests. An application on behalf of a man for sterilisation was not the equivalent of an application in respect of a woman; this was not a matter of equality of the sexes but a balancing exercise on a case-by-case basis. The court's task was to balance all the relevant factors and to decide what would be in the *best interests* of the person unable to make his own decision. There was no evidence that having the operation would have any effect on the care that this patient received, nor would it allow him any greater measure of freedom. If in the future his quality of life were to be demonstrably diminished because he was not sterilised that would be the time to seek a declaration that sterilisation would be in his best interests.

Thorpe, L.J., concurred and said that the evaluation of best interests was akin to a welfare appraisal in that it was necessary to draw up a balance sheet weighing the factors of actual benefit, such as the acquisition of foolproof contraception against opposing factors such as apprehension, risk and discomfort inherent in the operation. Accordingly, the Court of Appeal held that it was for *the court to decide* whether an operation to sterilise a person unable to give consent was in his best interests and the considerations, which were not all the same in the case of men and women, encompassed medical, emotional and all welfare issues. In these circumstances, sterilisation would not be authorised.

This is the first case where the court has been approached to grant sterilisation of an intellectually disabled *male* patient.

Liability for a failed sterilisation only for negligence or breach of contract

The basic principle in English common law is that, provided a duty of care has been shown to exist, liability for a failed sterilisation will not be imposed unless it can be established that the failure to achieve contraception was due to medical negligence or to breach of contract rather than to the possibility that conception might still occur after the operation as a result of the vagaries of nature (see Mason and McCall Smith (2002)).

Court must decide whether treatment is in the patient's best interests if patient lacks capacity—the hysterectomy case—*Re S (Sterilisation: Patient's Best Interests)* (2000) The Times, May 26, 2002

S, a woman aged 28, had a severe learning disability and was incapable of giving her consent to any medical treatment. She also suffered from a strong fear of hospitals. Her mother wished her to have a hysterectomy, both to end her heavy periods and to eliminate any risk of pregnancy. There was evidence that the periods caused S distress. S was currently cared for by her mother, aged 54, and was kept under close supervision, so there was little risk of pregnancy at present. However, her mother was finding it increasingly difficult to look after S and there was a plan for her to go into sheltered accommodation, where the risk of pregnancy might increase. S's mother sought a declaration that a hysterectomy was in her daughter's best interests and could lawfully be performed. The Official Solicitor opposed the application arguing that as an alternative, an intra-uterine device called Mirena, would significantly reduce S's periods, and provide adequate contraceptive protection. The insertion of the device would be less intrusive than the proposed hysterectomy but the device would have to be replaced every five to seven years. The mother's objection to the Mirena was that it was unlikely to end S's periods and that, because it was not a single procedure, would involve S in regular visits to the hospital throughout her life, causing her repeated distress.

At first instance, the two issues before the judge were whether it was in S's best interests to be sterilised in order to avoid the risk of pregnancy or to undergo therapeutic treatment to eliminate her menstrual periods.

Wall, J. granted the application, making a declaration that a laparoscopic hysterectomy could be lawfully performed on S; it was in S's best interests that her heavy periods should come to an end, and therefore the subtotal hysterectomy which would have the incidental effect of sterilising S, was in her best interests.

On appeal, however, the Court of Appeal held (per Butler Sloss, L.J.):

1. The decision of the judge was contrary to the expert evidence. The weight of medical evidence supported the less invasive method as the preferred option at least in the first instance, and the understandable concerns of a caring mother did not, on the facts, tilt the balance towards major irreversible surgery for therapeutic purposes.

2. The remedy proposed was out of proportion at that stage to the problem to be solved. Furthermore, a disabled patient has the right not to have drastic surgery imposed upon her unless or until it had been demonstrated to be in her best interests. The decision could not be allowed to stand.

3. The need for the best interests test in such cases had been first recognised in *Re F* (House of Lords).

4. Declarations should not be made as to the lawfulness of invasive treatment of incapacitated patients unless the treatment proposed passed the test of being demonstrably in the best interests of the patient.

5. It was for the judge, not the doctor, to decide whether a treatment was in the best interests of a patient, a decision which would incorporate broader ethical, social, moral considerations than those set out in *Bolam*, with the patient's welfare as the paramount consideration. Once the judge was satisfied that the options were within the range of acceptable opinion among competent and responsible practitioners, the *Bolam* test was irrelevant as to whether the proposed treatment was in S's best interests. The judge was therefore in error in his application of the *Bolam* test to his decision-making process and also in offering the mother the alternatives of the hysterectomy or the insertion of the Mirena coil; the best interests test ought to have provided the best answer, not a range of alternative answers.

6. It would have been within the best interests test to indicate that the less invasive procedure should have been adopted first and that, if it failed, it would have been appropriate to seek a declaration in respect of the proposed surgery.

Where a declaration is sought as to the lawfulness of proposed medical treatment for a patient unable to consent for herself, it was for the *court to decide* whether such treatment was in the patient's best interests.

PRACTICE DIRECTIONS on sterilisation of mentally handicapped persons in England

Several Practice Directions (also called Practice Notes) were issued by the Official Solicitor's Office to the English High Court during 1989-2001 in response to emerging case law. Of course, a Practice Note or Practice Direction does *not* bind the judges of the Family Division of the High Court. It is merely a guide as to best practice on a particular area of law and practice and the courts have not traditionally regarded such Practice Notes as mandatory, as *Re C* (1990) revealed.

The 2001 Practice Direction

The latest 2001 Practice Direction, issued in May 2001 (see [2001] *Family Law* 551), supersedes all previous Directions while replicating elements of the previous guide-lines; it extends to a wider range of medical and welfare disputes leading to litigation. However, it deals only with *adults* who lack capacity. In future, medical treatment or welfare disputes about children will be dealt with under the Children Act 1989 or the Court's inherent jurisdiction.

The 2001 Direction stresses that High Court approval is required *unless* there is a need for a therapeutic sterilisation, i.e. presumably, to cure or alleviate a medical condition. Otherwise, any cases 'lying anywhere the boundary should be referred to the court' (emphasis added). Obviously, someone from the Official Solicitor's office would have to decide whether a case was anywhere near the boundary or not. According to case law (*Sewell v Electrolux* (1997)) the court must resolve any conflict of expert opinion, but how would or could a judge decide in the marginal cases? As La Forest, J. put it so bluntly in the Canadian case of *Re Eve* (1986):

"Judges are generally ill-informed about many of the factors relevant to a wise decision in this difficult area. They generally know little of mental illness, of techniques of contraception or their efficacy. And, however well presented a case may be, it can only partially inform".

The 2001 Practice Note requires the likelihood of pregnancy as one of the considerations for whether the operation would be in the best interests of the patient. This must be 'identifiable' rather than 'speculative'. Yet is this is a defensible justification for authorising sterilisation? Again, the 2001 Note mentions as another component of best interests that the patient 'is having or is likely to have full sexual relationships'. Would this not be *Jeanette* Mark 2? Surely this was Jeanette's problem as a result of her lack of proper supervision. She was found in a 'compromising position' with a mentally (and physically) normal male carer. The point remains that sterilisation only removes the visible signs of the consequences of any sexual intercourse, such as pregnancy, but cannot protect a mentally· handicapped girl from sexual exploitation or rape. The medical opinion was in conflict in Jeanette's case but the court chose to accept the view that sterilisation was the only course of action left open and time was running out for the court to have the jurisdiction to make a decision, since it would lose its jurisdiction once Jeanette turned 18, which was a matter of weeks away. The notion of 'best interests' in this particular context remains, at least in cases like *Jeanette* (*Re B*) a matter for continuing debate.

8. DONATION AND TRANSPLANTATION OF HUMAN ORGANS

Background to organ transplantation

Organ transplantation is the medical procedure whereby living tissue from a human body is removed from that body and transferred to another part of that body or to another person; an example of the former is a skin graft. Where the transfer is from one person to another, the one supplying the tissue is the donor and the one receiving it is the recipient. The intention behind the transplantation is to replace a tissue that is no longer able to fulfill its original function efficiently as a result of disease or injury, with one that will. In Britain, and in most of the developed world, there is a shortage of organs for transplantation and the situation appears to be worsening. According to a British Medical Journal article, something like 1000 patients on waiting lists, die each year. The mortality figure worsens each year but the number of organs available for transplant remains constant. According to a British Medical Journal article published in June 2000, although 70 per cent of UK people claim to wish to be organ donors if eligible, only 20 per cent actually fill out donor cards.

Kidneys, livers, hearts, lungs, pancreas and bone marrow are the kinds of organs and tissues which may all now be transplanted, but there is no guarantee of success. Heart transplants have been performed on people whose hearts are so diseased that they cannot lead a normal life. The success of transplants over the last two decades has been far more than could have been imagined and today, the shortage of organs poses the main problem. Transplant organs could become available through xenotransplantation, (see below) or through donations between live donors and through donations from deceased persons.

Legal rights of property and the body

The law differentiates between live organ donations and cadaveric transplantations involving organs from cadavers or dead bodies. Commercial dealings are prohibited for both live and cadaveric transplants. What rights, therefore, does a person have in disposing of their bodies and body parts? What property rights, if any, exist in such tissue? Does anyone have a right of property in a corpse? English law does not strictly allow such a right (*Dr Handyside's Case* (1749)) yet it is possible to be convicted for the theft of a urine sample *R. v Welsh* (1974) or a blood sample: *R. v Rothery* (1976). Hospital post mortems are regulated by the Human Tissue Act 1961 (see below). Retention of body parts is legally permissible for 'therapeutic purposes or for purposes of medical education or research' provided the person in lawful possession of the body parts is unaware after making reasonable inquiry of any previous objection made by the deceased or his relatives. The Anatomy Act 1984 allows retention of body parts for teaching, studying or researching into morphology subject to the same conditions as above. A coroner may order a post mortem (under s.9: Coroners' Rules 1984) and following such a post mortem the coroner may direct the 'preservation of material which in his opinion bears upon the cause of death for such a period as the coroner sees fit'. As the law stands, the next of kin have no vested right to possession in the deceased's body (*Dobson v North Tyneside* (1996) Court of Appeal); only third parties, like medical personnel or the legal executor or administrator has any rights of possession and only on the context of burial. Parts of a corpse are capable of being property if they have acquired different attributes by virtue of the application of skill, such as dissection or preservation techniques, for exhibition or teaching purposes (see *R. v Kelly* (1998)). In such cases, someone who removed such parts without permission and for their own purposes, would be guilty of theft. The original possessor would then acquire rights of possession.

Consent required for lawful live organ donation

Organ transplants raise a fundamental question in medical law and ethics: the issue of consent. Any touching of a person, for example for an operation without that person's consent is unlawful. Thus, removal of organs without the donor's consent would constitute assault. Liability could be founded on the criminal or civil law of battery; but even if a person does consent, another principle arises, founded on public policy, namely, paternalism- that there may be times when an individual needs to be protected from himself. (but see the Human Tissue Act 2004: expected to be in force by April 2006)

Ethical and social perspectives

Jonsen in 'Ethical Issues in organ transplantation' in Medical Ethics (ed. Veitch) (1989) summarises various ethical and moral issues raised by organ transplantation, namely (i) it poses serious moral questions about the intrinsic morality of transplantation; (ii) the determination of the death of the source of a cadaveric organ; (iii) the right of persons to donate their own organs; (iv) the selection of recipients for scarce organs and the procurement and allocation of organs as a scarce social resource. Of these, the procurement of organs raises further issues: has there been free and informed consent; when does death occur, legally and medically? Death is now based on the brain stem death criterion but used to be based on heart-lung (or cardio-vascular) criteria. This shift in the criterion for death has implications for the supply of organs.

The case for and against permitting sale of organs

Arguments can be made for and against permitting the sale of organs; the main objection against such a practice would be the 'commodification' of the body/body parts so that the body would become a commodity, and merely a means to an end. Reasons to support such a practice are that the supply of organs might be increased, which would relieve the serious organ shortage and provide income for those who might sorely need it; conversely, respecting people's autonomy could mean allowing the donor who is perfectly willing to earn money from his sought-after body part, to do so. Additionally, offering a great deal of money for an organ might encourage people to pose serious dangers to themselves for the sake of earning a small fortune and the State might not wish to endorse such a policy.

The UK Transplants Support Service Authority (UKTSSA)

The UKTSSA was established as a Special Health Authority (SHA) in 1991 to carry out a range of support functions for transplantation, namely: allocation; information; transport; servicing Use Advisory Groups; maintaining national lists; maintaining databases for tracing, audit and research.

After a Review carried out in 1998/99 it was recommended that the UKTSSA continue with responsibility for these functions.

The Human Tissue Authority

This is a new body to be established under the Human Tissue Act 2004, (in force April 2006) which will advise on and ensure compliance with the 2004 Act, develop national operational procedures and guidelines and license activities which involve the use of human tissue.

LIVE DONOR TRANSPLANTATION

Ethical theories

A possible conflict between two types of philosophical theories may be identified: deontology v consequentialist theory. In deontology, a person's moral worth dictates decisions and it centres on moral imperatives. The principle of 'respect for persons' means that people should not be used as a means to an end. In consequentialist theory, however, utilitarianism is the watchword, which strives to maximise happiness and minimise suffering and proceeds on the notion of attempting to achieve greatest good of the greatest number.

An ethical question for the live donor is: How far is it permissible to expose one person to possible harm to benefit another person?

The legal position

The law on live organ donation is a combination of common law and statute. Both parties should give their consent and the consent of the donor would be invalid if the consequence of the removal of the organ is death. If a surgeon proceeds with the operation, he will commit murder or manslaughter. According to case law, it would be lawful to accept organ donation from an adult lacking capacity provided that donation would benefit that adult donor (*Re Y (bone marrow case)* (1996)).

See Professor Gerald Dworkin in "The law relating to organ transplantation in England" (1970) 33 Mod LR 353) for earlier suggestions for surgery in general and donor organ removal in particular, to be legal, emphasising the need for consent by the competent donor)
(see now The Human Tissue Act 2004 which makes consent the fundamental principle underpinning the lawful retention and use of body parts)

Common law position on removal of an organ from a live donor

If the adult is adult and competent-there must be consent to the removal of an organ; consent should also be obtained from the donee of the organ. This follows the general principle that consent is normally required for any medical procedure if the patient is competent and conscious. As far as the incompetent donor is concerned, the key issue is: *will the procedure benefit the incompetent donor?*

Re Y (1996)

This is a bone marrow transplant case, unique in its involving judicial authorisation of blood tests and bone marrow harvesting from a mentally incapacitated adult to a sibling based on the best interests test. Miss Y was 25 years old and had been severely mentally and physically disabled from birth. She had lived in care since 10 years old. Her sister, aged 36, (the plaintiff) suffered from a preleukaemic bone marrow disorder, and would suffer myloid leukaemia within three months. Miss Y's sister sought a declaration that it would be lawful to perform blood tests and possible bone marrow extraction upon Miss Y, despite the latter's inability to consent. A donation from a blood relative presented a 40 per cent cent of recovery for 18 months whereas a donation from an unrelated donor reduced that chance to around 30 per cent, as the most optimistic percentage.

Connell, J. held that the taking of blood tests and the harvesting of bone marrow from a person who is incapable of giving consent would be assault and illegal unless shown to be in the best interests of that person and therefore lawful. The question to ask is whether it would be in the best interests of the defendant for such procedures to take place. The fact that such a process would obviously benefit the plaintiff is not relevant unless, as a result of the intended donor helping the plaintiff in that way, the best interests of the donor would be served.

The court placed importance on several factors: (i) The intended donor derives a benefit from the visits which she receives from her family and involvement in family events; (ii) there is affection between mother and daughter; (iii) chances of survival would be greatly reduced if the transplant was not carried out; (iv) chances of semi-indefinite survival were good if the recipient survived the first six months after the transplant.

Could *Re Y*'s approach support organ donations by incompetent adults and children? This is probably doubtful. Andrew Grubb in his Commentary on *Re Y* (1996) 4 *Med LR* 204, gives several reasons why not: (i) *Re Y* is an unusual case where there was minimal risk to the donor, i.e. if there was a greater risk the court might not be so willing to think this organ donation was in the best interests of the donor e.g. where there is danger of the remaining kidney becoming diseased or damaged; (ii) evidence of a 'close relationship' with the patient which would be damaged, would be required; thus close relatives with severe mental disabilities or donations from babies appear to be discounted; (iii) the agreement of the donor raises difficulties-this would also exclude the very young or disabled; (iv) the donation would have a psychological benefit to the donor; (v) these cases fell into a special category that the court should therefore be involved, namely, for advice.

An American example

Strunk v Strunk (1969)

In this American case, the court authorised a kidney transplant from Jerry, a 27-year-old man with a mental age of six, to his 28 year-old brother who was suffering from kidney disease, after hearing psychiatric evidence of the 'extremely traumatic effect' that his brother's death would have upon him.

No legislative regulation on Bone Marrow Transplantation until Human Tissue Act 2004 comes into force (not before April 2006)

There is currently no specific legal regulation on bone marrow transplantation. Bone marrow is not covered by the Human Tissue Act 1989 as it does not appear to fit into the definition of s.7(2) of the Act as a 'structured arrangement of tissues which . . . cannot be replicated by the body'. However, when the Human Tissue Act 2004 comes into force, bone marrow transplantation will be covered.

Children as organ donors

Re W (a minor) (medical treatment) (1992) gives some indication on whether children would be permited to donate organs. Lord Donaldson, MR suggested that it is highly unlikely that even '*Gillick* competent' children would be permitted to donate organs (in the absence of parental consent) if the operation would not actually benefit the minor. Parental consent per se would probably not be good enough—the operation would have to be for the child's health or welfare.

Bone marrow donation between siblings is widely practised. In the USA, several cases have authorised bone marrow transplants, even kidney transplants (see *Hart v Brown* (1972)- between seven-year-old identical twins) but refused permission in the recent case of *Curran v Bosze* (1990) decided by the Illinois Supreme Court. This case involved twins who were three and a half years old and a 12-year-old child from the twins' mother's previous marriage. Permission was refused predominantly because the court held that there was insufficient benefit to the donor but there was also no existing close relationship between donor and recipient.

(see Human Tissue Act 2004, below)

Has the sale of organs ever been lawful in the UK?

It must have been, otherwise the British government would not have needed to pass legislation to prohibit exchanging money for the purpose of organ donation.

Unlawful act remains unlawful even if done with consent

R. v Donovan (1934)

The appellant was convicted by the High Court of indecent assault and common assault and sentenced to 18 months' imprisonment with hard labour for indecent assault and six months with hard labour for the common assault. He was given leave to appeal against his conviction.

The appellant appeared to be addicted to a form of sexual perversion and it seemed that he carried out a number of beatings on a 16-year-old girl, the prosecutrix, with her consent and compliance. The girl's married sister and a doctor later discovered the extent of these injuries. The girl testified she consented to the beatings with full knowledge of the appellant's intentions and without reluctance.

The Court of Criminal Appeal ruled that the prosecution had not been able to negative consent in this case but the correct question was: were the jury convinced that the blows were intended to cause bodily harm? If not, then they should not convict the accused. The appellant was accordingly acquitted on a technicality but the principles enunciated remain valid.

The Court of Criminal Appeal stated the guiding principles as follows: (i) If an act is unlawful because it is a criminal act, it cannot be rendered lawful because the person to whose detriment it is done consents to it (ii) No person can license another to commit a crime if the act was something wrong in itself.

Thus the prosecution need not prove absence of consent where an act has been wrong in itself but there are many acts which are in themselves harmless and lawful and which become unlawful only if they are done without the consent of the person affected. The onus of negativing consent then falls on the prosecution.

R. v Donovan establishes, inter alia, that an act unlawful in itself does not become lawful just because someone who has suffered from it has consented to it.

Limits to self-mutilation even in private

The principle in *R. v Brown* is: The common law does not afford unfettered licence for self-mutilation-in other words, there are limits to self-mutilation even when performed in private.

R. v Brown (1993)

This case involved sado-masochistic acts carried out in private. The House of Lords held that consensual sado-masochistic homosexual encounters which occasioned actual bodily harm to the victim were held to be assaults occasioning actual bodily harm, notwithstanding that the victim consented to the acts inflicted on him, because public policy required that society be protected by criminal sanctions against a cult of violence which contained the danger of the proselytisation and corruption of young men and the potential for the infliction of serious injury. A person could therefore be convicted for committing sado-masochistic acts even though they were committed in private, and the person on whom the injuries were inflicted consented and no permanent injury was inflicted on the victim.

Live donor transplantation is governed by the Human Organ Transplant Act 1989 until the new Human Tissue Act 2004 comes into effect

THE HUMAN ORGAN TRANSPLANT ACT 1961

Background

In the 1980s, it was discovered that there were donors selling kidneys for transplantation into those who had no genetic or other relation to the donor. There were several advertisements inviting Turkish people (among others) to come to England to make such donations. Three doctors who were involved were found guilty of serious professional misconduct by the GMC. The British government swiftly passed the 1989 Human Organ Transplant Act 1989. This is the current law until the **new Human Tissue Act 2004** comes into force, scheduled for April 2006.

The Human Organ Transplants Act 1989

This Act was passed to stop payments for organs which are then used for transplants; i.e. to criminalise and therefore prevent commercial dealings in organs throughout the UK. This Act therefore seeks to criminalise the commercialisation of live donor transplantation. In addition, the Act makes general provision to regulate transplants between living persons and for the creation of a statutory register of organ transplantation. It also covers organs from dead donors and applies restrictions on live donation of non-regenerative organs. Those who are genetically related must provide evidence of their relationship before proceeding.

Section 1 makes it a criminal offence to make or receive payment at any stage for the purpose of organ donation by the living. Legitimate expenses incurred by the donor are excluded.

Section 2 provides that a person is guilty of an offence if they remove an organ from a living person intending it to be transplanted unless the donor is closely genetically related to the recipient. However, donations between non-relatives are permitted with the consent of the Unrelated Live Transplant Regulatory Authority (ULTRA) (see further, below).

The 1989 Act makes no reference to minors. It does not, however, prohibit human organ donations from minors in principle, and this is also permitted under jurisdictions such as Canada and Australia. In reality, such cases are few and far between. The basic objective of the 1989 Act was therefore to stop the exploitation of poor people who could be pressurised into selling parts of their bodies for money.

Transplants between unrelated persons

For transplants between persons unrelated, permission can be given by the Unrelated Live Transplant Regulatory Authority (ULTRA), established by the Human Organ Transplants (Unrelated Persons) Regulations of 1989-Regulation 3-i.e. with full informed consent of the donor. Before ULTRA approves an application for donation by a living unrelated donor, it must be satisfied that: (i) No payment has been, or is to be, made; (ii) The person referring the case for consideration is the doctor with clinical responsibility for the donor; (iii) A doctor has explained to the donor the nature of the procedure and the risks involved in the removal of the organ in question; (iv) The donor's consent was not obtained by coercion or the offer of an inducement; (v) The donor understands that his or her consent can be withdrawn at any time; and (vi)The donor and the recipient have been interviewed separately by a suitably qualified independent person, who is part of the transplant team, and that person is satisfied that the above conditions have been met.

These conditions are equally important whether the donation is from a relative or from an unrelated donor.

Fetal transplantation

In Sweden, the USA and England, trials using fetal tissue for transplants into the brains of patients with Parkinson's and Huntington's Diseases have been carried out.

Adults lacking capacity as donors-BMA Guidance

In the section 'Adults lacking capacity to make decisions' the BMA Guidance states that 'provision must be made for those adults who lack the capacity to make an informed decision about organ donation . . . It should not be assumed that all people with learning disabilities are unable to make decisions about these issues, nor should it be assumed that they would not wish to donate organs after their death.' The Guidance continues 'Information should be provided in a way individual patients are able to understand and to allow them the opportunity to express their own views about organ donation.' It then considers the position of patients who 'lack all capacity' because they are in a coma or do not have sufficient capacity to make a decision about organ donation. The King's Fund Institute report suggested that adults lacking mental capacity might be considered 'presumed objectors' in a system of presumed consent. Here the BMA disagrees and argues that 'those who lack mental capacity should be given the same opportunities to perform altruistic acts and it should not be assumed that they would not wish to donate.' One should not presume to know the intentions of persons who lack mental capacity but what about patients who have never had the mental capacity to understand far less complicated matters, let alone human organ donation. The BMA Guidance also says that 'there must be established mechanisms for a proxy, or legal representative to opt out of donation on behalf of someone who is not mentally competent to make a personal decision.'

Comment

What does this Guidance mean? The current system in the UK is an *opt-in* system so consent is *never* presumed. Is the BMA suggesting that consent would be presumed because one cannot assume they would not want to donate their organs? This cannot apply to the patient with the mental age of four or five or to the PVS patient who has never expressed a view on organ donation while normal and before the onset of PVS. It must be equally dubious simply to assume that adults lacking capacity would wish to donate organs any more than adults with capacity, in the rest of the population.

Elective ventilation of patients close to death

The BMA Guidance suggests that another way of increasing the number of organs available for donation is by the use of elective ventilation. Elective ventilation involves ventilating a selected group of patients, who are in deep coma and close to death with no possibility of recovery, for a short period (usually only a few hours) before death is confirmed, to preserve their organs for long enough to prepare for their removal after death. Elective ventilation was introduced in Exeter with strict controls in 1988 and this led to a 50 per cent increase in the number of organs suitable for transplantation but the practice was stopped abruptly in 1994 when the Department of Health declared it unlawful. The law as it stands is that to protect people who are not competent to make decisions for themselves, procedures may only be undertaken which are necessary and are intended to be in the patient's best interests; any other intervention is unlawful.

Having reviewed this issue, the current BMA position is that there are 'too many ethical and practical difficulties for a change in the law to be recommended at the present time.' It declares, however, that if elective ventilation were to be permitted at some future date, strict safeguards would be needed.

THE DEAD DONOR-CADAVERIC TRANSPLANTATION

Donating of organs for therapeutic purposes after one's death

This would be permissible if there was an express request of the donor who is now deceased; or, in the absence of such a request, where reasonable inquiry reveals no objection to the same either by the deceased or by his spouse or surviving relatives.

In the UK, the removal of organs from people after their death is covered by the Human Tissue Act 1961 (the 1961 Act) (covering England, Scotland and Wales) and the Human Tissue (Northern Ireland) Act 1962. Once the patient is brain stem dead, transplantation can take place. The current definition of death allows for 'beating heart donors'. However, the **Human Tissue Act 2004** will regulate this area in the UK once it comes into force in April 2006.

The Human Tissue Act 1961 (the current law until the new Human Tissue Act 2004 comes into force)

> s.1(1) 'If any person, either in writing at any time or orally in the presence of two or more witnesses at the time of his last illness, has expressed a request that his body or any specified part of his body be used after his death for therapeutic purposes or . . . research, the person lawfully in possession of his body he may, unless he has reason to believe that the request was subsequently withdrawn, authorise the removal of . . . the specified part for use in accordance with the request.'
>
> s.1(2) 'Without prejudice to the foregoing subsection, the person lawfully in possession of the body . . . may authorise the removal of any part from the body for use for the said purpose, if, having made such reasonable enquiry as is practicable, he has no reason to believe-
> (a) that the deceased had expressed an objection to his body being so dealt with after his death . . . or
> (b) That the surviving spouse or any surviving relative of the deceased objects.

It might be necessary to hold an inquest, or a coroner's post-mortem examination in which case the Act states that organs or tissues may only be removed with the specific authorisation of the coroner. In Scotland, organs may not be removed in any case where the procurator fiscal has objected to their removal.

The person 'lawfully in possession' of the body-and it is by no means clear who this person or entity is-'may' but not 'must' authorise removal of the organ, suggesting there is some scope for discretion.

Areas of ambiguity

The 1961 Act is unsatisfactory and has widely been regarded as in need of reform. The loose wording of the legislation has led to difficulties in interpretation which will inevitably increase with advancements in communication technology. The Human Tissue Act 2004 addresses some of these ambiguities but not all of them.

As it stands, however, the meaning of making 'such reasonable inquiry as may be practicable' under the 1961 Act remains unclear. Does this include using the Internet or e-mail to attempt to contact every surviving relative? Should the view of a surviving relative, who might have been estranged from the deceased for many years, have the power to veto the donation of the organ? In the absence of clarifying legislation or regulations, practice has developed on pragmatic lines. The BMA Guidance asserts that it is generally accepted, though not beyond doubt, that where a patient dies in hospital, the hospital management is 'lawfully in possession of the body', until the executors or relatives ask for the body to be handed to them. When the person dies elsewhere, the person lawfully in possession of the body is considered to be a close relative or long-term partner. Again, a pragmatic approach has usually been taken in interpreting the phrase 'such reasonable enquiry as may be practicable' and in deciding which relatives' views should be sought. The BMA Guidance explains that in most cases, this will mean discussing the matter with those relatives who have been in close contact with the deceased in the period leading up to the death. These people will be asked about 'their own views, those of the deceased patient and whether any other relative is likely to object.' Medical and nursing staff will often have been in touch with potential organ donors who will frequently have spent some time in hospital before their death.

Seeking the consent of relatives has also become standard practice although the legislation only requires that the person lawfully in possession of the body has made enquiries to ensure that the surviving relatives do not object to the donation. The Department of Health Guidance 1998 says discussion with one relative will usually be sufficient.

Xenotransplantation or transgenic transplantation

There is also **Xenotransplantation** or **transgenic transplantation**-using other mammals like pigs to be harvested for making organs for transplant into human beings. Pigs' hearts have been used successfully for humans but there has not been any success with transplantation of other animal organs. Various problems may be identified:

(i) human beings might reject animal organs and contract animal diseases, which happened to a man in Pittsburgh who had been given a baboon's liver;

(ii) is it morally acceptable to transplant animal organs into humans?

(iii) it is argued that using animals for transplants causes them to suffer which overrides any benefit derived by human beings. Clearly, the risks to human beings of contracting animal diseases remains a problem. No cases of transplants between animals and humans have been reported in the UK.

As the population of the so-called 'aged' increases because of longer life expectancy (one national headline read: Today's babies can expect to live for 130 years (The Times) so there seems to be a greater need to replace diseased organs as well as using transplants to correct birth defects or the onset of cancer.

New guidelines were promised in 2000

In February 2000, the government announced that new guidelines are to be introduced preventing conditions being attached by relatives to organ donations following a government enquiry into the NHS organ transplant service, which was commissioned after a transplant co-ordinator agreed to conditions that a dead relative's organs be given to a white person. The government report calls for NHS staff training in race relations; criticises senior staff for allowing the practice of attaching conditions to organ donation; and condemns the NHS for failing to stop the practice earlier. Conditions imposed by relatives have included: organs only to be given to a child; that a smoker does not receive the organs of a non-smoker; and the organs of a drink driver not to be given to an alcoholic. In fact, racist pre-conditions would probably breach the Race Relations Act 1976 (s.20(1); s.31(1)) and would thus be unlawful.

Reforming the law

The British Medical Association launched a campaign in June 2000, for a 'presumed consent' to organ donation scheme to be implemented in Britain, under which it would be assumed that every patient wished to be a donor unless he or she had registered an objection. The BMA also called for an overhaul of the current transplant service and radically revising its co-ordination and infrastructure. In mid-2005, although waiting lists for transplants have grown slightly, there has been no corresponding increase in the number of transplants. The BMA also called for the introduction of a 'single, comprehensive piece of legislation covering all aspects of organ donation from both live and cadaveric donors'. To a certain extent, this has now happened with the passing of the Human Tissue Act 2004.

The Human Tissue Act 2004 (in force April 2006)

This Act makes **consent** the most important principle for the lawful retention and use of body parts, human organs and human tissue from the living or the deceased for specified health-related purposes and public display. It also regulates the removal of such material from the deceased. Note that removal of such material from the *living* will continue to be governed by the *common law*, under which it is an offence to interfere with a person's body without consent. The Act regulates removal, storage and use of human tissue (which is referred to therein as "relevant living material" defined as material which has come from a human body and consists of, or includes human cells) from the living. Here, cell lines are excluded as are hair and nail from living people. Live gametes and embryos are also excluded as they are already regulated by the Human Fertilisation and Embryology Act 1990.

But the Act makes it an offence to have bodily material (including hair, nail and gametes) with the intention of analysing the DNA, without the consent of the individual from whom it was obtained (or those close to them if they have died).

The Act lists the purposes for which consent is required in Sch. 1 and the consent required under the Act is called 'appropriate consent' which broadly means consent from the appropriate person as identified in the Act. Hence, in the case of a living child (incompetent or competent but unwilling to make a decision) the person who can give consent for lawful storage or use of human tissue is the person with parental responsibility (under the Children Act 1989).

The Human Tissue Act 1961 and Human Organ Transplant Act 1989 will be repealed when the 2004 Act is scheduled to come into force in April 2006.

9. THE END OF LIFE-EUTHANASIA AND ASSISTED SUICIDE

INTRODUCTION

What if doctors or other health professionals or carers/relatives bring about the death of a patient in a way that can be interpreted as merciful or compassionate, for example where a person who has been suffering severe pain for some time, requests relief or even permanent release from that suffering and the prognosis is that there is no realistic hope of recovery? In these circumstances, it is sometimes argued that it is more merciful to relieve that person's intense suffering even if by doing so, death might result-hence the notion of 'mercy killing', sometimes called euthanasia. A crucial ethical issue here is: when, if ever, is it permissible to terminate the life of a terminally-ill patient? The landmark House of Lords' decision-the Tony Bland case is one of the leading cases on this topic. Additionally, the possible impact of the implementation of the Human Rights Act 1998 (now more accessible to the UK via the European Convention) on the Bland principle, needs to be considered.

DEFINITIONS OF EUTHANASIA

The word euthanasia has been defined in many ways e.g. to refer to the deliberate ending of the life of a person suffering from a painful illness or: the means of inducing or bringing about a gentle and easy death; death without suffering. Davies in his *Textbook on Medical Law* (1998) suggests it might describe a positive act which causes death and could refer to:

(i)   a quiet, painless death;
(ii) the intentional putting to death of persons with incurable or painful disease or
(iii) the act of killing someone painlessly.

Active and passive euthanasia

Active euthanasia refers to any positive action terminating life. Such an action would have to be carried out with the deliberate intention of ending a person's life through, for instance, administering a lethal injection or a fatal dosage of medication but with the aim of relieving or ending that person' pain and suffering.

Passive euthanasia refers to the shortening of life through an omission to act, which appears to be allowed by English law in certain circumstances. Passive euthanasia refers to conduct such as withholding life-support treatment so that 'nature can take its course'. Despite several legislative proposals, active euthanasia is still forbidden by law, regardless of whether the patient has consented or not, and constitutes the crime of unlawful homicide (i.e. murder or manslaughter) in nearly all major jurisdictions.

Voluntary and involuntary euthanasia

Voluntary euthanasia is the situation where a life is terminated at the patient's request. There is also non-voluntary euthanasia, a term which has been applied to the termination of life of an incompetent patient, that is, a patient who is unable to make a rational decision about his life.

Involuntary euthanasia suggests ending the life of patient on paternalistic or other grounds while disregarding the wishes of a patient; this is certainly not regarded as lawful as it would be overriding the patient's autonomy.

One such form (called mercy killing) is where somebody, usually a relative, *deliberately* and *specifically* performs some act, such as administering a drug to accelerate death to terminate suffering. This may be described as active, positive or voluntary euthanasia. In law, however, this is still murder and as Devlin, J. put it in the Bodkin Adams trial: 'If the acts done are intended to kill, it does not matter if a life is cut short by weeks or months, it is just as much murder if it were cut short by years.': see *R. v Bodkin Adams* (1957). *Intention*, not motive, is the all-important prerequisite.

Thus, where a physician gives the fatal dose or injection at the request of a competent (rational), terminally ill patient who is in extreme pain, for the sole purpose of alleviating the pain, knowing that continued dosages will kill the patient, this has sometimes been called 'physician-assisted suicide', particularly in overseas jurisdictions, but it still constitutes murder. However, prosecutors have accepted a lesser plea such as manslaughter, as in *R. v Johnson* (1961). In the case of the relieving of severe pain of a terminally ill patient, the court might even accept a plea of diminished responsibility on the grounds of mental abnormality.

A right to life?

Medical technology now enables life to be prolonged but at what point should treatment cease?

It is frequently asserted that a very high value is placed in our society on human life. The 'right to life' has been much vaunted but what does it mean? One view is that it is the right not to be intentionally killed.

Article 2 of the European Convention on Human Rights states:

> Everyone's right to life shall be protected by law. No one shall be deprived of his life intentionally save in the execution of a sentence of a court following his conviction of a crime for which this penalty is provided by law.

The Burke Case (2005)—Appeal Court says GMC Guidance on withdrawing treatment is lawful

The High Court case of *R (Burke) v GMC* (2004), which went on appeal in May 2005, appeared to decide that a terminally ill man, Leslie Burke, 45, had the right to stop doctors withdrawing artificial nutrition or hydration treatment until he dies naturally. The GMC Guidance on withholding and withdrawing life-prolonging treatment was therefore amenable to judicial review in so far as it was erroneous in point of law. This case thus appeared to reinforce a right-to-live. However, the GMC won its appeal against the lower court ruling. The Court of Appeal, setting aside parts of the earlier judgment, ruled in July 2005 (see *Times*, 2 August) that the GMC guidance *is* lawful and that patients cannot be allowed to demand that a doctor administer a treatment that the doctor considers 'adverse to the patient's clinical needs.' However, doctors were still under a duty to perform reasonable measures for patients who wanted to be kept alive, regardless of their pain and suffering. Hence, if a doctor deliberately interrupted life-prolonging treatment in the face of a competent patient's expressed wish to be kept alive, with the intention of terminating the patient's life, he would have to answer to a charge of murder. Furthermore, the Appeal Court ruled that the GMC Guidance did not violate the European Convention on Human Rights. The Court was careful to reassure the patient in this case that he should not be apprehensive about his future treatment.

A right to die?

Is there a right to die? The Hippocratic Oath mentions good faith and the saving of life. This Oath, which is generally believed to date from the 4th century BC, only really represented the opinion of a small segment of Greek society. Thus the notion that life is sacred and the principle of the sanctity of human life, actually appears to date only from when Christianity became the dominant religion and introduced the principle of the inestimable value of each person's immortal soul. The 'right to die' is not really a clear-cut phrase as it could mean the right to reject medical treatment or the right to commit suicide alone or with someone's help.

Blood transfusions and Jehovah's Witnesses

In the case of an adult Jehovah's Witness who refuses a blood transfusion because of religious beliefs even if the adult will die without such a transfusion, the medical establishment has supported such patients' wishes but has occasionally changed its opinion on whether to support such a right based on religious beliefs.

In *R. v Blaue* (1975), the patient involved was a girl, aged 18, a Jehovah's Witness, who had been stabbed with a knife and sustained serious loss of blood from a pierced lung. When told she had lost a great quantity of blood and required a transfusion without which she would die, she refused on the ground of her religious beliefs. She persisted in her refusal, and also stated in writing that she had refused a transfusion. The doctors respected her views and she died the following day. The issue before the Appeal Court was whether the fact that the girl had refused a blood transfusion broke the chain of causation so that the stabbing by the appellant could not be said to be the operative cause of the girl's death. This argument was rejected by the court.

R. v Blaue suggests that the medical profession has been known to respect the wishes of an adult Jehovah's Witness not to have a blood transfusion based on religious convictions, despite their apparent reluctance to do the same when it comes to psychotically or cyclically disturbed children who assert the same right to die or adult women who refuse blood transfusions because they are purportedly Jehovah's Witnesses or 'born again Christians'.

Guidelines for treatment of Jehovah's Witnesses

The Association of Anaesthetists guidelines issued in 1999 declare that adult Jehovah's Witnesses should have the right to choose to die. These guidelines stress that to administer blood to a patient who has steadfastly refused to accept it is 'unlawful, ethically unacceptable and may lead to criminal and/or civil proceedings'. Jehovah's Witnesses were consulted during the drafting of the guidelines and have been advised to carry identification cards in case they are unconscious when the decision has to be made, or to make advance directives or living wills giving directions for treatment in these circumstances. In return, doctors are asked to take every precaution to avoid blood loss when operating on Jehovah's Witnesses and to consult the senior anaesthetist to determine whether a transfusion would be crucial. The guidelines stress that doctors should plan treatment of children well in advance, consult parents and allow enough time to apply to the courts if necessary.

Development of the definition of death in English medical law

There is a need to define death in some way in order to decide, for instance, whether there are any circumstances in which one may lawfully terminate the treatment of someone who has been in a coma, but not legally pronounced dead. Similarly, it needs to be established whether someone may be pronounced legally 'dead' before organs may be removed for transplantation. There is still controversy over the definition of death in certain circumstances and for certain purposes.

The cardio-pulmonary criteria of death was used for a considerable time before the 1960s, so that the death of a person was constituted by the irreversible cessation of breathing and heartbeat, that is, through a failure of the functioning of the lungs and heart. Subsequently, technology in the form of assisted ventilation and heart bypass machines undermined the previous criteria.

After several versions in the 1970s from the British medical establishment, the notion of 'brain stem death' was made a criterion of death, described as the 'irreversible loss of the brain stem'.

During the 1980s and 1990s, significant medical evidence contradicted the claim that brain death, as diagnosed by UK criteria, is the point at which all functions of the brain have 'permanently and irreversibly ceased.' A document was published in 1995 in the Journal of the Royal College of Physicians, entitled *'Criteria for the diagnosis of brain stem death.'* which stresses that the correct term is 'brain stem death' rather than 'brain death' and suggests a definition of death which will explain why brain death implies the death of the patient:

> It is suggested that 'irreversible loss of the capacity for consciousness, combined with irreversible loss of the capacity to breathe' should be regarded as the definition of death.

No statutory definition of death in English law

There is no statutory definition in English law and the courts do not appear to be unduly concerned about the definition of death, approaching it as an issue of fact determined by medical evidence.

Previously, death could be signified by the cessation of heartbeat and respiration and this was easily verified by physical examination. Now technology can keep people living longer or at least prolong the point of death. If technology keeps a patient going when his heart continues to beat on the machine but breathing has stopped and the brain has been irreversibly damaged, this can be very distressing to relatives, is bad for morale among the nursing staff, is costly, and might also be depriving someone of access to the life-support machine who might have benefited more from them. The rapid development in transplantation programmes led to the need for speedy diagnosis of death, so that once death was established, organs could be speedily removed from the body for transplantation, while they were still 'fresh'. In certain brain stem death cases, there appears to be a cessation of spontaneous respiration and instead of being followed by cardiac arrest, when supported by artificial ventilation, the heartbeat can continue for days and this will enable organs such as the liver and kidneys, to be maintained.

'**Brain Stem Death**' refers to the situation when parts of the brain which operate respiration and heart beat are dead and there is no electrical impulse. *i.e.* **irreversible loss of brain stem**

function. Consciousness or sensate awareness will have decayed. The patient has no capacity to live and will never recover it.

In a case reported in 1999, a young assault victim who was diagnosed brain stem dead is now communicating with carers. The case has reopened the debate on defining death.

Professor Margaret Brazier (in *Medicine, Patients and the Law*) argues that biologically, death is a process and not an event; different organs and systems supporting the continuance of life cease to function successively and at different times.

One needs to distinguish between two cases:

(i) where the life support machine is turned off because it is medically established that the patient is dead; and

(ii) where the machine is turned off because although the patient is still clinically alive, it is thought that no further justification can be found in continuing life support and so the patient ought to be allowed to die. Considerations here are: consent; the quality of life of the patient; the proper use of scarce medical resources.

Doctors should distinguish between their duties to a dying patient and the power to remove organs from such a person once that person is properly declared to be dead.

The anencephalic baby and brain death

The anencephalic child is born lacking most or all of a higher brain and is bound to die, usually in a matter of days or weeks. Such babies could be kept alive never to become conscious or respond to human beings. If other babies are born with intact brains, but defective hearts or kidneys, doctors may want to use organs from the anencephalic baby to save the life of the baby with other defective organs. Thus that baby must be ventilated, which poses a problem about the point at which he actually dies.

An anencephalic baby's brain stem may remain alive even when it has been ventilated. If brain stem death is inapplicable to such babies, should we accept that the lack of any higher brain function renders the baby as 'born dead'? Does that confuse euthanasia with defining death? The use of anencephalic newborns as sources of transplantable organs is one of the most controversial issues in medical ethics on both sides of the Atlantic.

Keeping such babies ventilated just to be organ donors might not be ethically defensible because this could be seen as using such babies as a means to an end (albeit helping others) rather than respecting them as ends in themselves. Anencephalic infants are not like other organ donors because it may be said that they are placed on life-support systems solely for the sake of others. If these babies are not usually resuscitated, intubated or placed on ventilators, is it justifiable to provide ventilation for them and regard this as proper 'treatment' for them?

THE ETHICAL DIMENSION

The two main ethical components relevant to the present context are: self-determination and autonomy, often labelled the so-called 'right to die'. It presents difficult questions for resolution by doctors of their role and duty as doctors. It inevitably raises issues of dignity and personhood and even requires the interrogation of what is the essence of a human being.

It is also relevant to consider notions of beneficence and autonomy. As we have seen at the outset of this book, one of the main medical aims is 'beneficence'—doing good to others; hence killing someone may not per se be seen as doing someone no harm! However, relief of pain and suffering is the aim of medical care or treatment; therefore relieving pain by putting an end to a patient's misery could be regarded as beneficent.

The second ethical component is autonomy and in the present context would mean that a person has the right to oppose treatment. The slippery slope argument has also been suggested: i.e. euthanasia is the start of the slippery slope-voluntary euthanasia in extreme circumstances will become euthanasia on request (as has happened with abortion). The even greater fear is that voluntary euthanasia will imperceptibly change to compulsory euthanasia for the handicapped and the elderly.

As the Report of the Select Committee on Medical Ethics 1994 expressed it 'The prohibition against intentional killing is the cornerstone of law and social relationships which protects each of us impartially, embodying the belief that all of us are equal'.

THE SANCTITY OF LIFE ARGUMENT

This is the principle that all life is sacred and it would therefore be morally wrong to take someone's life by withdrawing treatment of that person and other ways should be found to relieve suffering. Against this, it could be argued that the sanctity of life principle is not absolute and continuance of a life support system, for example, is not in the best interests of that patient, for example if that patient's quality of life would be very poor. The law now appears to adopt a qualified sanctity of life argument (as described by Stauch et al. *Sourcebook on Medical Law*); although life is given tremendous value, the courts might not see it as their function to preserve life in every case. (see *Re T* (1997) (the liver transplant case).

CRIMINAL LIABILITY

(a) Deliberate termination of the life of a patient
 Any deliberate action aiming to end a patient's life, for example by administering a lethal injection will lead to a prosecution for murder. English law has never sanctioned 'mercy killing' yet a patient may sometimes be given a high dosage of drugs as part of his medical treatment even if the incidental effect is to hasten that patient's death. The question is: whether this is murder or a form of euthanasia? All ethical codes reject euthanasia explicitly or implicitly.

R. v Cox (1992)

Dr Cox was prosecuted for the attempted murder of Lillian Boyes, a 70-year-old patient, who was suffering from an incurable and increasingly distressing form of arthritis. She made him promise that he would not let her suffer, and pleaded with him to put her out of her misery. She was suffering from the terminal stages of the condition and her pain could no longer be controlled by taking further analgesic drugs. He administered an injection of potassium chloride and Mrs Boyes died within minutes. Cox was charged only with attempted murder on the basis that Mrs Boyes' death could have been due to her illness, and she might have died at that time even without the poison being administered. The evidence indicated that the potassium injection could have no pain-relieving effect and it appeared to judge and jury that the potassium was the cause of death but it was not definitively established whether the injection was the operative cause of her death.
 The jury convicted Dr Cox of attempted murder and he was sentenced to 12 months imprisonment, which was suspended.

The principle was reiterated that it is unlawful to administer drugs to a patient with the object of bringing about that patient's death no matter how worthy the motive.

R. v Arthur (1981)

A newborn baby was born with Downs' Syndrome but there were, at this stage, no apparent further complications such as intestinal blockage. The consultant paediatrician in charge, Dr Arthur, having been told by the baby's mother that she did not want the child, prescribed 'Nursing care only' on the baby's chart. For this particular health authority, this meant that there would be no extraordinary attempts to revive the baby if it encountered any difficulties. The baby was fed with liquids and prescribed a pain-relieving drug which eventually produced broncho-pneumonia from which the child died. The doctor was reported to the police (by a member of the nursing staff; it has never been established who) and the doctor was charged with murder. In the course of the trial, medical evidence showed that the baby did have an intestinal blockage and would have died in any event. The prosecution therefore could not prove the cause of death and the charge was reduced to attempted murder.

The basic issue was whether the preparation and endorsement of the treatment by the consultant paediatrician amounted to an attempt to kill. The court asked whether the doctor had followed a procedure which could be supported by a responsible body of medical opinion-i.e. in accordance with the *Bolam* test. The jury thought that he did and although Farquharson, J. stressed that any profession cannot set out a code of ethics and say that the law must follow it, the jury unanimously acquitted him. The court stressed that there is no defence in law of mercy killing; active euthanasia is unlawful and punishable by a mandatory life sentence.

Acts and omissions-a convincing distinction?

The distinction drawn by the judge between acts and omissions certainly does not accord with the 1981 case of *Re B* (1981)(the Down's syndrome baby). In criminal law, a doctor in these circumstances cannot be liable under s.1 of the Children and Young Persons Act 1933 for 'wilful neglect' because he would not, in law, be regarded as having 'responsibility for the child'

since the section is limited to those having parental responsibility. Under *R. v Sheppard* (1981), the failure to provide
'adequate medical aid' has to be 'wilful' and 'cause the child
unnecessary suffering or injury to health'. In his statement to the
police, Dr. Arthur emphasised that the major aim of the
healthcare staff looking after the baby in this case was to relieve
distress in the child, which appears to have been accepted by
the jury.

(b) Administration of pain killing drugs for the purposes of
    pain relief

R. v Bodkin Adams (1957)

Dr Bodkin Adams was charged with the murder of an 81-year
old patient who had suffered a stroke. It was alleged that that he
had prescribed and administered such large quantities of drugs
(heroin and morphine) that he must have known that the drugs
would have killed her.

She was incurably ill but not terminally ill; She had left Dr
Bodkin Adams a chest full of silver and a Rolls Royce. Devlin, J.
introduced the *double effect* principle; i.e. if one act has two
consequences, one good and one evil, then the act may be
morally acceptable in certain circumstances, for example,
administering drugs to relieve pain but which would eventually
lead to death if administered in large doses. Devlin, J. declared
'No doctor, nor any man, no more in the case of a dying man
than a healthy, has the right to cut the thread of life,' but Dr
Adams was acquitted of murder on the grounds that the ending
of life was incidental to the relief of pain, which appeared to be
the primary purpose of Dr. Adams' actions. As Devlin, J. put it:

> 'The doctor is entitled to relieve pain and suffering even if
> measures he takes may incidentally shorten life'.

This is a good example of the statement of a general principle
(no doctor may shorten anyone else's life) qualified by an
exception-the double effect exception.

(c) Assisting suicide

An individual may end his own life but to assist in suicide
amounts to a criminal offence: see
Suicide Act 1962 s.2 (1) which states:

'A person who aids, abets, counsels or procures the suicide of another or an attempt by another to commit suicide, shall be liable on conviction on indictment to imprisonment for a period not exceeding fourteen years.'

Another form of assisted suicide is where a doctor furnishes the means to a patient that is not dying to kill himself. Hence, a doctor may provide a pill to a patient which the patient then takes, in the full knowledge that it will kill him, but the act of swallowing the pill breaks the chain of causation between the doctor's act of providing the pill and the patient's death. The doctor would then be guilty of an offence under s.2 of the Suicide Act 1961, which deals with criminal liability for aiding, abetting, counselling or procuring the suicide of another.

AG v Able [1984] Q.B. 795

The Voluntary Euthanasia Society produced a booklet entitled 'A Guide to Self-Deliverance' which set out various ways to commit suicide which was sold on request to members of the society aged 25 and over. A declaration was sought by the Attorney General that distribution of the booklet constituted an offence under the Suicide Act 1961. In order to find that an offence had been committed, the Voluntary Euthanasia Society must have intended to distribute the booklet to a person who, at the time of the distribution, was known to be contemplating suicide, with the intention to assist and encourage suicide by means of the booklet and that that person was in fact so encouraged and assisted.

Woolf, J. held that the sale of the booklet could be an offence but this did not mean that any particular supply automatically constituted an offence. On the evidence before the court, the declaration sought by the Attorney General was refused.

This case indirectly allowed the promotion of suicide and the requirements laid down are rather difficult to satisfy. However, such booklets are now available in ordinary bookshops and there is no attempt by the Euthanasia Society to sell such literature in any clandestine manner.

At the opposite end of the spectrum from the Sanctity of Life is the Quality of Life principle which states that life is not intrinsically of value but is made valuable from the life-holder's capacity for enjoying certain pleasurable states of consciousness which we associate with normal day-to day sensations of life.

AUTHORISATION OF NON-TREATMENT

The incompetent adult patient

Another tragic and extremely difficult area of medical law and ethics is the treatment of patients in a persistent (now also termed 'permanent') vegetative state (PVS). This is the condition where the brain expresses no evidence of activity in the cerebral cortex, the cognitive part of the brain. Difficult legal and moral questions are confronted in these sorts of cases because it brings into sharp focus the sanctity of life doctrine-should human life continue to be preserved, even when the patient is likely to continue to be in a comatose state, insensate, and totally unaware of anything going on around him or her, despite the continued functioning of organs such as the lungs and heart? PVS occurs when there is neurological damage to the cerebral hemispheres which govern voluntary action and consciousness so that the patient may be permanently unconscious. Such a patient is not brain dead as this entails the 'irreversible loss of the capacity for consciousness, combined with irreversible loss of the capacity to breathe' which may be identified applying the accepted 'brain-stem death criteria' (see Royal College of Physicians *"Criteria for the Diagnosis of Brain Stem Death"*,1995).

Royal College of Physicians: definitions of vegetative state

In 1996, the Royal College of Physicians defined the vegetative state as:

> "A clinical condition of unawareness of self and environment in which the patient breathes spontaneously, has a stable circulation and shows cycles of eye closure and eye opening which may stimulate sleep and waking. This may be a transient stage in the recovery from coma or it may persist until death."

The continuing vegetative state

When the vegetative state continues for more than four weeks, it becomes increasingly unlikely that the condition is part of a recovery phase from coma and the diagnosis of a continuing vegetative state can be made.

The permanent vegetative state

A patient in a continuing vegetative state will enter a permanent vegetative state when the diagnosis of irreversibility can be established with a high degree of clinical certainty. It is a diagnosis which is not absolute but based on probabilities. Nevertheless, it may reasonably be made when a patient has been in a continuing vegetative state following head injury for more than twelve months or following other causes of brain damage for more than six months.

In 1994, in the USA, pre-dating the College Report, the Report of the Multi-Society Task Force on PVS was published in the New England Journal of Medicine on the May 26, 1994. Its findings are similar and the only difference of substance appears to be that the periods before artificial nutrition and hydration might be discounted are shorter than those recommended by the College.

THE TONY BLAND CASE

In the early 1990s, the most significant 'right to life' or 'euthanasia' case to reach the House of Lords was the Tony Bland case see: *Airedale NHS Trust v Bland* (1993). The key issue was: whether it was lawful to withdraw the provision of food and fluid to a patient through a tube knowing that to do so would result in the death of that patient?

Airedale NHS Trust v Bland (1993)

Tony Bland, one of the victims of the Hillsborough football disaster of 1989, lay in a permanent vegetative state (PVS) for more than three years. Bland's brain stem was diagnosed as being still alive; however, he had suffered massive and irreversible brain damage. Medical opinion was unanimous that he would never regain any form of awareness. But he was not legally dead and was being fed by naso-gastric tube and not on a life-support machine, contrary to some reports. The Trust looking after him applied to the court (with the approval of the parents) that it would be lawful to withhold any further life-prolonging treatment and care, (which included artificial nutrition, hydration and antibiotics) thus allowing him to die.

In law, *cessation of treatment* is an *omission* and not an act; therefore it would not be a criminal act unless the doctors are under a duty to continue the regime. Since all hope has been abandoned and there is no longer a duty to continue hydration and nourishment, a failure to do so cannot be a criminal offence. The basis for withdrawal of treatment is what amounts to the best interests of the patient. Withdrawal would not be an offence if it was in the patient's best interests.

On the question of the acceptable course of action, the majority of the court accepted the test laid down in *Bolam v Friern Hospital Management Committee* (1957) whereby it was acceptable medical practice to withdraw medical treatment if a responsible body of medical opinion supported this course of action.

The ethical issue was clearly: did the principle of sanctity of life apply to the facts of *Bland*?

Legal issues

(i) Whether continuance of the treatment would, more than three years after the injuries which resulted in PVS, would confer any benefit on Tony Bland?

(ii) Was there a duty on the doctors to continue to treat the patient in these cases? If so, then it would not be lawful for a doctor who assumed responsibility for the patient to simply give up treating that patient. However, a medical practitioner is under a no duty to continue to treat such a patient where a large body of informed and responsible medical opinion believes that no benefit would be conferred by continuance of the treatment.

The House of Lords ruled that it was lawful to withdraw artificial nutrition and hydration from a PVS patient because continued intervention would confer no 'benefit' upon the patient and hence was not in his 'best interests'.

The House of Lords therefore held:

1. The object of medical treatment and care was to benefit the patient, but since a large body of informed and responsible medical opinion was of the view that existence in the persistent vegetative state was not of benefit to the patient, the principle of sanctity of life, which was not absolute, was not violated by ceasing to give medical treatment and care involving invasive manipulation of the patient's body, to which he had not consented and which conferred no benefit upon him, to a PVS patient who had been in that state for over three years;

2. That the doctors responsible for the patient's treatment were neither under a duty nor entitled, to continue such medical care;

3. That since the time had come when the patient had no further interest in being kept alive, the necessity to do so, created by his inability to make a choice, and the justification for the invasive care and treatment had gone.
4. Accordingly, the omission to perform what had previously been a duty would no longer be unlawful.

Tony Bland had no interests, said the Law Lords, because he was in PVS. The life-supports were withdrawn and Tony Bland later died as a result of renal failure. In this case, three of the Law Lords assumed that the doctor's purpose in withdrawing Tony Bland's tube-feeding was to end his life. Nevertheless, they ruled that, in the circumstances, it was lawful to do so.

Analysis of the Tony Bland judgments

Can death ever be in a patient's best interests?

Lord Browne-Wilkinson and Lord Lowry opined that if it could be established that life-prolonging treatment was no longer in the incompetent patient's best interests, such treatment would become an unlawful battery. There appeared to be a reluctance to apply *Bolam* but they did so anyway.

Lord Goff clearly adopted a strong *Bolam* line, saying "There is overwhelming evidence that, in the medical profession, artificial feeding is regarded as a form of medical treatment . . .". In even stronger terms, he stated that there was an 'established rule' that

> "A doctor may, when caring for a patient who is, for example, caring for a patient who is, for example, dying of cancer, lawfully administer painkilling drugs despite the fact that he knows that an incidental effect of that application will be to abbreviate the patient's life . . . Such a decision may properly be made as part of the care of the living patient, in his best interests, and, on this basis, lawful".

Lord Mustill did not support a best interests test. He was not impressed by the acts/omissions dichotomy and declared that 'the ethical status of the two courses of action is for all relevant purposes indistinguishable'. Indeed, he said, 'I . . . feel some reservations about the application of the principle of civil liability in negligence laid down in Bolam . . . to decisions on 'best interests' in a field dominated by the criminal law. I accept without difficulty that this principle applies to the ascertainment of the medical raw materials such as diagnosis, prognosis and appraisal of the patient's cognitive functions. Beyond this point, however, it may be said that the decision is ethical, not medical, and that there is no reason in logic why on such a decision the opinions of doctors should be decisive. If there had been a possibility that this question might make a difference to the outcome of the appeal I would have wished to consider it further, but since it does not I prefer for the moment to express no opinion on it.' He also expressed the view that the foundations of the courts' unanimous decision were 'morally and intellectually misshapen'.

Bland a landmark case

This case undoubtedly marks a watershed in English medical law. Before the Bland judgment, it was a felony to intentionally kill a patient either by commission (such as giving a lethal injection) or by omission (such as not taking steps to stop bleeding, omitting to provide insulin for an insulin-dependent diabetic or failing to provide necessary food and water to a patient). In the case itself, Sir Thomas Bingham, MR declared that "It is . . . important to be clear from the outset what the case is, and is not, about. It is not about euthanasia, if by that it meant taking of positive action to cause death." But Lord Goff of Chieveley clearly disagreed, saying: "To act is to cross the Rubicon which runs between on the one hand the care of the living patient and on the other hand euthanasia -actively causing his death to avoid or to end his suffering . . . It is true that the drawing of this distinction may lead to a charge of hypocrisy because it can be asked why, if the doctor, by discontinuing treatment, is entitled in consequence to let his patient die, it should be lawful to let his patient die, it should be lawful to out him out of his misery straightaway in a more humane manner by a lethal injunction, rather than let him linger on in pain until he dies."

The dilemma was summarised by Lord Browne-Wilkinson who said

> "the conclusion that I have reached will appear to some almost irrational. How can it be lawful to allow a patient to die slowly, though painlessly, over a period of weeks from lack of food but unlawful to produce his immediate death by a lethal injection,

thereby saving his family from yet another ordeal . . .? I find it difficult to find a moral answer to that question. But it is undoubtedly the law . . ."

His Lordship also said:

"Murder consists of causing the death of another with intent to do so. What is proposed in the present case is to adopt a course with the intention of bringing about Antony Bland's death. As to the element of intention or mens rea, in my judgment there can be no real doubt that it is present in this case: The whole purpose of stopping artificial feeding is to bring about the death of Anthony Bland."

Despite the fact that this case clarified the legal position of PVS patients there was still some uncertainty over withdrawal of treatment from non-PVS patients. Some of this uncertainty has now been removed by the House of Lords' decision in the Diane Pretty case (2002).

The dominance of Bolam

Four of the Law Lords regarded the Bolam test as a central criterion in determining the doctor's duty, namely in determining whether to continue treatment would be in the patient's best interests. Yet, as Kennedy and Grubb in *A Commentary on Bland* (1993) 4 Med LR 360, point out, the difficulty in using Bolam to determine the legality of a doctor's conduct as opposed to its reasonableness was highlighted by Lord Mustill when he observed that Bolam should be restricted to 'the ascertainment of the medical raw material such as diagnosis, prognosis and appraisal of the patient's cognitive functions.' It should not be used when the decision was ethical because there was 'no reason in logic why on such a decision the opinions of doctors should be decisive.'

The sanctity of life principle

The Court in *Bland* said the sanctity of life principle is not absolute; it does not in itself provide a complete answer; nor apply to force feed prisoners, nor justify compelling the keeping alive of patients who are terminally ill, where to do so would merely prolong their suffering. But it forbids the taking of active measures to shorten the life of a terminally ill patient. Although the judges identified *Bland* as a case in which sanctity of human life should yield to self-determination or best interests no judgment actually attempts to state the content of the principle of the sanctity of human life.

Ordinary and extraordinary care

The judges in *Bland* do not refer to this well-known distinction because, presumably, it takes them no further in determining what sort of care ought to be provided.

Acts and omissions

The Law Lords rejected the view that liability attaches only to acts but never to omissions. On the contrary, they make it clear that there could be liability even for an omission if a prior duty to act existed and was breached.

The Bland principle does not breach the Human Rights Act 1998

As a result of the implementation of the Human Rights Act 1998 in Britain the question is whether the Bland principle has to be reconsidered, particularly in relation to Art.2 of the Convention. In other words, does the 'right to life' under Art.2 negate the Bland principle? According to a recent case, the decision and approach taken in *Bland* is in accordance with Art.2 of the Human Rights Act. *NHS Trust A v Mrs M; NHS Trust B v Mrs H* (2000) (High Court) (per Butler-Sloss, P.) held that it was not correct to interpret Art.2 of the Convention to mean that a decision to cease treatment in a patient's best interests was intentional deprivation of life. Although the intention in withdrawing artificial nutrition and hydration in PVS cases was to hasten death, the phrase 'deprivation of life' had to import a deliberate act as opposed to an omission by someone acting on behalf of the State resulting in death. Treatment which was no longer in the best interests of a patient would violate that patient's autonomy even though discontinuance would shorten the patient's life. Article 2 of the Convention contained a positive obligation on a State to take adequate and appropriate steps to safeguard life but where a clinical decision had been made to withhold treatment on the ground that it was not in the patient's best interests, and the clinical decision was in accordance with a respectable body of medical opinion, the state's positive obligation under Art. 2 of the Convention was discharged. In the case itself, one patient had been in PVS for over three years, the other for ten months. The Court granted a declaration that it was lawful for the hospital trusts to withdraw artificial nutrition and hydration from both patients.

BMA guidelines 1999

The BMA's 1999 publication, *The Withholding and Withdrawing of Life Prolonging Medical Treatment*, accepted the Law Lords' definition in Bland that the provision of food and water through a tube is artificial and part of medical treatment. As such they could legally be denied to a patient. The BMA appeared to accept that the practice of legally withdrawing food and fluid from patients in PVS should not be subject to Court review.

So the BMA now suggests that the withdrawal of tube-delivered food and water not only from PVS patients but also from patients who are not terminally ill, such as those with severe dementia or serious stroke should not be subject to court review.

General Medical Council (GMC) Guidelines (August 2002)

For patients in the process of dying, this GMC Guidance states that the provision of hydration and nutrition may not always be appropriate. The key concern for the dying patient is the relief of distressing symptoms of thirst. The Guidance says that 'where death is imminent, in judging the benefits, burdens or risks, it usually would not be appropriate to start either artificial hydration or nutrition, although artificial hydration provided by. . . less invasive measures may be appropriate where it is considered likely to provide symptom relief. . . Where death is not imminent, it will usually be appropriate to provide artificial nutrition or hydration.' However 'circumstances may arise' where [it is judged] that a patient's condition is so severe and the prognosis so poor that providing artificial nutrition or hydration may cause suffering or be 'too burdensome in relation the possible benefits.' This GMC Guidance was challenged in the *Burke* case (2005) (see above under *A Right to Life*) which has now been held by the Appeal Court to be lawful and *not* in breach of the European Convention on Human Rights.

Expedited hearing-the Frenchay case

Bland was followed in Frenchay Healthcare NHS Trust v S (1994).

Frenchay NHS Trust (1994)

S, a teenager, took a drug overdose in June 1991 and consequently suffered acute brain damage; He was treated in hospital where he was diagnosed by the consultant in charge as being in a persistent vegetative state (PVS). He was fed through a naso-gastric tube in his stomach. The tube became disconnected and dislodged, probably as a result of his own movement. The consultant surgeon believed that the tube could not be reconnected and thought the only alternative was to insert another tube but took the view that continued treatment was not in the best interests of the patient. The hospital sought a court order that it would be lawful not to reinsert the tube.

The Court of Appeal held:

1. Although the time-scale had been compressed, the appeal should not be allowed simply on the basis that there had not been an opportunity on behalf of S for a full exploration of the facts. Indeed, there would be cases of acute emergency where it would be impossible that doctors should be obliged or able to come to the court and seek a decision.
2. The evidence of PVS in the case was not as emphatic nor as unanimous as it had been in Airedale NHS Trust v Bland [1993] 1 FLR 1026, but the evidence of those doctors who knew him best was convincing.
3. That it would be lawful not to reinstate the tube, thus agreeing with the doctor, stressing it was in the best interests of the patient and that there was no medical opinion which contradicted the medical opinion of the consultant in this case.

The Court agreed to grant a declaration at an expedited hearing.

Are the views of relatives of any significance?

In *Re SG; Re G* (1995) the patient, after a motorcycle accident, suffered severe head injuries and lay in PVS for three and a half years. Further brain damage was caused by cardiac arrest in hospital. The wife supported the action, but the mother opposed it and wanted treatment to be continued. The court opined that his mother's views were relevant but could not prevail.

The court therefore authorised the withdrawal of treatment.

One effect of *Bland* is that the courts will have regard to the wishes of spouses and parents but will not give their wishes a determinative effect. They do not have the ultimate right to decide on their relative's treatment.

Court the final arbiter

The principle that has apparently emerged from these PVS decisions is that the final decision on these sorts of PVS cases, lies with the court, not the relatives of the patient.

Re D (1998)

Sir Stephen Brown, P granted a declaration in this case that it would be lawful not to re-attach the feeding tube of a woman who had been in what was described as a 'near PVS' since September 1995. This decision did not appear to satisfy all the Royal College of Physicians' guidelines for the diagnosis of PVS and it coincided with a report in the media of another patient recovering some awareness after ostensibly being in full PVS for nearly eight years. This case, as in the *Frenchay* and *Swindon* cases, was decided at an expedited hearing after a problem developed with the patient's feedings tube of its own accord.

Patients cared for at home

Swindon v Malborough NHS Trust (1994)

The patient, a woman, had lain in an unresponsive state for two and a half years. She went into a coma after neurosurgery to remove a brain tumour, Her husband and children, who had strong religious faith, did not wish for her feeding tube to be unblocked when a problem arose without warning. They did not wish for her to be kept alive in her totally unresponsive state. Although only notified late on a Friday afternoon, the Official Solicitor was able to instruct an independent expert in rehabilitation to examine the patient, S, and to report to the hearing which took place before Ward, J. on the afternoon of the

Saturday. The judge granted the declaration authorising with-drawal of treatment asked for by the NHS Trust, even though the patient was being cared for by her family at home.

PRACTICE NOTE ON ADULT PATIENTS WHO LACK CAPACITY

Practice Note 2001

The most recent Practice Note, issued on May 1, 2001, see [2001] Family Law 551, replaces all preceding Notes and contains an Appendix on PVS patients. The main points of this latest Practice Note have been mentioned in the chapter on Sterilisation (see ch. 7). However, as far as PVS patients are concerned, the following should be noted:

1. The 2001 Note extends the guidance in the earlier Practice Notes to a wider range of medical and welfare disputes leading to litigation.
2. It deals only with adults who lack capacity. Medical treatment of children will be dealt with under the Children Act 1989 or the inherent jurisdiction in relation to children.
3. The claimant must adduce evidence from a responsible medical practitioner that the operation would not be negligent and that it is necessary in the best interests of the patient.
4. The discontinuance of artificial feeding and hydration for patients in a vegetative state will in virtually all cases require the prior sanction of a High Court judge: *Airedale NHS Trust v Bland* [1993] 1 All E.R. 821 at 833 and *Frenchay Healthcare NHS Trust v S* [1994] 2 All E.R. 403.
5. It says it is 'futile' to provide medical treatment including artificial nutrition and hydration, to a patient with no awareness of self or environment and no prospect of recovery. The purpose of the proceedings is to establish whether the patient is in this condition.
6. It is not appropriate to apply to the court to discontinue artificial feeding and hydration until the condition is judged to be permanent. Diagnostic guidelines and not statutory provisions and a precise label may not be of importance. The court's concern is whether there is any awareness whatsoever or any possibility of change.
7. The court's approach has been reviewed in the light of the Human Rights Act 1998 and held to be compatible with Convention rights. There has as yet been no decided case

dealing with the discontinuance of artificial feeding and hydration for an adult patient with any (however minimal) awareness of self or environment. (but see now the *Leslie Burke* (2005) case)

8. A diagnosis of PVS should not be made until the patient has been in a continuing vegetative state following head injury for more than 12 months or following other causes of brain damage for six months. The addendum to the review emphasises that there is no urgency in making the diagnosis and the assessors should take into account descriptions given by relatives, carers and nursing staff who spend most time with the patient.

9. As a minimum, it will be necessary to adduce evidence from the treating physician and a neurologist or other expert experienced in assessing disturbances of consciousness.

Two independent reports

The court will wish to see at least two reports from experts, one of whom must be independent of the treating clinical team and claimant. The Official Solicitor usually commissions the second expert report.

Claimants

. . . A claim may be brought by a family member or other individual closely connected with the patient. The claimant must also adduce evidence about the views of family members. The views of family members or others close to the patient cannot act as a veto to an application but they must be taken fully into account by the court: *Re G (Persistent Vegetative State)* [1995] 2 FCR 46 at 51.

The views of the patient and others

The Official Solicitor will investigate whether the views of the patient may have been expressed, either in writing or otherwise. The High Court may determine the effect of a purported advance directive as to future medical treatment . . . A valid and applicable advance refusal or treatment may be determinative. The patient's previously expressed views which did not amount to an effective advance decision will still be an important component in the best interests decision.

(see also the Mental Capacity Act 2005)

Physician assisted deaths

The major argument that dominates the debate on euthanasia is that if 'physician-assisted' deaths were allowed, doctors would assist in suicides in more and more dubious circumstances: i.e. if the doctor were authorised to carry out so-called mercy killings at the request of patients who were temporarily suffering from very low self-esteem, at which point could she decide that the treatment asked for would be in the patient's best interests? Hence, if one type of case may be lawful at the discretion of the doctor, how far should he be permitted to go? Would this not eventually lead to carrying out non-voluntary euthanasia as it is perceived happens in the Netherlands? The same slippery-slope argument could be applied to a carer wishing to terminate the life of a terminally-ill patient at the request of the patient.

Mental Capacity Act 2005 (MCA 2005)

This Act will come into force in April 2007 and is the 'culmination of efforts to enact wide-ranging legislation to deal with the mentally incapacitated to encompass the management and control of their financial affairs and of their healthcare and medical treatment.' (Laing, *"The Mental Capacity Bill 2004: Human Rights Concerns"* [2005] Fam Law 137). It provides a statutory framework to empower and protect vulnerable people who are not able to make their own decisions. It makes it clear who can take decisions, in which situations, and how they should go about this. It enables people to plan ahead for a time when they may lose capacity.

Guidance on the Act will be provided in a Code of Practice. People who are placed under a duty to have regard to the Code include those working in a professional capacity e.g. doctors and social workers. A draft was made available to assist Parliamentary consideration of the Act when in Bill form and is available on the DCA website (under "Mental Capacity Bill and supporting documents"). See also *www.dh.gov.uk* for further information on the MCA 2005.

The follollowing summary of the Act is taken from the Department of Health website: see *www.dh.gov.uk* with further information available from www.dca.gov.uk (the Department of Constitutional Affairs website).

The Act is based on a set of five key principles stated at Section 1:

- A presumption of capacity—every adult has the right to make his or her own decisions and must be assumed to have capacity to do so unless it is proved otherwise;
- The right for individuals to be supported to make their own decisions —people must be given all appropriate help before anyone concludes that they cannot make their own decisions;
- That individuals must retain the right to make what might be seen as eccentric or unwise decisions;
- Best interests—anything done for or on behalf of people without capacity must be in their best interests; and
- Least restrictive intervention—anything done for or on behalf of people without capacity should be the least restrictive of their basic rights and freedoms.

The Act puts into statutory form current best practice and common law principles concerning people who lack mental capacity and those who take decisions on their behalf. It will replace current statutory schemes for enduring powers of attorney and Court of Protection receivers with reformed and updated schemes

The Act deals with the assessment of a person's capacity and acts by carers of those who lack capacity

Assessing lack of capacity—The Act sets out a single clear test for assessing whether a person lacks capacity to take a particular decision at a particular time. It is a "decision-specific" test. No one can be labelled 'incapable' as a result of a particular medical condition or diagnosis. Section 2 of the Act states that a lack of capacity cannot be established merely by reference to a person's age, appearance, or any condition or aspect of a person's behaviour which might lead others to make unjustified assumptions about capacity.

- Best Interests—Everything that is done for or on behalf of a person who lacks capacity must be in that person's best interests. The Act contains a checklist of factors that decision-makers must work through in deciding what is in a person's best interests. A person can put his/her wishes and feelings into a written statement if desired, which the person making the determination must consider. Carers and family members now have a right to be consulted.

- Acts in connection with care or treatment—Under s.5, where a person is providing care or treatment for someone who lacks capacity, then the person can provide the care without incurring legal liability. The key will be proper assessment of capacity and best interests. This will cover actions that would otherwise result in a civil wrong or crime if someone has to interfere with the person's body or property in the ordinary course of caring, for example, by giving an injection or by using the person's money to buy items for them.

- Restraint/deprivation of liberty. Section 6 of the Act defines restraint as the use or threat of force where an incapacitated person resists, and any restriction of liberty or movement whether or not the person resists. Restraint is only permitted if the person using it reasonably believes it is necessary to prevent harm to the incapacitated person, and if the restraint used is proportionate to the likelihood and seriousness of the harm.

- Section 6(5) makes it clear that an act depriving a person of his or her liberty within the meaning of Art.5(1) of the European Convention on Human Rights cannot be an act to which s.5 provides any protection.

The Act deals with two situations where a designated decision-maker can act on behalf of someone who lacks capacity

- Lasting powers of attorney (LPAs)—The Act allows a person to appoint an attorney to act on their behalf if they should lose capacity in the future. This is similar to the current Enduring Power of Attorney (EPA), but the Act also allows people to let an attorney make health and welfare decisions.

- Court appointed deputies —The Act provides for a system of court appointed deputies to replace the current system of receivership in the Court of Protection. Deputies will be able to take decisions on welfare, healthcare and financial matters as authorised by the Court but will not be able to refuse consent to life-sustaining treatment.

They will only be appointed if the Court cannot make a specific, individualised decision to resolve the issues.

The Act creates two new public bodies to support the statutory framework, both of which will be designed to support the needs of those who lack capacity

- A new Court of Protection—The new Court will have jurisdiction relating to the whole Act and will be the final arbiter for capacity matters. It will have its own procedures and nominated judges.
- A new Public Guardian—The Public Guardian and his/her staff will be the registering authority for LPAs and deputies. They will supervise deputies appointed by the Court and provide information to help the Court make decisions.

The Act also includes three further key provisions to protect vulnerable people

- Independent Mental Capacity Advocate (IMCA)—An IMCA is someone appointed to support a person who lacks capacity but has no one to speak for them. The IMCA makes representations about the person's wishes, feelings, beliefs and values, at the same time as bringing to the attention of the decision-maker all factors that are relevant to the decision. The IMCA can challenge the decision-maker on behalf of the person lacking capacity if necessary.
- Advance decisions to refuse treatment—Statutory rules with clear safeguards confirm that people may make a decision in advance to refuse treatment if they should lose capacity in the future. The Act makes it clear that an advance decision will have no application to any treatment which a doctor considers necessary to sustain life unless strict formalities have been complied with, namely: that the decision must be in writing, signed and witnessed. The directive must also contain an express statement that the decision stands "even if life is at risk".

 A criminal offence

 A new criminal offence will exist under this Act, of ill treatment or neglect of a person who lacks capacity. A person found guilty of such an offence may be liable to imprisonment for a term of up to five years.

Source: Department of Health website *www.dh.gov.uk*

TERMINAL ILLNESS

Withdrawing treatment v actively terminating life of terminally ill

The Diane Pretty Case (2002)

Diane Pretty, 43, was paralysed and suffering from motor neurone disease, a degenerative and fatal illness. She only had a short time to live and faced the prospect of a humiliating and distressing death. She has full mental capacity but her physical incapacity prevented her from taking her own life without assistance. She requested her husband to carry out this process and he was willing to do so, provided he would be immune from prosecution under s.2(1) of the Suicide Act 1961, whereby aiding and abetting the suicide of another is a crime. The DPP refused to grant that immunity. The Divisional Court refused judicial review and the issues involved a consideration of whether there would be a breach of the Human Rights Act 1988 (in force in the UK through the European Convention). The House of Lords ruled that there had been no breach of Convention rights because:

a) Art.2 (right to life) enunciated the sanctity of life principle, protected the right to life and guaranteed that no individual should be deprived of life by intentional human intervention; it could not be interpreted as conferring a right to assisted suicide; the state had no positive duty to recognise such a right.

b) Art.3 (prohibition of torture or inhuman or degrading treatment) did not encompass a right to die; the UK was not obliged to guarantee the right to assisted suicide.

c) Art.8 (right to respect for private and family life) did not relate to the manner in which an individual chose to die.

d) Art.9 (freedom of thought) could not be used to justify conduct which was prohibited by the criminal law.

e) Art.14 (prohibition of discrimination) did not apply since no other Convention rights were engaged.

On appeal to the European Court of Human Rights, the decision was upheld, with the Court unanimously declaring that there had been no violation of any Article of the Convention.

What about an adult patient of sound mind with a terminal condition who requests the hospital treating her to withdraw her life-supports because she no longer wishes to live? Would the hospital be assisting in the patient's suicide if it complied with the patient's wishes?

Ms B's Case: Re B (Consent to Treatment: Capacity) (2002)

Ms B, aged 43, was paralysed from the neck downwards with no prospect of recovery. However, she could be admitted to a spinal rehabilitation unit with a view to rehabilitation into the community. She declined to participate in this and asked for the ventilator which was keeping her alive to be disconnected. At a hearing held at the patient's hospital bedside, Dame Butler Sloss, President of the Family Division, found the patient to have capacity and therefore lawfully able to refuse treatment. She was, of course, merely requesting discontinuance of treatment already in place, rather than refusing to have any treatment *per se*. The patient was subsequently transferred to another hospital where the life supports were removed and she died peacefully.

Distinction between Diane Pretty and Ms B

These cases illustrate that in English law, it will be permissible to withdraw life-support and allow a terminally-ill adult patient to die at that patient's request provided that patient is of sound mind whereas the court will not allow a positive act to be carried out (e.g. through lethal injection) to actively terminate a terminally-ill adult patient's life even when that patient requests such termination, and is also of sound mind. The distinction between acts and omissions remains important in these cases.

What if a terminally ill patient wishes to go abroad for the purpose of having an assisted suicide legally and her husband wishes to assist her in travelling abroad? Would the local authority in whose area the patient resides be obliged to prevent this assisted suicide being carried out abroad? *Re Z* (2004) appears to have answered these questions. The Court *retains a discretion* whether to prosecute those who assist in the suicide process in the case of a terminally ill patient, for example, by taking such a patient abroad: *Re Z* (2004).

Re Z (2004)

Mrs Z was a middle-aged woman with a terminal illness who wished to travel to Switzerland in the company of her husband, to have an assisted suicide. The husband informed their local authority that he wished to assist her in here intentions and the question arose as to the extent of the local authority's duty in these circumstances where a criminal act (assisted suicide) might be perpetrated.

The issue which arose for determination was: what was the extent of the duty owed by a local authority when the welfare of a vulnerable person in their area was threatened by the criminal (or other wrongful) act of another.

The Court held: The local authority incurred duties to: (i) investigate the position of a vulnerable adult to consider what was her true position and intention; (ii) consider whether she was legally competent to make and carry out her decision and intention; (iii) consider whether any other (and, if so, what) influence could be operating on her position and intention and to ensure that she had all relevant information and knew all the available options; (iv) consider whether to invoke the inherent jurisdiction of the High Court so that the question of competence could be judicially investigated and determined; (v) in the event that the adult was not competent, to provide all such assistance as could be reasonably required both to determine and give effect to her best interests; (vi) in the event that the adult was competent, to allow her in any lawful way to give effect to her decision although that should not preclude the giving of advice or assistance in accordance with what were perceived to be her best interests; (vii) where there were reasonable grounds to suspect that the commission of a criminal offence might be involved, to draw that to the attention of the police; (viii) in very exceptional circumstances, to invoke the jurisdiction of the court under s.222 of the Local Government Act 1972.

The local authority's duties did not extend any further. In the instant case, although they had power to seek to continue the injunction under s.222, they had no obligation to do so. Further, the court should not seek to continue the injunction of its own motion in circumstances where no-one with the necessary standing sought any such order, where the criminal justice agencies had the requisite knowledge and power, and where the effect of the injunction was to deny a right to a seriously disabled but competent person that could not be exercised by herself by reason only of her physical disability. Accordingly, the injunction would be discharged.

Scarce resources and quality of life

There is the usual concern with the allocation of scarce health care resources-should we be spending a lot of money and resources in preserving life of persons who is no longer enjoy any sort of quality of life or should these limited resources go into promoting the health of someone who can still enjoy a reasonable quality of life?

ADVANCE DIRECTIVES

An advance directive is a declaration made by a competent patient in advance of his death stipulating the nature of the medical treatment he wishes to have in the event he becomes incapable of expressing his intentions. It can be in the form of a document (usually called a 'living will') which sets out an individual's wishes in the event of incompetence and the occurrence of medical conditions or precipitating events. On the other hand, an individual may appoint someone to act as proxy (i.e. confer an enduring power of attorney) by which he appoints an agent to make decisions on his behalf during any future period during which he is disabled. It may include a refusal of treatment but it can also authorise life-prolonging treatment but cannot require that such treatment be given. Such directives could be general or specific, oral or written. If oral statements uttered in times of stress or anxiety are accepted as authentic, there is potential for exploitation and questions of proof may present insuperable difficulties for relatives, and in some cases, may even endanger the life of the patient.

Until the Mental Capacity Act 2005 comes into force in 2007, the UK will have no legislative framework to give effect to advance directives or to define their scope, but the legal position of the advance directive is that they will probably have legal effect provided they satisfy the requirements laid down in *Re T (Adult: Refusal of Treatment)* (1992) namely that it must be 'clearly established' and 'applicable in the circumstances' [of the particular case]. Doctors will also have to consider the true scope and basis of the decision expressed and must ask whether the patient has refused consent to the treatment or procedure which it is desired to carry out. Lord Donaldson stressed that what really matters is 'the declaration by the patient of his decision with a full appreciation of the possible consequences, the latter being expressed in the simplest possible terms'.

The key concepts underlying these directives are:

(a) a patient has the right to refuse medical treatment, including life-saving and life-sustaining treatment, which refusal should be respected and complied with by the patient's doctor's (see *Ms B*'s case (2002)) and
(b) provided certain requirements have been fulfilled, a person can make valid and enforceable treatment decisions in anticipation of future disability.

Of course, it will be difficult to devise a document which will be free from different interpretations if words such as 'grave' and 'severe' are used.

Another concern is that the patient might have changed his mind in the period between making the living will and the onset of the illness or the incapacitating event.

The only official formulation appears to be a Practice Note [1994] 2 All E.R. 413 which states:

> "The views of the patient may have been previously expressed, either in writing or otherwise. The High Court exercising its inherent jurisdiction may determine the effect of a purported advance directive as to future medical treatment . . . the patient's expressed views, if any, will always be a very important component in the decisions of the doctors and the court".

Two of the Law Lords, Lord Keith and Lord Goff, in Bland's case indicated that the advance directive had legal status. However, their comments were arguably *obiter*. Davies in his *Textbook on Medical Law* (1998) argues that although Lord Keith found support for the potential legitimacy of an advance declaration of refusal of treatment in the cases of *Re F* and *Re T*, there are still questions which will require resolution before it would be possible to decide whether such a directive will apply to or bind those who may be considering treatment in the future.
(see now The Mental Capacity Act 2005)

RECENT DEVELOPMENTS

Assisted Dying for the Terminally Ill Bill

The new Assisted Dying for the Terminally Ill Bill came before Parliament in 2004 and this seeks to legalise assisted suicide and also purports to make provision for terminally ill individuals to receive pain-relieving medication. It aims to enable a competent adult who is suffering unbearably as a result of a terminal illness to receive medical help to die at his own considered and persistent request, and to make provision for a person suffering from a terminal illness to receive pain relief medication. It remains to be seen if this Bill will become law and the form it will eventually take.

10. EXAM TIPS, ADVICE ON ASSIGNMENTS AND SAMPLE QUESTIONS

Some courses/modules use a combination of forms of assessment-an essay and a 'closed book' examination instead of only the traditional three-hour or two-hour examination, where you have to choose certain questions to be answered from a selection. If your particular course uses the traditional exam assessment, you will find it useful to bear in mind the following:

Revision for examinations

1. Revise **early** (as you follow the course) and revise **often**. This means that instead of waiting for all the teaching on the course/module to be completed, you should be going over the material that was covered in lectures and seminars, every week and at least every two weeks; make sure you also revise at the end of the First term/semester.
2. Summarise the main points from a lecture and /or seminar/tutorial in a separate set of Revision Notes which you should then revise from just before the examination. Discuss topics with colleagues whenever possible. Use vacation times sensibly-you can still have Easter Day and three days off for Christmas!
3. In your exam answers, be sure to refer to, discuss and link any relevant ethical principles which may be relevant to the issues you have been asked to analyse: e.g. to the sanctity of life and quality of life principles when discussing handicapped newborn babies and patients in PVS,

autonomy when discussing consent, or the double effect principle when discussing 'physician assisted suicide'.

4. Consult **past years' exam papers** (these may be available on the internal university website) to get some idea of the structure and types of questions that tend to be asked. Are they just essay-type questions (e.g. 'The shortage of human organs for donation must be addressed by more drastic measures'. Discuss) or a combination of essays and 'problem questions' i.e. a factual situation requiring you to give specific and detailed advice on with the usual rubric: 'Advise X'. An example would be:

Mrs X, aged 65, who has a history of mental illness, consults you as her legal adviser and tells you that she consented to an operation to ease the pain in her back. In response to a question, she was assured by her doctor that it was a straightforward operation with minimal risks. However, the result of the operation is that she is now paralysed down one side of her body. She wishes to know what her legal position is and against whom she can seek legal redress.

Advise her.

A suggested Answer Plan might be to:

(i) identify the key issues that have been raised (Consent; disclosure; negligence/ assault/ battery? Therapeutic privilege?)

(ii) discuss each issue citing the relevant cases (*Sidaway, Chatterton v Gerson, Gold v Haringey, Blyth v Bloomsbury,* etc.) applying the legal principles to the factual situation.

(iii) discuss who can be sued and on what basis; (e.g. vicarious liability?)

(iv) discuss the remedies that might be available (damages?)

5. Find out how many questions you are required to answer in the exam and plan to be able to answer at least two more than required, so that you can pick the questions you can answer best. This will be the kind of question where you can not only cite the leading cases and statutes accurately but in which you can also refer to some academic commentary to enhance the quality of your answer and make some good points.

6. At the examination, **read each question carefully.** Then **read it again.** Plan your answers in bullet-points and make a rough note of the time you need to stop writing

for each question before you start writing. Leave yourself some time at the end to have a quick check of the answers to pick up inadvertent errors in spelling or simply to make potentially illegible words legible! You never know, legibility might make the difference and endear you to the marker(s)!

ADVICE ON ASSESSED ASSIGNMENTS

1. Read through any published assessment criteria in the Course/Module Handbook. Check the word limits and do not exceed them (except by a very small margin, if at all). Check if footnotes and the Bibliography count as part of the word limit. Decide which style of referencing you will be using, i.e., numbered sequential footnotes (literally, at the foot of the page) or referencing within the text, e.g. citing 'Mason and McCall Smith (2000)' which is linked to a full reference in your list of references at the end of the essay under the heading References. Thus:

References

Brazier, M Medicine, Patients and the Law, 1992, Penguin, at p.75
   Jones, M 'Informed consent and other fairy stories' (1999) 10 Med LR 103, at p.105
   This list would not be required if your text already has numbered footnotes at the foot of the page on which they are cited.

2. Remember your Bibliography (full list of references) should be the final list of references at the very end of the essay, arranged alphabetically, by surname, thus:

Bibliography

Brazier, *M Medicine, Patients and the Law,* 2nd edition 1992, Penguin
   Kennedy, I and Grubb, *A Medical Law,* 3rd edition 2000. Butterworths
   Mason, JK & McCall Smith, *RA Law and Medical Ethics,* 5th edition, 1999. Butterworths

3. Consult some journal articles (cited in book lists or footnotes in the articles) relating to the particular topic you are researching for the assignment. Sift through the

material and select what you think is most relevant to the question being asked. Use sub-headings if you think they help to clarify the text. The Introduction should clarify any technical terms the question might contain and identify the main issues raised and the ethical issues that might be relevant.

4. Use suitable quotations but do not use too many. Remember that there is no 'model answer' as such to the question. This is not what is expected at the university/ HE level. The examiners want to see a well-structured, logical, well-presented essay which addresses the issues raised by the question, is free from careless typographical errors (check your spelling! Or have it checked!) sticks to the question, and puts forward an approach based on the student's research. The work has to cover the most important possibilities and issues raised by the question, supported by a case analysis and/or citation from some (at least a few!) published academic commentaries (journal articles) which move the essay along, or enhance the level of discussion, but still be within the word-limit, i.e. concise. Make sure your personal commentary, which should be balanced and supported by well-argued reasons, is also included, particularly at the very end of the essay, where you are offering an approach to the question being asked.

5. End with a strong conclusion and an opinion about the question asked, making sure it is preceded by well-balanced arguments.

SPECIMEN EXAMINATION QUESTIONS

1. Discuss, with reference to decided cases, the extent to which English law permits the refusal of medical treatment in relation to adult patients. How is this situation different from the withdrawal of life support to an adult patient who is disabled or in a coma? Evaluate the legal and ethical implications of the leading cases, *Re Z* (2004) EWHC 2817 (Fam) and the possible impact of the Human Rights Act 1998.

2. (a) Alfred has a serious kidney condition that requires a kidney transplant. He wishes to know the legal position on a number of queries which he raises with you because:
   (i) he believes he can purchase a human organ on the Internet; and

(ii) he knows a doctor who says he is able to obtain a replacement kidney for a fee.

Advise Alfred on the relevant law and ethical issues that might arise from these situations.

(b) What measures will be implemented in the UK in 2006 to regulate the storage, use and removal of human tissue from deceased persons and human organs for transplant?

3. Is there a duty under English law to preserve the life of severely disabled newborn children?

Critically discuss, from ethical and legal perspectives, the English judicial approach to this situation, with reference to leading cases, paying particular attention to the significance of parental wishes regarding the medical treatment of severely disabled newborn children. Is the *David Glass* case (*Glass v UK* [2004] Lloyds LR 76) of any significance in this context?

Answer either (a) or (b)

4. (a) (i) Brittany has just given birth to a baby as part of a surrogacy arrangement. However, soon after the birth, she decided that she did not wish to hand over the baby to the commissioning couple, although she has already been paid £8,000 and has been promised another £30,000. She also wishes to go and live with her sister in New Jersey, in the United States, and wonders whether American law is similar to English law.

Advise Brittany on her legal position in the light of English law and the American case of Baby M (*Re M* (1988)109 NJ 396).

(a) (ii) If Brittany had not changed her mind, would the commissioning couple have been legally entitled to adopt the child in England?

OR

(b) Is there a 'right to reproduce' under English law? Has the legal position been affected by the Human Rights Act 1998? Is there a right in English law to artificial or assisted reproduction or the right to 'posthumous reproduction' using sperm from a dead donor as in the Diane Blood case (*R. v Human Fertilisation and Embryology Authority ex p. Blood* [1997] 2 WLR 806)?

Answer either (a) or (b)

5. (a) Critically consider the extent to which an unborn child may be seen as having been accorded legal status in English law, with particular reference to leading cases such as *AG's Reference (No.3 of 1994)* [1997] 3 All ER 936 and the leading caesarean section cases.

OR

(b) Critically evaluate the 'best interests' test in relation to the sterilisation of mentally incapacitated patients with reference to *Re B (A Minor)(Wardship: Sterilisation)* [1988] 1 AC 199 and related cases.

Answer either (a) or (b)

6. (a) Is it sometimes permissible to breach the duty of confidentiality? Critically consider medical confidentiality with particular reference to leading cases based on the 'public interest' and the issues surrounding HIV positive patients.

OR

7. "The Gillick case was heralded as a landmark decision for children's rights. However, in the case of teenagers, their right to refuse consent to treatment has been totally ignored by the courts and suggests that for them, the Gillick principle has been somewhat undermined."
Evaluate the accuracy of this statement, with reference to decided cases decided after *Gillick* and any relevant legislation, giving reasons from an ethical and legal viewpoint as to whether you support the English courts' approach.

APPENDIX

MEDICAL LAW AND HUMAN RIGHTS

Throughout medico-legal situations, autonomy, respect for persons, paternalism, doing good and not doing harm, the sanctity of life v. the quality of life conflicts, and notions of 'best interests' will be ever-present. Human Rights have once more returned to the forefront in the UK, as a result of the entering into force of the Human Rights Act 1998 in England and Wales on October 2, 2000 which enables the European Convention on Human Rights to be pleaded in domestic courts.

IS THERE A RIGHT TO TREATMENT?

Withdrawing or withholding of treatment will not breach Art.2 (right to life) of the European Convention on Human Rights (ECHR) provided it is in the patient's best interests. No case law to suggest that an individual may demand the right to life-saving treatment; moreover, any such right would be constrained by the resources available (*Osman v UK* (2000) and negated if the treatment would be futile (*LCB v UK* (1998) 27 EHRR 212; see now *R (Burke) v GMC* (2005) *Times*, 2 August)

It is unlikely that patient's relatives have the right to demand certain treatment for the patient but if a legitimate expectation had been created by the Health Authority for the provision of that resource then it might be a breach of Art.8 for the Authority subsequently to withdraw that resource: *R v North and East Devon ex p. Coughlan* [1999] Lloyds LR Medical 306. Prima facie, Art.8 does not impose a positive obligation to provide treatment: *North West Lancashire HA v A,D & G* [1999] Lloyds LR, Medical 399.

R (Burke) v GMC (The Burke Case) (2005) Times, 2 August - GMC Guidance does not breach Human Rights Convention- Court of Appeal

(the man who wished not to have his treatment withdrawn even after he might no longer be able to communicate his wishes)

The Court of Appeal ruled in July 2005 (see *Times*, 2 August) that the GMC guidance (on the circumstances in which life-prolonging treatment in the form of artificial nutrition and hydration could be withdrawn from a patient) is lawful and did not violate the European Convention on Human Rights. Patients cannot demand that a doctor administer a treatment that a doctor considers adverse to the patient's clinical needs. But doctors who sought to interrupt a patient's life-prolonging treatment against the patient's expressed wish to be kept alive, with the intention to terminate the patient's life, would have to face a charge of murder.

A RIGHT TO LIBERTY AND SECURITY OF THE PERSON

H. L. v the UK (The *Bournewood Case*) (2005) European Court of Human Rights

The European Court of Human Rights held that the informal admission of a compliant adult patient who lacked capacity to decide about his psychiatric care, constituted an arbitrary detention that breached Art.5(1) (unlawful detention); the absence of effective legal procedures to review such informal detentions was in breach of Art.5(4); the detention of this particular patient was not in accordance with the procedure prescribed by law; the doctrine of necessity was insufficiently precise in its scope to prevent arbitrary application of its criteria.

A RIGHT TO REFUSE TREATMENT?

Art.8 might arguably be used if a patient is treated without consent since the right to respect for one's private life covers physical integrity. Art.9 might be invoked in the first instance if someone is treated against her stated religious beliefs, for example a Jehovah's Witness who is given a blood transfusion.

Art.3 (prohibition of degrading treatment) is the provision which might be invoked in cases like *St George's NHS Trust* (the Collins case) if a case of enforced caesareans is claimed.

An anorexic patient treated (or fed?) without her consent might also cite Art.3 but the 'best interests' test and the right to life would have to be considered and weighed in the balance.

The competent adult patient's right to refuse treatment even if she was severely physically disabled, appeared to have been affirmed in *In re B (2002) Times*, March 26, but in fact, Ms B was asking doctors to withdraw the treatment already begun.

(*Ms B v An NHS Hospital* [2002] 2 All ER 449)

CONFIDENTIALITY

The relevant provision is Art.8 of the ECHR (now part of English law under the Human Rights Act 1998) which states:

1. Everyone has the right to respect for his private and family life, his home and his correspondence.
2. There shall be no interference by a public authority with the exercise of this right **except** such as is in accordance with the law and is necessary in a democratic society in the interests of national security, public safety or the economic well-being of the country, for the prevention of disorder or crime, for the protection of health or morals, or for the protection of the rights and freedoms of others.

Thus Art.8 is *not* an absolute right; it may be restricted in accordance with the provisions of Art.8(2). Medical records are part of a person's private life, thus disclosure of a patient's records would breach Art.8. (see *McGinley v UK* (1998) 27 EHRR 1.)

STATUS OF THE UNBORN CHILD /RIGHT TO LIFE?

Art.2 'everyone's right to life shall be protected by law' according to *Re MB* (1997), *Paton v UK* (1980), and the fetus is not entitled to protection prior to viability; so 'everyone' does not, *per se*, include a fetus. Abortion law is therefore not affected, as such, by the Human Rights Act 1998.

CHILDREN AND HEALTHCARE

Art.2 of the ECHR (the 'right to life') could be invoked by a child who claimed that certain medical treatment was needed to save her life. (e.g. see *Re C (A Child) (HIV testing)* [2000] 2 WLR 270). Note that in the now famous 'conjoined twins' case (*Re A (Children)* [2001] FLR 1) the court held that the death of Mary as the result of the separation operation could not be regarded as inhuman and degrading under Art.3 or a breach of the right to life under Art.2. If a child is given treatment against its purported religious beliefs, for example if its parents are Jehovah's Witnesses who object to the treatment, conflict arises between the right to life and freedom of religion (Art.9). The court must then decide which right prevails. Provided acting 'in the best interests' is said to be the court's approach, it usually means that there is no breach of any Human Rights provision.

If a case similar to *Re T* (the liver transplant case) [1997] 1 All ER 906 arose again, Art.2 might well be invoked but the best interests approach would have to be discredited or negated before an appellate court would overturn the lower court's decision.

R. v Portsmouth NHS Trust ex parte Glass [1999] (The David Glass Case)

The European Court of Human Rights unanimously held that the NHS *did* breach the right to respect for private life, as guaranteed by Art.8 of the European Convention on Human Rights. This breach took place when the hospital authorities decided to over-ride the mother's objection to the treatment proposed for her severely disabled son in the absence of authorisation by a court.

STERILISATION OF THE MENTALLY DISABLED

Art.12 provides that 'Men and women of marriageable age have the right to marry and to found a family, according to the national laws governing the exercise of this right.' Note that the provision talks about the right to marry *and* found a family (i.e. conjunctively) so that the two rights do not appear to exist independently. See also *R v Secretary of State for Home Dept ex parte Mellor* (2001) 2 FLR 1158: Court of Appeal held that Art.12 did not create a right to be enabled to procreate. Thus there is no absolute 'right' to found a family.

Art.8 declares the right to respect for private and family life but Art.8(1) is subject to the qualification in Art.8(2) (reproduced above, under Confidentiality).

ASSISTED REPRODUCTION AND SURROGACY

Art.12 (the right to marry and found a family) presupposes that the persons involved are of the opposite sex (see also *Cossey v UK*). The question also arises over an AID-conceived child.

In *X, Y and Z v UK* (1997) 24 EHRR 43, X was a transsexual (from female to male) who had cohabited with Y, a woman, for some years. In 1992, through artificial insemination by donor (AID), Y gave birth to Z, and X was refused permission to be registered as the father of Z. X, Y and Z claimed that the refusal to register X as the father of Z was a breach of Art.8, i.e. an infringement of their right to respect for their family life. The European Court of Human Rights held that since the States could not agree how the law should treat the child conceived by AID and the role of the father in such a case, the UK did not breach Art.8 by not recognising X as Z's father in these circumstances.

EUTHANASIA AND ADULT PATIENTS

Under Art.2 is the 'right to life'. Yet, in *NHS Trust A v Mrs M; NHS Trust B v Mrs H* [2000] 1 All ER 801, the court held that an omission to provide treatment by the medical team will only be incompatible with Art.2 where the circumstances are such as to impose a positive obligation on the State to take steps to prolong a patient's life. Art.2 therefore imposes a positive obligation to give life sustaining treatment where, according to responsible opinion, such treatment is in the best interests of the patient but does not impose an obligation if such treatment would be futile (*LCB v UK* [1998] 27 EHRR 212, EComHR)

'An insensate patient suffering from PVS has no feelings and comprehension of of the treatment accorded to him or her. Art.3 does not in my judgment apply.' per Butler Sloss, P in *NHS Trust A v Mrs M; MHS Trust B v Mrs H* (2001) (above). By analogy, Art.3 would not be breached by the Tony Bland (*Airedale NHS Trust v Bland* [1993] AC 783) ruling because of the 'best interests' approach and *LCB v UK* (1998) (above).

A NHS Trust v D [2000] FLR 277 (decided before the HRA 1998 came into force) -Cazalet, J granted a declaration that doctors do not need to treat a severely disabled child with artificial ventilation and that there can be no Art.2 infringement here because the treatment as advised is, in the light of the order he proposed to make, in the best interests of the patient concerned.

A RIGHT TO ASSISTED SUICIDE?

Re Z (2004) Med LR 257 (the terminally ill woman wishing to go to Switzerland to have an assisted death)

The Court ruled in relation to the 'right to life' under Art.2 that this right does not assume primacy over rights of autonomy and self-determination. Whilst Art.2 imposed a duty on the State to protect life, it did not create a right to die. The Court retains a discretion whether to prosecute those prepared to assist in a suicide.

EUTHANASIA AND SEVERELY DISABLED NEWBORN CHILDREN

Art.3 (prohibition of torture, degrading treatment) includes the right to die with dignity (per Cazalet, J in *A NHS Trust v D* [1997] 24 EHRR 423).

But, apparently Art.3 requires the victim to be aware of the inhuman and degrading treatment which he or she is experiencing or at least be in a state of physical or mental suffering: per Butler Sloss, P, in *NHS Trust A v Mrs M; NHS Trust B v Mrs H* [2001] 1 All ER 801. Newborn children would certainly not fulfil this requirement.

INDEX